For Ellen Coolidge Burke Library

Letters to Virginia

Bart Winters   12/15/2010

Letters to Virginia

Correspondence from three generations of Alexandrians before, during and after the Civil War

Barb Winters

Acclaim Press
MORLEY, MISSOURI

Acclaim Press
— *Your Next Great Book* —

P.O. Box 238
Morley, MO 63767
(573) 472-9800
www.acclaimpress.com

Design: Tiffany Glastetter
Cover Design: M. Frene Melton

All images, unless otherwise indicated, are courtesy of the Local History/Special Collections Department of the Alexandria, Virginia Library. Picture of Joseph Eaches courtesy of Donald M. Robey.

Letters to Virginia: Correspondence from three generations of Alexandrians before, during and after the Civil War / compiled by Barb Winters.
    p. cm.
  ISBN-13: 978-1-935001-63-8 (alk. paper)
  ISBN-10: 1-935001-63-9 (alk. paper)
  1. Eaches family--Correspondence. 2. Tackett family--Correspondence.
3. Fendall family--Correspondence. 4. Alexandria (Va.)--History--
19th century--Sources. 5. Alexandria (Va.)--Social life and customs--
Sources. 6. Alexandria (Va.)--Biography. 7. Virginia--History--Civil War,
1861-1865--Sources. 8. Virginia--History--19th century--Sources.
9. American letters--Virginia--Alexandria. I. Winters, Barb.
  F234.A3L48 2010
  975.5'03--dc22
                                    2010043520

First Printing: 2010
Printed in the United States of America
10 9 8 7 6 5 4 3 2 1

Contents

Dedicated to Rita Williams Holtz for her researching expertise, knowing where the photos were buried and her support and encouragement through the three years it took to write this book.

Cast of Characters

All of the people in this book are referred to by their first names or nicknames. Therefore, the following list is compiled in the same manner, regardless of family affiliation. More specific dates of birth, death and marriage may be found in the Family Trees.

Ann Eaches – 1797–1850. A Quaker, the wife of Joseph and mother of nine children.

Benjamin Fendall – 1851–1923. Eldest child of Townshend Fendall, he became City Engineer of Baltimore. His son was also named Benjamin but was called Mason.

Carrie (Caroline) Eaches – 1837–1866. She was the eighth of the Eaches nine children. She was a devout Quaker who married Thomas G. Russell of St. Louis, had three children and died of cholera.

Charles Tackett – 1848–1910. The younger brother of Jack Tackett. Harriet was his wife, who had a son, Lawrence, but nothing was found regarding his father.

Daniel Eaches – 1832–????. The black sheep of the family. Believed by historians to have died before his father, he was actually disowned, per Carrie's letter in 1864.

Eliza Eaches – 1822–1907. She married Townshend Fendall in 1850, had four children (one died at two days old), became a staunch Episcopalian and a pillar of strength to her brothers and sister. Both her sister, Carrie, and her daughter, Nancy, named a daughter after her.

Florence Mason Fendall – 1855–1941. Ben Fendall's wife and the name of their daughter, who died of cholera just shy of eight years old.

Hector Braden Eaches – 1840–1875. The youngest Eaches, Hector was an artist who painted a much admired portrait of Robert E. Lee. He was wounded in the Civil War and ended up spending it in several federal prisons. Carrie named her son after Hector.

Jack (John) Ford Tackett – 1847–1908. Jack graduated from VMI with distinction as a civil engineer but joined his father's business to help out. It was a huge mistake and he would pay for it by living apart from his beloved wife, Nancy Fendall, for most of their married life. His letters, however, were passionate and informative. In spite of all his efforts, he died penniless.

James Eaches – 1817–1847. Eldest of the Eaches, he was not very successful as a portrait artist. He has only one letter in the collection.

John Eaches – 1835–1868. He was an alcoholic and served most of the Civil War, like Hector, in prison. After the war he found fault with every job he had and was still adrift when he died. The Eaches brothers, except Thomas, all died in their 30s.

John Edward Tackett – 1822–1910. Jack's father, he had a dry goods store for many years in Alexandria. He outlived two of his three children.

Joseph Eaches – 1794–1857. Joseph was from a Loudoun County Quaker family but fought in the War of 1812, became a flour merchant, moved to Alexandria in 1818 and was involved in a dozen organizations, including becoming the mayor from 1843–1846.

Katherine (Kitty) Brastow – 1860–???? Will Fendall's second wife, she had two sons and invested in property Will told her he owned, which he did not.

Lily Chalmers Fendall – ????–1910. Will Fendall's first wife had three children: Marion, Algernon and David.

Mary Eaches – 1820–1858. Mary's life is a mystery. The only signature here was on a will, written 10 days before she died, two weeks after her father.

Nancy Lee Fendall – 1853–1940. Nancy was the only daughter of the Fendalls. She married Jack Tackett in 1883 and turned a house he bought, in 1890, into a boarding house, in order to help pay the bills. They had three children. One – Eliza – died of cholera at 14 months.

Nancy Lee Fendall Tackett – 1887–1959. Not a misprint. Nancy's daughter was given the exact same name as her mother. She never married and actually ran the boarding house when Nancy was away and after Nancy died.

Sophie Ford Tackett Blanton – 1892–1985. Sophie was the third daughter of Nancy. Sophie married Stanley Blanton in 1918 and had two sons.

Stanley Gifford Blanton – 1890–1941. Stanley was in the army and a teacher of cadets so he was stationed all over, including in Puerto Rico, where his and Sophie's second son was born. They were in San Francisco when Sophie's mother died.

Tom (Thomas) Eaches – 1824–???? Tom married Mary or Molly in Louisville, KY and they had three children: Hester, Ewing and Kate. Hester died before Ewing was born. The Kentucky census does not list Tom after 1870 and the other two children were wards of the state in the 1880 census. Tom remained loyal to the government during the war but he and Hector remained friends though he and John did not.

Towny (Townshend) Fendall – 1813–1893. Towny married Eliza Eaches in 1849. He was an officer in the Farmer's Bank when it was closed during the Civil War. He was unemployed for five years. He sent his wife and children to Maryland during the war and wrote letters describing how the South was winning every battle and how "foreign interference" would soon join in their cause.

William Eaches – 1826–1856. William was an entrepreneur who invested in real estate. Unfortunately he did not live long enough to reap the rewards of his labor.

Will Eaches Fendall – 1856–1936. Unlike his namesake, Will was a con artist who fleeced his sister, Nancy, and their mother out of money entrusted to him. Nancy and his brother, Ben, had to sue him to receive anything. He married two rich widows – Lily and Katherine. He lied to his second wife about property but whether he cheated his first wife is unknown. Will had no children of his own that are known.

Map of Residences

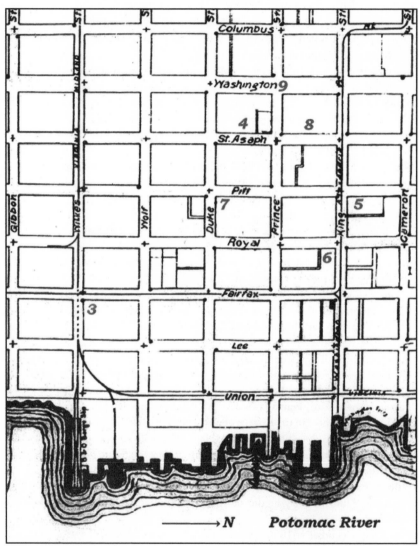

Identification of Number on Map: (1) Eaches residence, (2) William Eaches and Will Fendall residence, (3) Fendall residence, (4) Tackett residence (pictures on page 143-144), (5) Location of Tackett and Marshall Store (pictures on page 158-159), (6) 100 Royal Street Market (picture on page 17), (7) Location of St. Paul's Church, (8) Columbia Fire Company (picture on page 18), (9) Confederate Statue (picture on page 33).

Prologue

This is the true story of three generations who lived in Alexandria, Virginia from before, during and after the Civil War and World War I. It is an intimate tale of their lives and loves, told by them through hundreds and hundreds of handwritten letters they left behind, uncensored and unread until the 21st century. In effect, their diaries, where they tell of their trials and triumphs, passionate love and longing and what life was like for people who lived during those times in America. They also divulge their deception and inter–family betrayals.

In today's world of instant messaging, letters are becoming obsolete. People are communicating more than ever, but via e-mail, cell phones or other electronic devices. All those words of love, congratulations, joy and sadness are lost in the ether that surrounds us. Soldiers, as well as astronauts, "write" home by zapping their thoughts through space at the touch of a button, their words then buried in a machine with a limited capacity and life span. Finding abandoned boxes of letters covered with cobwebs is a rare occurrence today and that is a great loss to future historians, as history is lost with them.

The over 800 letters and other memorabilia were dropped off at the Local History/Special Collections Department of the Alexandria (VA) Library in 2000. From them we learned that among them were two artists, two Confederate soldiers, a mayor of Alexandria, a governor of Maryland, a banker and a dry goods merchant, Quakers and Episcopalians. We also learned of the life and times, religion, politics and philosophy, love and abiding relationships and got a look into the private thoughts of three families who survived the worst of times but rarely knew the best.

There were wills, including those listing slaves as property; locks of hair and Confederate Bonds; a land lease, expenditures (business and personal) and tax receipts; pamphlets collected from Alexandria to Europe; an inventory of estates and a division of assets; a thank–you letter from Robert E. Lee for blankets and an Oath of Allegiance from a Confederate soldier in 1865; postcards, photographs and World War I documents; wedding presents and a marriage book; and most telling of all, inter–family squabbles over money and inheritance.

The letters, resealed in their original envelopes by the passage of over a century and mixed together haphazardly, had to be read to determine if they were of any historical interest to the library. In the process they exposed an intimate insight into the private lives of these three families.

Alexandria waterfront during the Civil War.

Alexandria waterfront a few years after the Civil War.

They also revealed the lives of those who lived, loved, worked and died when we were a young nation. Not distracted by uncountable venues of entertainment and lacking modern conveniences, their daily lives were a constant struggle to survive obstacles and diseases forgotten today. In the 1800s cholera wiped out the young and old, babies died from teething, consumption felled many and people witnessed war in their back yards, not from across an ocean.

Though forays would be made to other locations, Alexandria, Virginia would be their bedrock, the home to which most would return and be buried. Seventeen–year old George Washington assisted in surveying the town in 1749. On July 13th forty–two lots were auctioned off and construction of houses began on the banks of the Potomac River but it was 30 years before the town was incorporated. By then the town had enlarged its boundaries. Some streets were paved with cobblestone but most were dirt. Keeping the streets clean was particularly difficult, since transportation was live horsepower and garbage was tossed in the street.

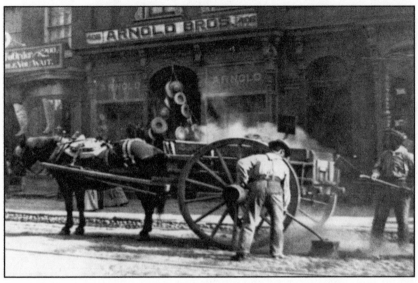

Street cleaner had a full time job as garbage was dumped in the street and horses were the method of transportation.

The city survived the Revolutionary War and helped elect their townsman as the first president of the new country. They were, however, ill prepared for the War of 1812, during which the British burned Washington, D.C. and looted stores and warehouses in Alexandria, destroying the town as a major seaport. The Civil War would take a different kind of toll, not from naval bombardment but from an invasion. Abe Lincoln was not about to leave his front door unguarded so Alexandria would become the reluctant host to thousands of Federal soldiers and would be occupied longer than any other city.

Before the first shots were fired on Fort Sumter on April 12, 1861, Alexandria had paved most of its streets, established banks and newspapers, built shipyards, foundries, a cotton factory, one of the largest breweries in the South, a furniture factory and some fine homes in which to house that furniture. It had also opened a slave market in the 1820s and by the 1830s

300 block of Cameron Street. Note the cobblestone street.

was the largest slave trading center in the United States.

Slaves picked the cotton and tobacco in the fields and slaves or servants did the cooking, washing, ironing and general cleaning in the city. No matter how fine and grand the outside of a house appeared, cooking was still done over an open fire or on a wood–burning stove or oven. Today we turn a knob to determine the temperature, from 200° to 450°, in order to correctly cook chicken, a soufflé, biscuits or potatoes, without a second thought. But how did they get precise temperatures when using coal or wood fire? And how did they maintain that temperature? The pots and pans were hung from hooks. Only the wealthy had cupboards in which to store these and refrigerators were not available even for the rich until the next century. Root cellars were used for fruit and other perishables but meat or fish of any kind had to be purchased daily at the grocers.

Water was drawn from a pump in the kitchen or from one outside. The city also installed them at various street corners, where slaves or servants would haul buckets to the pumps to fill, then haul them back to the house for cooking and washing. Or they could buy water for one cent a bucket, from "water carts," which consisted of a hogshead on two wheels, according to the *Alexandria Gazette* of April 24, 1890. As there was no running water and what was pumped was cold, bathing was not a

14

common ritual. They believed in Godliness but cleanliness was not always next to it. When Jack Tackett lived at a hotel in Norfolk he had a wash stand with a bowl, filled from a pitcher, just like he had at home.

Hotels were no different than the homes from which their patrons came. Even at Jack's handsome house in Alexandria, there was no indoor plumbing, no faucets or flush toilets. There would have been an outhouse (or privy) in the back yard and chamber pots for use indoors. If the latter were built into a stand (like a potty chair for children), they still had to be emptied each day. These accommodations, which are actually quite advanced for some parts of the world today, seem primitive to us but were what our ancestors used. Even hotels and restaurants had outhouses. The only difference was in the number of occupants each could seat or how fancy they were. Some had lids for the seat, some included smaller openings for children, some had shelves and some were not much different from the bright blue Port–a–potties one sees dotting the landscape at large outdoor events. Rich and poor alike used chamber pots, though those of the rich were usually more ornate. Before toilet paper was produced, in 1857, all kinds of material was used, including newspapers, lace, hemp, wool, even shelled corncobs. But the most ubiquitous was the Sears Roebuck catalog.

Elsewhere in the bedroom brass beds were popular, as was flowered wallpaper and stained glass lamps, which burned oil or kerosene. Velvet drapes with ball fringe, overstuffed chairs and sofas, sideboards and grandfather clocks were fashionable; so were landscape paintings or portraits. Rugs were cleaned with a broom or taken outside, hung over a clothesline and beaten, since the carpet sweeper – the precursor of the vacuum cleaner – was not yet available. Every room had a fireplace or cast iron stove, the only method for heating a house until the mid 1880s. Cooling a house was more of a problem. Air conditioning meant opening the windows but even with cross ventilation Alexandria's summers were so hot the ladies of our families spent them elsewhere.

Alexandria had – and still has – a preponderance of row houses. Even today new housing often consists of townhouses with shared side walls. The major difference is now they frequently have a built–in garage and some suggestion of a front yard. When Alexandria was built, the front door of these houses opened directly onto the sidewalk, with only one step. Most also had an outside entrance to the cellar, for delivering coal or wood.

In the 1840s and 1850s most women made their own clothing, though there were also many tailor shops. Tacketts dry goods store carried fabric, not ready–made clothing. The sewing machine was invented in 1846 but it was after the Civil War before it appeared in homes. Zippers, snaps and safety pins were unknown. Men's shirts were pulled over the head and were long enough to sleep in. They had removable collars that were washed more often than the shirts. Men's trouser's had a front flap, fastened by three buttons across the waistband. Suspenders held up the pants. Long underwear, of varying weight and tied at the ankles, was worn year round to protect legs from wool fabric. A matching ensemble of coat, waistcoat and trousers was called a "ditto suit" and did not become fashionable until late in the century. A tall or wide–brimmed hat topped off a man's ensemble and our gentlemen were sure to have had a pocket watch on a chain.

Ladies wore voluminous skirts over several petticoats, a chemise and a corset, stiffened to provide the proper shape. Pantalettes – two separate leggings tied to the leg or buttoned to the corset – were worn under the fuller skirts. Hoop skirts made these attachments necessary as the skirts tended to expose more than intended. The hoop was also a form of air conditioning, holding the heavy fabric away from the body and allowing air to circulate beneath it. The long full skirts, with or without hoops beneath them, swept the floor; they also swept the sidewalks. Petticoats were meant to hold the skirt away from the body and keep the inside of the skirt clean. Clothes were brushed or steamed many times before they were washed, as washing was a major operation, done entirely by hand over a washboard. Everything was hung on a line to dry, even in the White House. Flat irons, heated on a stove, ironed out the wrinkles.

Closets were not yet built into bedrooms. Clothes were hung in wardrobes or on hooks but even the middle class usually did not have an extensive collection of clothes. Nancy Lee Tackett may have been an exception as she had a ready supply of fabric at hand from her husband's store. All our ladies "dressed" for tea, which was a daily occurrence, and of course one had to have a Sunday best outfit, even for the children.

These were the conditions under which people lived in the 19th and early 20th centuries. Fortunately for us the only means of communicating with family and friends during those times was by letter, which is why we have the life stories of the Eaches, the Fendalls and the Tacketts. They begin in the 1830s and cover over a century. We will learn of their dreams and aspirations, their deep and abiding love, their hopes and fears and how they lived, day to day. They become flesh and blood, a combination of greed and graciousness, devotion and disgrace, passion and penitence and all the other characteristics of mankind. They also epitomize the strength and endurance people had to have to survive those times.

The birth, wedding and death dates were determined primarily by notations within the letters and obituaries. Census records were used to establish addresses and the identity of residents, slaves or servants but usually not for ages, as these were sometimes guessed by census takers. Letters are translated exactly, with misspelled or abbreviated words. Some of the spelling may have been customary at the time so "sics" have generally been omitted. Otherwise they would clutter up the story. Including all the letters would have taxed the reader, so excerpts from the most informative and revealing have been used, with the dates indicated. Letters are not numbered for, as already mentioned, not all the correspondence is used. Salutations and sign–offs are seldom included, especially if they were the same in every letter. The author also begs your indulgence for the lack of citations throughout this book. Relating the lives of the Eaches, Fendalls and Tacketts could not have been done if time were taken to cite every fact found within and there are no footnotes. Explanations are given in parentheses instead.

As you read the letters, think about how this collection came to be in the garage of the great-great-great-great-granddaughter of Joseph Eaches. How did it start? The oldest letter in the collection is from Elizabeth Dade Fendall to her husband, Benjamin Truman Fendall III, dated November 13, 1817. She was in Alexandria but there is no indication where he was located. In the letter Elizabeth bemoans: not hearing from her brother and fearing he is dead; receiving a note from the Potomack Bank which she could not pay; asking Benjamin to advertise for William, a slave; noting his sister is in bad health and she is growing sick.

So, how did that letter start it all and why did Benjamin keep it? And where? In a locker? In a drawer? He must have taken it back home with

100 Royal Street Market

him and that would mean Elizabeth would have been the keeper of the letter. Did it have some special meaning to her or was it just a coincidence the letter was kept? And why did she keep Book of Private Devotion belonging to her sister, Mary Dade, from 1836?

Even more puzzling is the next contribution to the collection, which is the only letter surviving from James Eaches to his father, Joseph, dated April 15, 1838. There is a big gap until we have an inventory of Benjamin's estate, dated November 22, 1851. (He died in 1849, one year after Elizabeth.) His will, dated June 15, 1848, was also included, as were the wills of five other Fendalls or Tacketts. Beginning this same year, correspondence started to fill whatever receptacle held all of the above. Here, too, there was no apparent arrangement to the collection, no clue as to who might have been the collector or collectors in each family, no way to know why some letters were kept and others apparently were not. And why, as it moved from one household to another, did no one take time to read any of the letters?

Among letters from Townshend Fendall are those from Carrie, Hector and John Eaches, from 1848 to 1865, along with US Government $5 and $10 bills, financial papers, diaries, Confederate Bonds and Lease of Land in Spotsylvania County. Not only did the collection gather goods from over the back yard fence of the families, it seemed to have no boundaries and when the Tackett letters were added to the mix the diversity of material exploded. But somehow it all ended up, piled helter-skelter in

Columbia Fire Company at 109 South Street Asaph. Now a fancy brasserie.

several boxes, covered with over 150 years of dust, in the garage of the great-great-great-great-granddaughter of Joseph Eaches until she dropped it off at the Lyceum in Alexandria and they brought it to Local History, where it remains today, albeit now arranged in order. All the images in the book, unless otherwise noted, can also be found in the library.

Local History/Special Collections frequently gets a box of private papers or letters kept by someone whose descendants then bring it to the library. This usually contains material from two or possibly three generations of the same family but never before did Local History receive such a vast and varied collection as this, encompassing three generations, three families and over 150 years of history. It is a story that begs to be told, so let the story begin.

Letters to Virginia

*Correspondence from three generations of
Alexandrians before, during and after the Civil War*

The Eaches

Joseph Eaches, a future mayor of Alexandria, Virginia, went off to fight in the War of 1812, even though he came from a Quaker family and was barely 18. He joined Captain Blimcoe's 57th Regiment Virginia Militia as a

private. It is not known whether this was an act of patriotism or he was after the promised bounty of 160 acres of land. *The War of 1812: Virginia Bounty Land & Pension Applicants* indicates he never applied for the land, possibly because it would have been in Arkansas, Illinois or Missouri. He returned home to Loudoun County, VA and married Ann McCormick, November 27, 1816. She was three years younger and a practicing Quaker. They had a mill in Waterford, Virginia that specialized in fine cloths, but moved to Alexandria by 1818, where he became a dry goods merchant.

Joseph Eaches, courtesy of Donald M. Robey.

Joseph wore many hats in Alexandria. He was a collecting agent for the Light House, a flour merchant, a director of the Alexandria Library Company, secretary of the Potomac Fire Insurance Company, a Worshipful Master of Washington Lodge #22, the mayor of Alexandria from 1843 to 1846 and, at the time of his death, the president of the Alexandria Canal Company. He and Ann had nine children and lived at what is now 912 Cameron Street. Ann died July 4, 1850 and Joseph on December 19, 1857. Both are buried in the Quaker Cemetery, Oaks of Ivy Hill, in Alexandria.

All of the above tells you what Joseph did and where he lived but says nothing about what kind of man he was. For that we need to read his letters. Although there is not very much correspondence from Joseph it, along with his will and other information, provides a glimpse into the kind of father he was. There is only one letter from his eldest, James, on April 15, 1838, thanking his father for "forty Dollars of United States notes" with which he will pay two weeks rent and use the remaining $22 for a few articles and his travel expenses home. James was 21, a struggling portrait artist living in New York. His dreams of staying at home would not be realized as his health forced him to move to Tallahassee, Florida. He died September 3, 1847, 10 years before his father.

Joseph would help support at least two more of his sons, William and Hector. In 1850 he assigned William the amount due Joseph "from the United States for extra compensation due to me as Collector of the Customs

for the District of Alexandria under the Act of July 1840." William was 24 and on the way to becoming a successful entrepreneur. He invested regularly in stock of the Alexandria, Loudoun and Hampshire Railroad Company and in 1853 he purchased 219 South Alfred Street, with some financial assistance from his brother–in–law, Townshend Fendall. William then renovated it and leased it as a boarding house. Unfortunately, he died of consumption (TB) February 26, 1856 but the property did not revert to Townshend until 1883 and was subsequently replaced.

Mary, probably born in 1820, also succumbed to TB, on January 2, 1858, two weeks after her father. There is no record of her being married or anything about her life. The only footprint she left in this collection is her will, written the day before she died, in which she left her sister, Carrie, $150 (equivalent to $3550 today) and brother Hector $100.

Joseph had left three tenths of his estate, after all debts and expenses were paid, to Mary. He then divided the rest amongst his other children as two tenths each to Caroline (Carrie) and Hector and one tenth each to Thomas, John and Eliza. Carrie's and Hector's shares were to be held in trust until they came of age or if Carrie married before then. The will specified the principal was to be used for their benefit during their minority, as his Executors might deem advisable. Carrie was 20 and Hector 17 by then.

Except for the provisions in his will, there is no record of Joseph helping out his daughters financially. The presumption then was they would marry and their husbands would care for them. Eliza, the second daughter, married Townshend Dade Fendall in 1850 (at 28) and seems to have been a pillar of strength to her brothers and younger sister. They exchanged dozens of long letters, many of which were descriptive of the times and the hardships they endured. She appears to have had strict rules for her children but correspondence indicates those rules were not always followed, especially by her daughter.

The birth date of Thomas Eaches, another son, is a matter of dispute, depending on what source is used. 1824 and 1833 are both given. All that is known for sure is he moved to Kentucky, married and had at least three children. One was a son, Ewing (as per his letter March 13, 1863, to "sister" stating "Just arrived. A fine boy without any name but doing well.") Unlike brothers John and Hector, he was a Union man but that did not affect the relationship between him and Hector. There are only three letters from him or his wife, Mollie, but they at least indicate he was a man of means and generous with his funds. The first letter described his circumstances. It was written on November 26, 1856 and was from Mollie:

> "Mr. Eaches was duly installed in the Bank of Louisville on Friday as chief bookkeeper with a salary of $1200 a year [equivalent to $27,386 today], he seems to be delighted with the plan and

most agreeably situated with all the Bank officers which is quite a desideratum to his happiness in business life, as nothing is calculated to insure ones health and spirits so much, as associating in the daily walks of life with agreeable companions which seem to add a charm more than anything else can do."

It is not known when Thomas died but it was probably between 1867 and 1870. He was an executor of his father's will so he was still living in 1857 but, like another brother, Daniel, he disappears from the record books available here. That's not the last we hear of Thomas, however, as he was maligned in several letters from brother John, whom Thomas would label "the prodigal son." Judging from letters from other members of the family, John could more properly be labeled the lost sheep. He was at least a thorn in his father's side, as evidenced by a note around 1855, when John was in his early 20s:

"How can you possibly act as you do? You know that for two days a policy has been wanted for Mr. Wade, but you neglect it and leave the office. Oh! My son - if you knew the anguish of heart your conduct gives me I cannot help believing you would reform. Come down after dinner. Your distraught and affectionate father Jos Eaches"

As later letters from John reveal, he never did reform. His next letter in the collection does not surface for two years so it's time to introduce the rest of the family. The third daughter, Carrie, was born in 1837 and died, suddenly,

Caroline (Carrie) Eaches (Mrs. Thomas Russell)

of cholera before her 30th birthday, leaving three children and a distraught husband behind. She poured out her feelings and news about others in her letters, including one lamenting her third pregnancy. Hector, the last of the Eaches, was everybody's darling. He became a portrait artist, like his brother James, but seems to have achieved more fame than fortune in his brief life. He was born in 1840 and died in 1875. The letters of these two provide most of the information about the family's activities.

At seventeen, Carrie's letter (April 29, 1854) to her sister, Eliza (now Mrs. Townshend Dade Fendall), was typical of teenage girls. She rhapsodized over the expensive wedding presents of Rachel, a mutual friend in St. Louis, who was married at "approximately a quarter before six" <u>in the morning</u> [underlined by author]:

"Rachel's presents are perfectly elegant. She received a handsome plated tea service, a solid silver pitcher, an elegant set of black lava from Ned Miller, a beautiful pickle stand, books, variety of spoons, fish knives, cake do [?], salt spoons & mustard, two very handsome napkin rings, solid silver crumb scraper, berry spoons, brush and comb - shell, from Maude Miller, which I suppose must have cost at least ten or twelve dollars. Cousin Charlie gave them the gas fixtures valued in Philadelphia at $50 of course here they would be worth much more. Cousin Sarah has furnished her house most elegantly, hair cloth and rose wood, thro'out. She is with out exception one of the luckiest girls I ever heard of. Cousin Sarah told me the other day she was going to give me $10, to get a handsome organdy. She and Rachel have been kind to me and seemed to be fond of me. I have tried to have nothing to do with the affair in any way, have had little to say about it to any one."

The last line does raise a tantalizing thought, especially since the nuptials were so very early in the morning. The identity of "Cousin Sarah" is not known but there was a tendency to call many "cousins," whether related by blood or not. Carrie was obviously having a grand time in St. Louis, attending receptions and a Fancy Ball, among other activities.

"Last evening I had the privilege of inviting some of my particular friends to tea. I asked five or six girls that have been kind and attentive and after tea some of my particular gentlemen friends. We had an easy and charming time, all passed off well, delightful supper, cream, water, ice cake and champaign after tea."

Perhaps one of the "gentlemen friends" was her future husband.

"Received seventy five dollars from brother Tom after constant writing and he promised to send more in a few days. I bought with it a dress and shawl, have two dollars left so you see how money flies here. My dress is very pretty double skirt barage, blue midriff, my shawl white barage, handsome deep border and fringe."

Barage was a sheer, woven fabric, made of cotton, silk or wool. Mary Lincoln used it.

On January 28, 1856, Carrie wrote to…

"…my darling Hec. It snowed here last Sunday week all day and drifted in some places as high as ten feet. Cousin Lute lost his way completely and was compelled to stop at two or three houses on the way as he said 'to gain his breath.' He gave us a most terrible account of his troubles.

"My letters 'tho not so interesting as those of my sister come often. Your letters are very pleasant I enjoy them much – I feel all the time dear brother as if I would give one of the things I prize most to see you – but one Sunday night about two or three weeks ago I felt as if I would give all my earthly possessions to see you. I felt as if I could not wait for summer to come. I miss you particularly on Sunday. I believe no changes have taken place in the family since your departure but the loss of Mary and aunt Amy to me are serious losses, for I'm sure we will never again get two such good servants."

The Eaches, being Quakers, not only did not have slaves but in the *"Slave Manumissions in Alexandria Land Records, 1790–1863"* there is a notation indicating Mary and Eliza Eaches freed a "mulatto in consideration of sundry small sums of money at various times to us paid."

On December 13, 1856, one year before he died, Joseph wrote to Hector, though it was "a great labour for me to write." Hector, not quite 17, was living in New York but still relying on his father for sustenance. He was living with friends of the family. Joseph wrote of his concerns.

"I wish you to let me know if you were admitted into the academy and whether or not you have yet prevailed upon any good artist to receive you in his studio, if you have Who? and on what terms? if you have not what is the prospect? how do you like New York? and how are you getting along in drawing? I am very feeble but for two weeks have been able to attend my office – rest of the family about as usual – present my respects to Mr. & Mrs. Sands and family – The children join me in love to you – with my prayers for your welfare. Your affectionate Father, Mr. Eaches"

Signing full names to letters, regardless of the close connection between writer and recipient, was common in all three families. The next letter from Joseph is dated March 25, 1857, addressed to "My Dear Son."

"I did not receive your letter of the 20th until this morning…I now send you herewith enclosed a draft for $60 – all your expenditures are approved and your forgetfulness about the time of the rept [repayment] of your former draft excused. It gives me heart felt satisfaction that so far I have had so much to approve and so little to complain of in your conduct and feel great confidence that you will not depart from the correct course you have so far pursued.

"I wish you to paint something handsome and such as will be pleasant to your friends. How long do you think of remaining in New York? I suppose it is scarcely necessary for me to request you to stick closely to your work and not get in the habit of being dilatory and wasting time. Do you think you will be able to paint portraits next summer for pay? Will you take any from life in New York? The health of the family is about as usual. I am sometimes better & at others worse. No great change since you left us."

On April 23, 1857, the last letter in the collection from Joseph to Hector, he wrote:

"I enclose $50 with which you will please pay Mr. Hicks and remain until the 1 of July though I would be greatly comforted by your presence at home since John is away. My health very little changed. Mary has been confined to bed three or four days, is better to day...I close in haste Affectionately Your father Jos Eaches"

Carrie confessed her desire to become a Quaker to Hector and shared the latest news about John in her letter of the 26th:

"I suppose sister Mary told you Johnnie had left us. I received a letter from him yesterday he is delighted with all the Ewings, particularly Nellie, of whom you have heard me speak so frequently. He has already lost his heart with her I believe. Says he intends going to Church with her every Sunday and has formed many other good resolutions which I hope he may never abandon. God grant that this move may be the means of saving him from eternal ruin."

[To save the reader wondering what the 'eternal ruin' is, Carrie identifies it as alcohol in her letter to Eliza June 21, 1865.]

"Dear Hec I am desirous of connecting myself with the Church (Quaker) this July but I feel such a sense of unworthiness sometimes and such a fear that I may not conform to those solemn vows that I will think it necessary to make that I am sometimes at a loss what to do. I wish you were here to tell me your experience for I feel, tho' you are so much younger, you are serving God daily in your heart, and I so frequently do worry but I pray for that Divine assistance which alone can lead me into the path of righteousness. There is not a day that the thought of my unworthiness and wretchedness of heart does not arise and bid me seek at once a rest for my weary soul – but yet I do not seem to improve for I am constantly doing something I have to regret. I have had a wish to join the Church ever since you did and I have so often regretted that I did not do it then. Oh my darling brother, I wish you were with me now. Pray, my dear brother, that the right spirit may move me to this all important step, and that I may set an example worthy of a Christian."

John now appeared on the scene in three letters to his father and sister,

Eliza Fendall. The first was written to "Pa" June 14, 1857, from Louisville, KY, where he had been staying with Thomas and Molly. He was 21 or 22 at that time.

"I recd your letter to day & must thank you for taking the trouble to write to me, as I know in your feeble state of health you write with difficulty. You remarked that you were pleased with all you had heard about me. I have started here to do well, if attention to business &c will do it & I think I will succeed, & hope I may yet be a comfort to you in your old age, & do credit to myself & family. You can rest assured that I will never go astray, though we are all human & liable to err, yet I <u>will</u> resist all evil temptations & be a <u>man</u>.

"I feel much more happy than when I had no <u>regular</u> employment, for now I know that if I don't do the right thing it is all over with me. I have a <u>character</u> & <u>name</u> to make here & I intend to do it & hope that you may live to see me a prosperous & useful citizen of Old Kentuck. My monetary affairs are at present rather in a bad condition & have had to make several small draws on my banker (Tom) with whom I have never made any deposits but he is good enough to help a friend in need."

On August 7, 1857 he wrote Eliza:

"You are aware that I am not pleased with my present employers by any means, they don't suit John, <u>sure</u>, they are two of the meanest men I have met with for some time, all they think of is that almighty dollar and whats more, how to keep it, & as to taking any interest in the welfare of a clerk, they never think of such a thing; now these

Eliza Eaches (Mrs. Townshend Fendall)

things are <u>so</u>. I have done all kinds of work since I have been with them & the more I do I find the more I have to do, so I have just come to the conclusion that I'll do no more; to give you an idea of what they <u>would</u> have me do if they <u>could</u>, but they <u>cant</u>, Goddard yesterday asked me to drive a two horse wagon to the RR Depot with part of a machine in it, which I was to help unload. I told him that I did not agree when I started with them to become a wagoner & that I most assuredly would do no such thing. He then said he had done it, I said I never had nor never would, so there it ended. I don't like to see a young man cut up & fly off for trifles & I am one who will not do it, but I thought the time had arrived when I ought, in justice to myself, to let them see that I was no lackey & that I would not do <u>anything</u> they might ask of me, no matter what. I could give you many instances of the same kind but it is needless, as I have long ago formed my opinion of the men & intend vacating the Southwestern Agricultural works of Messrs Munn & Co as soon as I can find employment elsewhere, but not until then, as 'funds' wont permit. If I can find no employment here in the fall I think I'll strike Westward ho! I understand this business very well & ought to have a good salary, or anyhow a much better one than I now receive, but I am content with what I have as I have no board to pay, but suppose I had? Whar would I be? Echo answers, whar? I answer no whar; look on the bright side my boy & 'trust to luck' you will say, well I will & I'll bet a horse I come out 'right side up.'

"'Old Kentuck,' as Mr. F calls Mollie, is well, & just one of the best little women in these parts. Tom is in high glee, having gone to housekeeping, he is rather verdant yet but that will soon rub off, they all come to John to know this that & the other. I'm head man, do the marketing & various other things 'too tedious to mention.' M says she don't know what she'd do with out me; I am glad I can do all these little things for her for she is certainly as kind to me as I could wish. . . I must stop as it is Saturday evening & I have my time book to get up, pay the hands &c. . . Yours, JM Eaches"

On May 8, 1858, John wrote to Eliza from St. Louis, MO that he had…

"…received an appointment on the Pacific RR & have every reason to hope it is permanent though I am now so used to disappointment, it seems as though I ought only to retain the place a month or so & then be discharged. Still I hope I will be able to keep the place & save a little money, a thing I have never yet been able to do. My pay will be $1.25 per day, Sundays included, I paying my own board, which will amount to from $12 to $13 per mo. I leave St L on Monday."

A letter from Thomas to Hector, 18, who is in New York and, as usual, short of funds, included comments about their brother, John. It was dated July 12, 1858, seven months after the death of their father.

"Don't talk to me about 'selfish motives.' I know you well enough boy, & that you are 'all right.' I enclose $20 with the greatest pleasure & care no more about it than so much dust, indeed I feel it to be my <u>duty</u> to help my brother who is <u>trying to get along</u> & when ever you are <u>short</u> I do assure you it will afford me real pleasure to give (or loan on your own time) whatever you may require, if I can raise it without my own creditors being kept from their dues. I am desirous of sending the first spare $50 to Carrie which I think I can do about the 1st of Aug. Dr. Ewing and myself agree that any brother who would not help another <u>is a dog</u>, provided that brother be worthy of help but really between you & I John hardly proved himself so. I heard from him at Franklin Missouri, Pacific RR some month or two ago & that is the last, & my only hope is that having 'filled his belly with the husks that the swine do eat' he may, like the prodigal son, return if not to his father's house at least to his senses.

"I will scold Mollie about not answering your letter but you may rest assured she loves you, letter or no letter. She is anxious for me to be an Episcopalian but that is not likely, as I am a Baptist in sentiment all over, if not in practice, yet whatever we may be we should love one another but love our Maker above all."

When Joseph died the family fortunes declined but, whether due to the inexperience of youth or the temptations of the big city, Hector appeared unaware of the change in financial circumstances. He was studying under a Mr. Hicks (probably Thomas Hicks, well–known contemporary painter) in New York and apparently was not as economical as his father had hoped he would be. In 1858 he moved to the Oriental Hotel, where he described the boarders as "living like fighting chickens." Money, or more accurately the absence of it, seems to have plagued him throughout his brief life. He frequently beseeched his brother–in–law, Towny, for funds (as well as his brother, Tom), until Towny reminded him his own finances were limited.

Within a year of the death of their father, Carrie and Hector went to Louisville to live with their brother, Tom. Carrie was now 21 but Hector was only 17 or 18, still subject to the decisions of Joseph's Executors. In November 1858 Carrie wrote to Eliza from Tom's house in Louisville they were having "very merry times every evening after tea. Sister Mollie plays while Hec and I dance or Hec and Tom play a game of seven–up while Mollie and I sing." All is not fun and frolic, however, as she wrote:

"…I am compelled to be quite economical. I do not like to impose upon brothers' generosity. He has already given me a handsome dress. By the way, if you can dispose of the old dress &c (which I left in your care) in a profitable way the proceeds will be very acceptable for I have but ten dollars left of my money and I wish to keep that much to <u>help</u> to pay my way to St Louis should I go."

In her postscript she added:

"Hec is very anxious to get to work. Wrote brother Towny some time ago to send his paints which have not yet been received. Brother Tom says he will write you soon. Cousin Liz of course will send you my last letter in which I give an account of the grand ball. I did not taste a drop of anything to drink, nor dance, because I desire if I possibly <u>can</u> to resist all such temptations with the desire to set a good example to those most dear to me."

Carrie obviously made it to St. Louis because on August 30, 1860 she married Thomas G. Russell of that city and had a baby girl, Dora, in July of 1861. Hector established a portrait studio at 471 Main Street, as listed in the Louisville City Directories of 1859–60–61, but on June 7th of 1861, two months after the Civil War had begun, he wrote a letter to Eliza from New York, stating:

Hector Eaches, self-portrait

"After many efforts I've at last succeeded in getting some work & am consequently in much better spirits & feel able to compose myself long enough to accomplish a letter…have been hard at work all day on a portrait which I've just commenced. Not a particularly interesting subject – a course tho' rather handsome man, with strong marked features & imposing monstrous side whiskers. I have another commission to be commenced about the 1st of the month. I have, as usual, numerous others in prospect, but if I get one order out of half a dozen prospective ones I'll consider myself fortunate. I think, on the whole, however, that things look very well for me.

"I have hopes of reaping quite a harvest this summer, from the numerous southern visitors who flock here during the summer months. I painted some time ago two or three portraits, for parties of considerable influence in Ala & Ga & they were so much pleased that they promised to do all they could for my reputation. I am happy to be able to say that in no single instance have I failed to give perfect satisfaction, not only to the parties immediately interested, but to all their friends to whose criticism my works have been submitted, since I've been here & so my patrons all predict for me a brilliant future, but I don't expect ever to be very brilliant & will be satisfied to be solid & substantial.

"With regard to my habits of life &c, I hope you will give yourself no uneasiness. I'm living a quiet, orderly life & am trying hard even to be systematic. The older I grow [he's now 21], I think, the greater my tendency to be quiet & settled, & I think I only want a moderate share of Fortune's favor, to make me comparatively happy & enable

32

me to conduce to the happiness of others, & be a correct & proper citizen."

Fortune's favor would not smile upon Hector's future. There is no letter explaining why, but on October 25, 1861, he enlisted in the Alexandria Rifles, Co A, 17th VA Infantry, C.S.A, in spite of being a Quaker, who oppose war. His brother, John, had joined the Army of Missouri in April. Both of them would become prisoners and be shuttled from one camp or hospital to another for the war's duration. The first of their wartime correspondence came from Hector, to his sister, Eliza, July 11, 1862. He was at Fort Delaware, called Fort Delaware Death Pen by Confederate prisoners. It had one of the highest mortality rates of any Civil War prison.

"The fortune of war has given me a berth in this <u>pleasant summer retreat</u> as a prisoner of war. I was wounded (not dangerously) & taken at the battle of White Oak Swamp [generally referred to as Frayser's Farm] last Monday week. It is a great consolation to me in my captivity that my misfortune has given me the opportunity of communication with the loved ones at home.

Confederate Statue

"Thus far God has mercifully preserved my life through all the dangers & hardships of the field, though I have been twice shot & have, in each successive battle, seen many of my bravest comrades fall around me. My wound is healing & my health good – the hope of seeing you all again has shed a cheering ray over my spirit in many an hour of gloom & trouble & I fondly cling to that hope.

"Please write to me immediately as I may be moved to some other place. Direct to Hector B. Eaches, prisoner of war, care of Captain A. A. Gibson, Fort Delaware. I have written 'as much as the law allows' & must close. Most affectionately your brother, Hector."

His next letter to Eliza was written July 25, 1862.

"Your kind letter of 15th came like a blessed ray from the hallowed sunshine of home to lighten the gloom which oppresses me here; the happy scenes it called to mind, the pleasant phantoms memory summoned from the buried pleasures of the past, as I lingered long upon its contents, cheered & comforted me til these pleasant fancies vanished one by one & gave place to the harsh realities around me. Since that letter I have rec'd two from bro Towny, one with regard to the box, & the other enclosing $5, for which I am very much obliged to him. Today I am in receipt of a letter from dear Carrie – imagine how it delights me – as long as I am so blest my troubles will sit less heavily upon me, & now for the information you desire –

"Thos Fitzhugh is the son of Aunt Mary Dade's sister & is from Culpepper. Dr. T enquires with regard to Wert & Vernon Ashby, R. H. Green & Stringfellow; the two former were not taken with us most probably escaped, the R. H. Green referred to, who I suppose is Robt G of our company, has been absent from us for a long time on account of sickness. There is a Stringfellow, a prisoner with us, son of Robt S of Culpepper; also, from Alex, John Horseman, son of Elijah H, lives on Royal bet King & Prince. Charles Greenwood has a widowed mother living in poverty, cor Queen & Royal, Thos Cross, son of R. Y. Cross, Wm Murry, an Irishman.

"Please advise their friends of their whereabouts if possible & see if any thing can be done for poor Greenwood's mother. These boys are greatly in need of clothes & money & have friends who could furnish them. The box was duly rec'd & I enjoyed examining its contents very much, especially little Nan's hemming [Eliza's daughter]. God bless her. Your affectionate bro, Hector."

Hector was exchanged and sent to General Hospital #7 in Richmond. A letter from John to Hector brings us up to date on his whereabouts. It was dated January 15, 1863 and sent from City Hall Hospital in Jackson, Mississippi.

"Dear Brother, I very unexpectedly met Mr. Wilmer McLean this morning and he has kindly offered to try and deliver you this, so I avail myself of the opportunity to drop you a line to let you know that I am still in the land of the living though in poor health. I am now detailed in the hospital on account of ill health, my lungs are too much effected for me to perform camp duty. I have a comparatively easy time as I have only to see that the work in the kitchen and dining room is done properly and dispense out the rations, call the roll of the convalescents daily, etc.

"I understand from Ned Miller that he delivered to my Lieut for me from you, some months ago, a letter and I was very much disappointed when I called for it to find that he had lost it. I was in the hospital at Corinth at the time and the contemptable (sic) little upstart would not take the trouble to bring or send it one mile. I have written you several times since but have never been so fortunate as to receive a letter from you.

"I joined the Army of Mo first under Genl Jeff Thompson in April 1861, was with him two or three months, all of which time had no tent to sleep under except that so much talked of 'Canopy of heaven,' which will do well enough in a dry beautiful midsummer night but to take it in April with a cold nasty disagreeable rain it is not so pleasant. Finding Jeff could not board me I concluded I would take a transfer to the 1st Mo Regt from St. L, then in the service of the Confeds and since then I have been in that Regt.

"I have written to sister Eliza today and Mr. McC. I think that he can get it to Alexa for me. I am exceedingly anxious to hear from some of you and if I can hear from you I will try to get a furlough and come on to see you, provided I can get my bounty clothing money and service pay, which in all amounts to upwards of $125.00. I have drawn no pay for some time and am rather hard up for clothing, etc. and nothing to buy anything with.

"I want to know something about the Alexa boys and what they are doing and have done in the army to distinguish themselves. I know they will do their duty. What are you doing in the army or out of it? Praying for your health, and that you may live through this glorious struggle for liberty. I remain as ever yours, John M Eaches."

Hector now wrote Eliza from Richmond, January 22, 1863:

"My joy at being released from the miseries of Fort Delaware was mingled with deepest regret at the idea of not being able to hear from you any longer as I could do while there. We departed from that delightful locality rather sooner than expected, so that I could not receive any answer to my last letter if one was written. I have read again & again those sweet messages of love I received from home & remembered how they lightened the burden of my pain & sorrow & how they seemed to me like gleams of light beaming kindly & cheeringly upon me through darkness & gloom of my spirit, from some brighter sphere.

"I have not been in active service since my capture, my wound having unfitted me for it. After my return I hobbled about here as best I could on two rough ill–made crutches for some weeks & then got a furlough of sixty days which I spent very pleasantly in N. Carolina & in Petersburg. At the end of that time I returned to report myself for duty & being considered still unfit for active field service was detailed as draughtsman in the Ordnance Dept in this city, where I have been ever since & may be kept during the winter.

I have thrown aside my crutches & walk quite well, though I can not go very far without suffering some pain from the bullet which is still in the joint of my leg.

"I am quite pleasantly situated here being in the office with one of the best boys in our company, Charlie McKnight, who was in Alex some time ago, having been captured at Williamsburg, where he lost his arm. I have a room in the house of a German doctor, where I have the finest possible opportunity of pursuing the study of German, of which I am very fond, under the auspices of an old German friend who has a room next to me & is also in our office. I talk German with him during the day & read the German pacts with him at night & enjoy it exceedingly.

"I have drawn a pleasant picture of my present life but I have not pointed to the dark shadows which, alas! have recently fallen upon it. First came the bitter faith which broke the heart of the kindest & dearest friend I had on this side of the lines & whom I loved next to my own sister & called by that fond name, because she was as a sister to me (I mean bro Tom's sister–in–law Mildred, whose mournful history you have probably heard ere this, whose noble husband Gen'l Anderson fell at Sharpsburg & whose child died a few days after), & separated her from me, she having gone home shortly after his death to her parents. And then poor Rannie Fairfax, my noblest, dearest, earliest friend was taken from me, killed instantly at the battle of Fredericksburg & I was one of those who let his dear form down into the cold grave & it seemed to me almost as if I were burying my own heart under the dull heavy cloak we threw upon his coffin.

"I had a letter from sister Mollie to day. She & all the family were well. She had heard from dear Carrie who was also well. Please send this or a copy to dear Carrie as I have only time to write one letter which must do for both. I remain affectionately Yr Bro Hector."

Carrie wrote Hector from St. Louis, on February 18, 1863 to tell him of the birth of a son she intended to name Hector. She, her husband and 19–month old daughter, Dora, are "boarding in a very pleasant family home & when I was sick no relations could have taken better care of me." Thomas wrote to Eliza from Louisville, March 13, 1863:

"As it is bed time and Mollie has retired you must excuse my brevity. I decline discussing politics [he remained a Union man] as I suppose you understand all about it from 'The Gazette.' To be sure you live on 'The Sacred soil,' but we Kentucky folks are more or less deluded with the idea that we know a thing or two as well as other folks…I am disgusted with the politicians and 'Pledged to no party's arbitrary sway I follow truth where ere it leads the way.' However, that's what everybody says. Mollie's love to all & a kiss for the children.

"P.S. Just arrived! A fine boy without any name but doing well. I am Your affectionate brother Thomas."

Among the more than 800 letters in the collection, two of them were "burn me" letters. The first of these came from Carrie to her sister, Eliza, in which she poured out her unhappiness over being pregnant again so soon. The second will come from Eliza's daughter, Nancy Lee Fendall Tackett, who was embarrassed about expressing her physical longing for her absent husband, Jack. Fortunately, neither Eliza nor Jack followed these directions and we become privy to these intimate feelings but Nancy Lee's daughter, Sophie, did dispose of her mother's correspondence and we can only guess what she might have written in them. The most poignant of all is from Carrie to Eliza in June 1863. She marked it "Private."

"Dear sister, I will try and divert my mind for a short time by writing to you tho I feel I must dwell upon the thoughts that I would wish to banish. I have been awfully sick all morning and have had no return of my monthly sickness which are pretty sure indications that I am in the same unenviable condition that I was this time <u>last year</u>. I do not know what sort of stuff I can be made of. I never before have felt so rebellious. I am getting more and more prolific every year, only thirteen months difference this time.

"I had hoped to be spared this Summer for I did suffer so much last, was so fat and growing to be quite a full habit. I weighed some weeks ago and weighed 135 lbs. Of course my present condition has not yet affected my weight for when I came from New Orleans I was still heavier. If my strength will only be increased with my weight I shall be thankful but I feel my spinal bone give way already, the lower part of the bone upon which I fell once when a child and could scarcely move for a while. It is always very weak from the beginning of pregnancy. Sometimes I can scarcely walk. Tom seems very much distressed that I have to go thru all of this suffering so soon again but I tell him if he had only given me his sympathy about two months ago it would have done me some good. It is too late now. Tho sympathy is very acceptable it cannot relieve me.

"I do not wish you to breathe this to any one. No one here knows it, tho they are all the time questioning me. Sarah happened to be spending the day here the last time I was sick and just a month after she asked me if I had had a return. I told her it was not time yet and I do not tell cousin Nell or any of the rest because they scold at me for not preventing it, and it is bad enough to have to suffer without bearing the blame of others.

"We are blest in so many respects and there is no commandment

in the Bible that would justify our keeping children out of this world, but every encouragement to multiply and replenish the earth and I begin to think sometimes that it is intended that Tom and I should colonize somewhere out here and build up a small settlement. Lamentable as it often seems to have to suffer so, we have much fun over all our babies. Some of the members of our Church seem to think I am the wonder of the age that I can accomplish so much, but I know if I trust in the Lord He will strengthen me.

"Last evening I invited all the Millers and Appletons to tea, we had a fine oyster supper, hot waffles, beaten biscuit, Sally Lunns (which I pride myself upon making), fine apple and cream with my own make of fruit cake. After tea hot whiskey punch. We had a very jolly time, they all laughed and said it was a jolly Presbyterian party. Tom has a quiet manner but he is full of fun and mischief and teases me considerable about being such a good <u>breeder</u> as poor Miss Mary used to say.

"I fear I will not see you this Summer, do not know when I will ever be in a condition to travel. I have to <u>travail</u> at home. My dear little "Leet" has been quite sick. I very much fear that weaning him will serve him as it did Braden. This is a doleful letter but I may feel more resigned to my fate by the next time I write. Please <u>burn</u> this as soon as read. Love to all from your devoted sister, Carrie."

John was transferred to Fort Delaware, as a POW. Several of his letters to both brothers– in–law (Townshend Fendall and Thomas Russell), as well as to his sister, Eliza, survive and relate what life was like in a prison camp. It is here that John displays deep animosity against brother Tom, from whom, in June 1857 he "had to make several small draws on my banker (Tom) with whom I have never made any deposits but he is good enough to help a friend in need." The following year Tom called John "the prodigal son" and hoped he would "return if not to his father's house at least to his senses." Those two fragments of correspondence are the only clues to this mystery we have.

On July 16, 1863, from Fort Delaware, John wrote Towny:

"I received your highly prized letter some time since and would have answered immediately on receipt but waited expecting daily to receive the bundle which you said you sent pr express. I am sorry to inform you that I have never seen nor heard anything of it. I feel confident that it is some where on the road for I know if it ever came to the Fort I would have received it from the Officer. I was very sorry to hear that you were out of employment and trust you may soon see a better day and live in peace and plenty again. [Townshend's unemployment situation is described in the chapter on the Fendalls.]

"I have written two letters to Tom since I have been a prisoner and can hear nothing from him. I suppose he thinks (although my brother) I deserve nothing from him but silence and contempt because he's a Union man and I a poor <u>God forsaken Rebel</u>; well 'let him rip,' I'll never bother him again while I live for any thing, all this I of course take back if he has not received my letters, but it seems strange after writing two letters I have not heard from him.

"I don't want you to send me any thing for I can get along somehow without and I am fearful you have not much to spare from what you say. I will try and weather it through with what I have until (if ever) I am exchanged, when that will be, God knows for I don't but I am afraid not soon… In haste as ever Yours JM Eaches.

To Eliza August 1, 1863:

"I rec'd your kind letter of July 19th and also $5.00 some days ago, for which accept my thanks. I was glad to hear that the bundle returned safely and can't understand who sent it back and by what authority, as it never came to this post. I rec'd a box of clothing from Carrie to day exactly suited to my wants, so I am at last comfortably fixed in the clothing line, though I am sorry I did not receive the handkerchiefs that dear little Nannie hemmed for me. I would have appreciated them highly, tell her I thank her for her kindness to 'Uncle Jonnie.' Tell Ben to write to me. Am truly glad Hec is in a good situation and thank God his life has been spared doubtless for a good purpose. I trust Mr. F has employment by this time or soon will have. I trust I may some day have it in my power to repay partly if I can his many kindnesses to me, would that our brother Tom were more like him. I cannot help speaking thus, Tom has treated me as no brother of <u>feeling could</u> treat another, have never heard a word from him, expect I never shall, the day may come when he will regret it. Love to all, as ever yours JM Eaches."

To Thomas Russell, on August 1, 1863, he wrote:

"I received your esteemed letter of 24th and also the clothing &c, for which accept my sincere thanks; the articles sent exactly suit my wants even to the fine comb which I doubt not dear Carrie put in, tell her I am sorry to say I made use of it immediately on receipt, and found it an admirable weapon with which to attack the creeping foe. I killed and captured the whole community at one fell swoop! should any again appear I shall exterminate the race entire.

"My health remains 'in status quo' am thin and poor in flesh but am thankful that my health is as good as it is when I see so many others worse off. Carrie and I have or had a <u>brother</u> in Louisville Ky,

I want to know if he has forgotten <u>her</u> as he has <u>me</u>. I wrote to him <u>twice</u>, before troubling you or Mr. F concerning my situation, have received not a <u>line</u> from him. He could have let known at least that he had no longer a brothers feeling for me. Your friend JM Eaches."

To Eliza on September 19, 1863:

"We rec'd orders late this evening to be prepared to leave in the morning, whither we go I know not, but hope to 'Dixie' for exchange. I think it probable that we will only be removed to some other place better adapted for wintering prisoners than this, this of course is only surmise of my own as none of us know certainly anything concerning our destination; should we still be kept in the Federal lines I will let you hear from me on my arrival at our next prison. Should we be exchanged I shall not have the pleasure of your correspondence, which has been a source of great pleasure to me during my imprisonment and although I shall not have that pleasure I would rather be denied the pleasure than to remain in prison to enjoy it."

[Mail could be sent and received between Alexandria and Federal prison camps or from Union soldiers but those in confederate territory, be they friend or foe, could not communicate because Alexandria was occupied by the government. If John were sent back to the Confederate Army he would not be able to write to or hear from his family any more.]

"I know you will ever think of and pray for your brother and forget and forgive him many errors. I trust I may be spared to see you 'Towny' and the dear children again, should we not meet on earth, God grant we may meet in a better world. Mr F has been a brother to me indeed, even more than one, for I am sorry to say that Tom has proved himself <u>less</u>, have never had a word from him; shall never forget the <u>unkindness</u> of my brother and will always remember the kindness of my true brother 'Towny' with pleasure Affectionately your, JM Eaches."

By September 22, 1863, John was at Point Lookout, Maryland, a newly constructed POW camp situated at the junction of the Potomac River and Chesapeake Bay. Originally a resort area the site was leased to the government in June 1862. Officers lived in the former hotels and cottages while POWs were housed in tents. There were nearly 4000 POWs there. It was an especially brutal place to be in winter. "According to official records, between November 1863, and February 1864, more than 540 southern men confined at Point Lookout perished from their new environment." *Portals to Hell: Military Prisons of the Civil War* by Lonnie R. Speer.

John wrote Eliza:

"I wrote to you a few days ago from Fort Delaware informing you that we would leave there the next day, which we did, and arrived here yesterday after a pleasant trip on salt water. I was much surprised and gratified to meet some of my old Alex friends here who belong to the VA army, they inform me that Hec is yet in Richmond and all speak highly of him. I wrote to Carrie, informing her also of my intended departure. I wrote to her some time before informing her that I stood greatly in need of various articles, among them a pair of shoes and a hat. In my last letter I told her she need not send them and that if she had she could write and have them returned, or forwarded to me if I was not to be exchanged; for fear I should not receive them. I would like very much to have a pair of No 8 shoes, some heavy cotton socks and a hat. I see the boys receive various kinds of 'nice things' in the eating line, and as you made the offer to send me something in one of your letters, when I was sick, I will accept it now and think I can enjoy it better, as my health is good compared with what it has been; have no idea of course how long we will remain. Address Company E (prisoner of war) 3d Division, Care Capt Patterson Provost Marshall Point Lookout Md. As ever yours JM Eaches."

October 1, 1863, again to Eliza:

"I rec'd your note and the articles I requested yesterday and assure you that they were thankfully rec'd. The shoes are just the thing and will do me all winter. Have not had the pleasure of encasing my feet in such a pair for many a day. I divided with at least a half dozen Alexandrians who have been exceedingly kind to me, among them Mr Kidwell and Mr Taylor who were small boys when I left home. They would not let me pay for my own washing or rather would not let me wash my clothing but had it done for me. I sincerely hope Mr. F will get into some business yet and that times will be as they once were with you. I would rather by far that I could lend you a helping hand than to have to call upon you in your present circumstances for favors, and trust that the day may yet come when I may be able to reciprocate.

"You remarked that you thought this a more healthy place than Fort Delaware. I like it in every respect far better, the water and 'grub' is better and things much nicer than at Fort D. We have more ground to walk about, it seems less like a prisoners camp than any place I have yet been confined to, the Officers too and men seem to grant us all privileges in their power, we take a bath daily in the bay if we wish, which I do, and I find it beneficial both to health and cleanliness. Of course it also plays the mischief with one of the soldiers greatest enemys, 'grey backs,' or body lice of which I am now entirely rid."

On October 26, 1863, John wrote:

"I hasten this evening to drop you a line as letters after this date will not be allowed to be sent, though of course you can, I suppose, write to me. The mail will be only stopped for a short time but should you not hear from me you will know the reason."

Then, on November 2, 1863, he wrote Eliza:

"I wrote you a few days ago stating that the mail had been discontinued for a time. I now write per Mr Taylor, formerly of Alex, who will mail this in Baltimore if it is permitted to go. Continue to write to me, and let me know if Tom knows whether I am here or not and if he ever rec'd either of my letters. I wrote to him you know when I was suffering for clothing. If he did hear from me I want to give him a piece of my mind, he has acted in a pitiful manner. I will be pleased on receipt of a heavy rough blanket, never mind how old. Yours JM Eaches."

To Eliza again, December 2, 1863:

"…sending something to eat, send it, and nothing else. It will be very acceptable at the present time, as none of my 'mess' have had any thing from home for some time. They have been receiving plenty of 'good things' from home until lately and of course I shared with them. Send no bread as it is apt to spoil before it arrives. Here is what I want, any Butter, Tobacco, Cheese, Coffee (ground) and anything else that will not require cooking that you see fit. I have a <u>very bad</u> cough it troubles me much at night. Am glad to hear from Hec. I wrote to him for flag of truce, have had no answer. I got $5.00 from the Provost M for the boots as I was not allowed to receive them. Aunt Mary sent me a coat and pants & $5.00. I could not wear the pants, too small. As ever affectionately Your JM Eaches."

On December 21, 1863, John wrote:

"I am happy to inform you that I expect to leave in the morning for 'Dixie,' several Alexans leave with me. I don't know whether there is to be a general exchange or not, only about seven or eight hundred are going as I understand. Out of forty six men captured from my Reg't (1st Mo) there are only <u>four</u> of us left to return to Dixie, the others all having taken the oath. I would like to hear from you if I get safely back to 'Dixie,' a letter addressed to me at Richmond would be forwarded to me. I do not intend to return to the western Army. I shall apply for transfer to the VA Army when I arrive in Richmond, suppose you can write per flag of truce."

Aboard the "Flag of Truce boat" near City Point, VA, December 26, 1863:

"I am aboard the boat bound for Dixie, expect to be in Richmond to day, spent Christmas aboard with soldiers 'grub' for my Christmas dinner. How different from Christmas' past, but would not have asked to have spent it more pleasantly as the thought of my return to my dear old native state was pleasure enough after a captivity of over seven months. I wrote to you the day before I left Point Lookout, that I expected to leave, requesting you to write to me at Richmond. I would like to hear from you. I never heard a word from Tom during my imprisonment."

This will not be the end of John's incarceration nor the end of his problems. At this point a letter turns up from Carrie to Eliza, dated February 12, 1864, in which a mystery figure appears – a man identified simply as "D." In reading all the letters chronologically it was easy to become familiar with the nicknames and abbreviations used to designate family members but there had never been a reference to anyone as "D," until now. The answer may lie in the unwritten past. In the Eaches family tree a son, Daniel, appeared in 1832, then vanished from the record books. All researchers presumed he died at a young age, since he was not listed in Joseph's will, which included everyone else. But suppose, instead, he had left the bosom of his family and committed something to bring shame on them and had, for unknown reasons, suddenly reappeared in their lives. Suppose he was not the prodigal son but the profligate one who did not die before his father but was deliberately disinherited. It would explain the trepidation both sisters felt at his reappearance.

"My dear sister, I rec'd your letter yesterday enclosing one from D – and was really surprised, could not have been more so if we had received intelligence from one whom we knew to be dead. As regards my writing, I am very indifferent except on your account and I do not see why a letter from you writing what you advise me to write would not do quite as well, if not better, than from one from me. I wrote him <u>five years</u> ago and he took no notice of it until now. Still I would gladly correspond with him if I felt I could do him any good. I will write just as soon as I can and tell him as you say, tho I think it just as incumbent upon you to write for thro me he must know you are still in Alex if I say 'it is doubtful whether you will remain there' as you state. And now he must know of my whereabouts and is as likely to visit me as you if he were reformed.

"I know not that he is improved and dread the idea of beholding one who has brought such trouble upon us and thru whom we have dearly loved. He seems to take it for granted that all things are just as when he left us. It is sad to see how little he is prepared for these great changes. I suppose the uncertainties of the future seldom trouble him. It seems strange how such characters turn up. They are like bad pennies but God in his mercy no doubt spared them that they may turn unto him and live.

"Oh! How rejoiced I would be to know that those of us who are left were his own children. I do feel so much every day I live the vanity of all things earthly. If we have nothing to make us happy there is always something to cloud and darken our pathway. I do wish I could live alone for Heaven that all that I do and say could be with the view of glory for my Maker instead of for our own comfort and gratification. I want to live most for Christ and try to be nearest to him but I find time to do but little except for those immediately around me, tho if I do my duty faithfully and with the right spirit towards my own, God will approve it tho I might do that and more as others have done.

"I have not been well for several days. Have been suffering much with piles and such a weakness in the lower end of my spirit that I limp all the time, do not pretend to walk much even about the house. I do want to see you all so much sometimes, but will never be able to go without Tom, tho he gives me permission to go yet would be very disappointed if I should really make up my mind to go without him for he often speaks of ladies here who leave their husbands to go East as not caring for them or they would not go.

"I do hope you will not allow yourself to be troubled in regard to D, tho I know how you feel there where you are, surrounded with so many sad associations. I do wish you could have some change of scene. It would do you so much good. If Tom were only rich I should just send on a few hundred and bring you all out to spend the summer. We have not got a house yet but are looking out for one. Tom wants much to get fixed. He is fearful I may have a frolic in the wrong quarters. Much love to dear brother and the little ones. I should be perfectly easy as regards D. I do not believe he will venture home. Ever your devoted sister, Carrie."

If this is, indeed, the missing Daniel it explains why all the amateur and professional genealogists in the past 125 years have not been able to find him. **They didn't have this letter.** It was dumped in a box, along with hundreds of others, then kept in various basements, attics or garages while its contents were forgotten, its writer had died and was buried, until it finally resurfaced in 2000. And that's why old letters are so valuable.

Hector reappeared on the scene. It was October 23, 1864 and he was in Richmond, hard at work revising and correcting his painting of General Lee, which is apparently being received with "unqualified approbation of most of the Richmond critics, & several 'gentlemen of the press' & also a number of Genl Lee's intimate personal friends & staff officers. They have done me the honor to pronounce it the best picture of the Genl that has been painted." He wants to keep it on exhibition until it becomes known, thereby increasing its value.

> "I was very glad to learn from your letter that John had started out to try & do something for himself, tho' I'm afraid Baltimore will present fully as many temptations for his weakness as Alex. I rec'd a letter from him written from King George & wrote one soon after, to meet him in Baltimore as he desired. I wrote what I thought best calculated to appeal to his manly pride (which I believe he has in some degree, appearances to contrary notwithstanding), & to arouse whatever there may be of slumbering ambition within him, tho' I believe nothing anyone can say is likely to have much effect in such cases. Words have but little weight, in the moral balance, against passion & habit.
>
> "I rec'd a long & very agreeable letter from Carrie the other day, it breathed a very cheerful spirit. It is a great comfort to know she is so happy & comfortable in her married life. She sent me a picture of herself, which discovers scarcely a trace of the revolving years. It seemed to me much the same face that smiled upon me eight or ten years ago. I would judge from it that she was quite fat & in excellent health. I wish I could hear that your health was equally good. I hope your indisposition is only the effect of trouble & excitement & will soon pass away."

On March 30, 1865, 10 days before Grant and Lee met at the Appomattox Court House, he wrote to Eliza:

> "Mrs. Meade expects to leave here for the north tomorrow & I profit by the occasion to break the silence which has so long existed between us & which has kept me in a state of painful suspense about you all, which is only occasionally relieved by favorable reports of persons coming through the lines. I have written you several letters before which I was satisfied you never received & I had concluded there was very little satisfaction in writing & never even knowing if the letters were rec'd. Truly between us there is a 'great gulf fixed.' I cannot but repine at the stern necessity that separates us so widely.

"God grant it may not be long. It is so strange to think that we have not seen each other for seven long years. Alas, we must all have changed in that time but the children particularly. I'm afraid I should hardly recognize my little Nannie in the half grown girl, or my little nephew Willie in the stout boy that I might expect to see now, if I could be at home again. As for Ben I suppose he is quite a man & recognition in his case would be entirely out of the question. Can't you find some means of sending some photographs by which I may familiarize myself with faces which, dear as they are to me, time must have rendered almost entirely strange? I haven't seen a picture of you or any of the family to console me for the pain of absence.

"I have now a very pleasant position in the Engineer Corp as draughtsman & asst & am getting along very comfortably, being well clad & well fed, which is as much as a soldier ought to expect. John is here too, in hospital. Of course I see him often, tho a deep ravine which separates the one of 'seven hills' on which he is, & my abode, renders a trip from one to the other quite an undertaking & forms no small barrier to our intercourse. I'm sure he would have written too, but I have been unusually busy for some days & could not find time to let him know Mrs. M was going. He is constantly talking of home & consoling his spirit with blissful imaginings of a happy reunion of those who are still left to make life dear. His health, tho still bad, is much better than at the time of his return from prison. His return, by the way, was entirely unexpected to me at that time & you may imagine my surprise & emotion when a man whom I did not, at first, recognize (he was so changed by time & disease) walked into my office one day & proclaimed himself my brother, but gradually his face became more familiar & now seems to me about what he was seven years ago, except for ill health. I am still unable to exert my leg very much without pain. Sometimes it troubles me a good deal but I'm very fortunate to get off as well as I did with it. The ball is still in the knee but I have good use of the leg."

From John, in Richmond prison April 15, 1865:

"I am again a prisoner of war, was sick in the Hospital when the city surrendered. I am yet at the Hospital but understand will have to go to Libby prison tomorrow or take the oath. I prefer the former. Hector is in our lines somewhere safe he was well when I last saw him the day before I left."

He took the oath May 20th.

Libby prison originally housed Union prisoners and shared its reputation with the infamous Andersonville. After Richmond fell to the Federal Army

46

the prison was used as a depository for Confederate POWs. Hector had moved on to Charlotte, N.C., as indicated by his letter to Eliza of May 25, 1865.

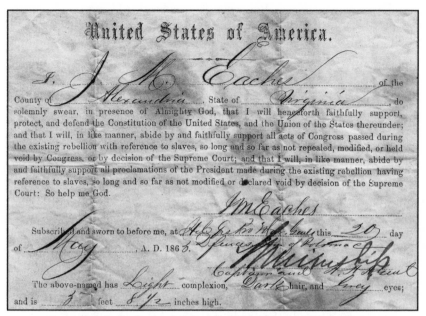

Oath of Allegiance taken by John M. Eaches, May 20, 1865.

"After a long wearisome journey from ill-fated Richmond & the painful experiences that usually attend refugees from oppression in these days of trial & misery in the land, I finally arrived in this place, weary & heart–sick as you may imagine, & here I have been ever since, finding it impossible to get across the Mississippi as I expected. I am here, as it were, by the force of inertia, existing almost as a thing without volition. The dearest hope of my soul crushed out I have little heart for any thing just now. I have no definite plans for the future but I do not think this country can hold me long if I can get the means to leave it. I have still visions of Italy & art & it may be an occasional recurrence of those silly boyish hallucinations about fame etc. At any rate I think if I could get to Europe & bury myself in the study of art I might in a measure forget my country's humiliation & my sorrow & feel that I had some object in life which I can't feel here because I have no longer an interest in the country except that which binds me to family & friends & what comfort I may derive from that is only by sufferance.

"I have heard nothing of John since I left Richmond. I am very anxious to hear from him particularly as I did not have time to see him before I left, the move was so sudden, but I expect you have seen him before this point. I don't think he could have come in this direction, & if paroled in Richmond he would be likely to go to Alex. I believe there is no regular mail to this place yet, but suppose there will be soon. I send this by a friend to be mailed in Richmond. I do hope it may reach you. Ever your devoted brother Hector."

On June 12, 1865 Hector again wrote to Eliza:

"I wrote you two or three weeks since. As I mentioned in that letter, I have no definite plans for the future but my chief desire, at present, is to leave the county & to that end I shall work if I can find employment but the country is so nearly impoverished by war & the existing 'law of the land' that I fear it will be a long time before art will flourish to any extent in this atmosphere. Seeing some prospect of patronage here, I think of staying some weeks & then if I find it unprofitable I will try Richmond where I have many friends & would probably be more successful.

"The hard experience of the past four years & my present adversity have rendered me quite practical & prepared me to leave the dreams of Fancy for stern Realities. I cannot but feel that the prospect before me is rather a dreary one. The path of my future life is likely to prove rugged & toilsome I think. In the present state of things it will require a struggle, perhaps, to live & much more, to satisfy the demands of an ambition, natural to my age & profession. However, now that I have, in a measure, recovered from the kind of mental paralysis which I felt in common with many other devotees to the cause of Southern Liberty, upon its sudden ruin I feel prepared for whatever may be before me & stand, like David Copperfield, with an imaginary axe, ready to hew down the great trees in any reasonable–sized 'Forest of Difficulty.'

"...I am very anxious to see you all but don't know when it may be convenient or advisable for me to go to Alex. I have heard nothing from there for a long time & know little about the state of things, the number & temper of the union people, the policy of the yankee authorities towards southern people, etc. I hope you will soon enlighten me on these points. Tell me something of Carrie when you write. I am very anxious to hear from her. Have you seen or heard from John? I left him in the hospital in Richmond & was unable to see him, my departure was so sudden & unexpected. I supposed he went to see you after the yankees came in but have felt much anxiety about him.

"I have just recd a most affectionate letter from sister Mollie, written nearly two months ago, a few days after Gen'l Lee's surrender. She begs me to come to Louisville & live with her & writes with so much earnestness that under different circumstances I would go but as it is I could not reconcile my mind to the idea of going back there. I should be so glad to hear from brother Townie personally. When you write, send letters as far on as possible by private opportunity, if you have any, as I hear the mails are very uncertain. Please write several without waiting answers, that I may at least get one. Hector."

Judging by Carrie's next letter to Eliza, written June 21, 1865, it didn't take John long to revert to his old habits, once he took the oath and was released from prison. Carrie's 10–page letter indicates Tom is not doing very well, either, and Eliza's husband, Towny, is still unemployed. Carrie's third child, a daughter, named after her sister, Eliza, is one year old.

"My dear sister, I was greatly pained to hear of our poor unfortunate brother's conduct. I had looked for it but not to the extent he has gone. Such base ingratitude I never knew. I just took a hearty cry, just to think of your having all this to bear with your numerous other troubles. I have not the least patience with John. There is no reason in him, he only came home to talk of his being anxious to see us and loving us so much and then returned to disgrace us. Had I known he was acting in this way Tom [her husband] should not have sent him one cent. He does not deserve a place to lay his head. What is there in our brothers that induces them to act so!

"I feel sometimes when I think of all we have passed thro as if I could send every drop of liquor into the river. I can assure you I shall not write to John about the money nor do I wish one cent more spent for him. If he has determined to be a vagabond let him be one. It nearly breaks my heart to think of his course, but God I feel knows we have done all that we could and He in His mercy has spared his life and brought him back to friends who would do all they could for him but I am sure none of us have means to throw away on him. It is just as much as Tom can do to support his immediate family, increasing as rapidly as it is, and assist his father when he can, but we are willing to do all we can for the boys if they are deserving. We would deny ourselves comforts to gratify them.

"Tom is very anxious to have Hec come out here, thinks he would do well and he would forward money to pay his way out. Tom often reminds me of dear brother Towny, he is too generous for his means and a great hand to go around and repair things and make little conveniences. He says if John were to come to the city he would just see him on a boat and persuade him off or force him off, that he would not allow him to come to the house at all to annoy me, that he knows I could not stand it and I am sure he would for he has no sort of patience with or sympathy for such characters.

"I never want to see him again unless he reforms and there is less

hope of one reforming from drunkenness than from any other vice. I am very sorry you ever allowed him to return until you knew he had reformed. I feel that I have borne enough of his conduct in other days. Alexandria has been the cradle of all our woes.

"As to brother Tom's assistance he is a good deal worse and I guess has spent all he has. I do not know how he is doing now but a year ago when his wife was here she was about to separate from him. I do hope that dear Hec may be able to resist all such temptations, that God will strengthen him and throw about him the everlasting arms of love when in the way of sin. Dear boy, he has his peculiarities but I hope he will never have this vice. We must do all we can to keep him employed for Satan oftimes leads captive those who are unemployed.

"Give much love to dear brother. I do not see how he can keep up his spirits as well as he does. I am very well for me just now and am soon to have the trial of losing an English nurse who has been with me but one month and I am delighted with her, like her better than any I have ever had with one exception, but my troubles are nothing to yours. I really do not see how you can endure your trials, dear sister.

"Tom sends much love and sympathy to you all. As to my not telling him anything, we do not keep a single thought one from the other. You cannot imagine two persons more devoted and wrapped up in each other than we are. He said yesterday he felt sometimes that he was making too much of an idol of me and if I should die he would want to be buried in the same grave. Now I know he is sincere for he seems to live for me alone. His children are always secondary. He says if I should go away from him a week he would be perfectly unhappy. Oh I am blest in such a husband. You know I am so dependent upon love, tis my very live. Your devoted sister, Carrie."

Carrie's husband now sent word to Hector, August 23, 1865:

"Carrie is especially desirous for you to come out to St. Louis to live & set up in your profession, in all of which I most heartily agree with her, think this is a fine opening for you, the leading artist De Franca having lately died, offers a fine chance for one of your attainments. We will be only too happy to have you put up at our house and make yourself perfectly at home should the 'needful' not be at your finger ends we will open a 'borrow & loan a/c' if you say so.

"This is to be (is now) in a very short time the New York of the west & it is therefore in my estimation the place for you, besides you will make many sympathizing friends, especially if you bring that picture you left behind at Richmond along with you. Think you would have your hands kept full duplicating it & which would be an opening for other items. We heard you were the most popular man in Richmond amongst the fair sex. If you were here would doubtless do you no harm. At all events you are at liberty to make merchandise of such material when you can.

"It is a cause of much gratitude that you were spared thro the danger & forces of the past four years & although it not be worth emotions of pleasure that you look back upon them, still let us hope that the future in the happy circumstances in which you may be placed you may with more readiness be enabled to forget the past & all that has been disagreeable attaching to it. Let us hear from you at a very early day – Yr brother, TG Russell."

Hector, back in Richmond on September 15, 1865, informs Eliza:

"I have at last arrived in this place safe & sound. I have been expecting to come here for the last month & that is why you have not heard from me before. As the mails between here & Charlotte are so unreliable I thought I'd better wait & write from here. I rec'd only one letter from home while in C – & that was from John. Tell him if I don't see him soon (which I expect to do) I will answer.

"I rec'd a kind letter from Carrie & also one from Mr. Russell, asking me to come to St. Louis. I think strongly of going as besides the pleasure I should have in seeing Carrie again, it would probably be a fine opening for me in my profession as Mr. R. says he knows I would meet with every encouragement, especially with my portrait of Genl Lee, which the critics of the city have done me the honor to say is the best ever taken of him. If I go to St. L. I will stop in Alex to enjoy the pleasure that I have been so long looking forward to, that of seeing you & your family. I hope to see you any how soon, but for the present you know, I must go where there is a probability of my making something.

"I sold one picture of Genl Lee in Charlotte for $200 [$2680 today] but my expenses for board &c. there & clothes &c. have nearly exhausted that. I want to stay here some time yet to get a portrait of Genl Johnson, who is here. He has promised me a sitting. I may also be able to sell some copies of Genl Lee. Of course I will be at considerable expense here & as I have little money I will ask you to get brother Townie to send the value of my stock, if it is worth anything. If not I may be able to raise enough to go on, for the present somehow. I can borrow what I want here if I choose, but don't like to.

"And now, my dear sister, I will take this occasion to prepare your mind for some apparent changes in my life & character, which I have hesitated to speak of before, perhaps from a sort of moral cowardice, because the subject was unpleasant to me & I did not know how much more so it might be to you & now I do not know how the honest statement I am going to make to you may effect (sic) you towards me, but I must do it any way.

"As you know, when I was about fourteen or fifteen, without experience in life & with little judgment of my own, I connected myself with the church, under the influence of one of those hallucinations of mind to which very young people are too often subject. I have since discovered in myself tastes & feelings, entirely at variance with religion & have long since determined, after careful consideration, that honesty required that I should no longer profess what I could not feel, nor wear the guise of Religion without her spirit & now, should we meet, you may expect to see in me neither saint nor an infidel nor quite a <u>monster</u> either, I hope, but a plain rather good hearted youth, fond of society & pleasure & in most respects like other youths of his age & condition whose best moral quality, perhaps, is a desire to be honest & who prays that whatever else he may be, he may, at least, never be a hypocrite. & now, dear sister, with much love to Bro. T. & family, believe me, as ever, your affectionate Brother Hector."

Apparently Eliza, an Episcopalian, was dismayed over Hector's decision to leave the Quaker Church, though her letter is not among the collection. In his response to that letter, written October 2, 1865, he tried to allay her fears about any changes in his personality due to his leaving the Quakers. He also expressed his wish he could be of more help to her regarding John. It is an incredibly forthright and caring letter.

"I was much pained to learn from your letter that you were in so much trouble & particularly to think that I should have contributed to the measure of your sorrow. Do not, I pray you, my dear sister, torture yourself unnecessarily on my account tho heaven knows I do not pretend to have anything to boast of in the way of morals, yet I think I may venture to console you with the assurance that my case is not so dreadful as you seemed to imagine, to judge from the first part of your letter.

"I am not the slave of any bad passion or habit, except such minor ones, perhaps, as procrastination. I believe I have passed that age when such influences are likely to gain sway over the mind. I think I may say without flattering myself much, either, that my habits are quite as common as those of numbers of young men whom I see every day doing things that I could not reconcile with a Christian devotion & who are yet very regular in their attendance at church & at the communion & apparently zealous in all the external exercises of religion, bear a good reputation & are regarded as great sources of spiritual comfort to their devoted parents & sisters.

"I might live in the same way & my kind, confiding sisters be none the wiser but this is a role in the drama of life, to which I could not school my heart if I would. I have no wish to deceive myself or anybody else into a false belief as to my spiritual condition. I have not been able to shut my eyes to the fact that my tastes & feelings, as well as my actions, were not consistent with the Christian profession & therefore I have long since ceased to make such profession as the only honest course for me to pursue.

"I cannot help regretting deeply that I was ever led into a false conviction on this subject, tho I can hardly consider myself responsible for what I did, through the influence of the sincere but mistaken zeal of others, when I was too young, really, to judge for myself. But let us drop this subject now, dear sister. It is painful to me because it seems to be so to you. Let us drop it then, with the assurance on my part that you shall not find me a less devoted brother, because I have the misfortune not to be the pure Christian your fond fancy pictured me.

"I have been thinking, ever since I read your letter, how I could help you in your troubles, particularly about John. I don't know what can be done with him now, but one thing is certain – he must not be allowed to distress you any longer. I'm afraid he is without principle or feeling. If I could raise the money I would come home & send him off somewhere myself &, if necessary, go with him. I may be able to sell my picture here & if I do, I will come at once & do what I can. If I could come now I would only be another burden to you (for I've no idea that I could make any money in Alex) & heaven knows you have enough.

"How is your health now? I do trust you may regain that at least soon. How is brother T's foot? I hope it improves. I hope he did not allow my stock business to trouble him. I had no idea how he was afflicted or I should never have mentioned it. It has occurred to me that if he should be able to get it, it might help to get John off somewhere. I would gladly give all I can scrape to that end for I know that as long as he stays in that town he will do just as he does now. He often spoke of going west again during the war. Said that country suited him exactly. It would be well to remind him of the charms of western life, I think & if we can, get him back there, where he can't trouble anybody but himself. I will certainly do all I can to accomplish it.

"I believe I would like you to send this letter to Carrie, if you choose. I would like her to see the first part of it as I wrote to her on the same subject & have been so long without an answer that I don't think she rec'd it & I don't care to write again about it but I want you both to learn to think of me as I am, not as I ought to be, before we meet. Adieu, with love to all from Your affectionate Brother Hector."

John seemed unable to comprehend the negative feelings his siblings had toward him and his drinking for he continued to pursue their financial assistance to help him find employment. From Lothian, in King George County, MD, on October 10, 1865, he wrote Eliza:

"I arrived here, after a pleasant ride, on Wednesday last and will leave this morning for Baltimore, where I hope to be able soon to find employment. Ashton does not want me to leave him. He has made me a first rate offer, which I certainly will accept if I can raise about $300 [equivalent to $4100 today] by spring. His offer is this, I am to furnish a team of two horses & one plow only, he furnishes two teams, one ox & one horse team. He also has four work hands who will be supported out of next year's crop. He feeds them and furnishes everything until our next year's crop is made. I am to be at no expense, other than the team & plow, this year. I think we could do well and 'all hands' are pleased with the proposition. The servants are all fond of me, as Ash says, and want me to come. I could not do better, you see we have no hire to pay the servants, only feed and clothe them, which does not amount to a great deal in the country. Ash seems to be very fond of me and says there is no other man with whom he would be willing to live. Ashton has to leave this place by Jan 1st, he has already rented another beautiful place, near the Rappahannock, which contains about four hundred acres, two hundred of which is open land & very rich. He will move in a short time and wants me to return soon and help him to move and fix up the farm. He rents his own farm out as there is no comfortable dwelling on it.

"I am fearful from what I hear that it will be a very difficult matter to get a situation in Baltimore, but of course I will try. If I do not succeed I shall return to King George. Ask Mr. Fendall if he knows of any one from whom I could borrow $300. I can give 'first rate' security. Ash, who you know, is worth five times that amount, will endorse for me so the party lending it will be perfectly safe. I would want it for one year from about the 1st of Jan 66. I am confident I can make the money and if I do not raise the amount I will not be able to accept Ash's offer. I will never have a better chance. If I succeed and go with him next spring, we will lease the farm for four or five years. Mr. Turner, the owner, has agreed to let us have it for that length of time if we wish it.

"I have I think started with the determination to do the right thing. All I ask is a start and as I expect to work hard myself I am not fearful of not doing well. Other men are here renting land, with not half of the advantages which I would have, and are making a good support and money, and I <u>know</u> with energy, sobriety and industry I am <u>bound</u> to succeed. [Of course, it is his lack of sobriety that is the root of his problems.] A farmer's life is the one I wish to lead. I know

I would not be contented in town. It has been my intention to settle in the country and had I obtained a situation in town I only would have held it long enough to have made money enough to buy me a team & plow.

"I wrote quite a long letter to Hector on the 8th and expect an answer on my arrival in Baltimore. I addressed him at Richmond, where I suppose he is. I would like very much to see him before he goes west and may possibly go to Richmond if I do not succeed in obtaining employment in Baltimore. My love to Mr. F. and the children. Say to Mr. Fendall that he will confer a favor if he will find some one who will let me have the $300. I will of course give my note with Ash to endorse. I can give other security, perfectly good if required. I do not expect to remain in Balto more than a week so you will please answer immediately. My address is Care of Smoot Harbersham & Barrett, No 79 Exchange Place, Baltimore. John"

Hector's response to John's letter is quite a contrast to his previous comments about his brother's chances of improving his lot in life. On November 27, 1865 he wrote Eliza:

"I had a letter some time ago from John. It was chiefly about a business arrangement he proposed he enter into with his friend Ashton Dade, which depended on his getting a wagon & team, upon which Mr. D. proposed to give him an interest in the profits of his farm, John to assist in its management. He wrote to know if I could in any way help him to raise $300 for his purpose, which I could not as you will readily imagine, tho' if I had it or could raise it in any way I'd be glad to do it for a prospect, even, of his doing well. Have you heard anything of it at all? Do write to him, if you know where he is, or to Mr. D. to learn what you can & enlighten me about the farming arrangement & also his reported engagement with Miss D. He may do well yet & if there is any prospect of his doing anything in the way of farming really, I may be able to help him after awhile as I have some influential friends here tho' nobody has much money in this quarter now."

John was buried in the Oaks of Ivy Hill Cemetery on May 1, 1868, but there is no information as to how he died, whether he found sobriety down on a farm or fell "off the wagon" there, married and had a family or died fatherless, as all but one of his brother's did. No further information on Ashton Dade was in the collection, either, though it is interesting his surname was the same as Towny's mother. Meanwhile Hector was hard at work laboriously making copies of his painting of Genl Lee, hoping to sell them at comparatively low figures. He was trying to make enough to spend Christmas with Eliza and her family, though whether he succeeded or not is another unknown. Some time between the above letter and February 14, 1866, he moved to Baltimore and wrote Eliza:

"I am sitting in the midst of a pile of letters, all calling for immediate answers, in a state of desperation at the idea of such a task. Among them is one from Carrie just rec'd, in which she very kindly encloses me $10. It was almost entirely of a religious character & contained very little about herself, or family, in a temporal point of view & tho' it was very kind & good, I confess I could have wished that some little of its spiritual character had been sacrificed, to make room for some few points of earthly interest with regard to her health, the children &c. As she says nothing to the contrary, however, I take it for granted they are as well as usual.

"I have also a letter from Miss Nimmie Fairfax, telling me that Genl Lee will be willing to sit for me whenever I go to Lexington. I think I'll go as soon as my picture is sold, which I hope will be very soon. I have been much delayed by waiting for a frame which was not finished until last Saturday. My friends here have thought best to put the picture up for raffle at $500 believing it will bring that tho' I don't think it will, but we are determined to try it & if it doesn't bring that to take less.

"I write with only one eye open, the right covered with a handkerchief to exclude the light. It has been more painful than usual for the last two days, probably owing, in a measure, to a large boil on the end of my nose, a very handsome ornament, as you may imagine, now in full bloom, being of a purplish red hue, with two charming little white spots in the middle, hurting awfully & thus beautifully illustrating the mournful moral that youth's <u>brightest blossoms</u> are not without thorns."

Hector probably suffered from blepharitis, an inflammation of the eyelids. It is a common eye disorder today but may not have been properly diagnosed or treated in the 1800s. It affects people of all ages but is not contagious. It would, however, be very inconvenient for an artist to be infected with it.

"P.S. Feby 15th – Your letter of 13th was rec'd last night in which you express surprise at my having stayed here so long. I have done so for several reasons. In the first place, I thought it better even to be at some expense & attend to the raffle of my picture myself, than to leave it entirely to others, who however much interest they may seem to feel in it, cannot have as much as I, & consequently are not likely to exert themselves as much, as my former experience has plainly taught me. Besides, I think there is a very fair prospect of my getting a good deal to do here, by staying awhile, & making acquaintances among the wealthy people, some of whom have already assured me of a liberal patronage if I would locate here. I have certainly been here much longer than I expected & been at considerable expense. I had to stay several days at the Hotel before I found a boarding house, which was a very expensive business, $4 per day.

"The long delay in getting my picture ready for exhibition was on account of the frame, as I mentioned before. I had much trouble about it & was at last very unfortunate in my selection. In fact, I think I was decidedly swindled. The man in whose gallery the picture is, offered to make me a very handsome frame for $14 but required a week to do it in. Unwilling to wait so long, I spent several days in looking for one ready made, finally found one which, tho' not entirely to my taste I thought would do, so I bought it in my haste for $12, but found it afterwards, upon closer examination, to be an old frame & so imperfect as to be unfit for use, but fixed up so as to be very well calculated to deceive a careless eye, in such a subdued light as the store afforded. I tried to get the man to take it back even at half price, but he refused so I had to make the best of it, which I did by putting it in the hands of the first dealer, to have it entirely renewed at an expense of $10. So I lost a good deal of time & money by being in too great a hurry."

Hector's problems, although huge to him, were insignificant compared to those Carrie would face in six months. Cholera was the scourge of the 1800s and it would hit the Eaches hard. Eliza would lose her sister, Carrie, and two grandchildren to the disease. The most devastating loss of all would be of Carrie, for she left behind three children under the age of five. There are those who would argue the loss of a child is the most difficult to bear but all of the families believed when a child died, he or she went to a better place and was spared the traumas every life experienced in growing to adulthood. Losing a mother, however, created an additional burden on children and their father, removing their anchor and cutting them adrift. Nowhere was that more evident than in the letter Thomas Russell wrote to Eliza on Friday, August 17, 1866, one day after Carrie died of cholera. His distress is evident, not just in his words, but in his handwriting, which became illegible at times.

"My dear Sister, You of all others can properly appreciate my feelings at this time. Your dear sister & my dear <u>wife</u> is no more. She died this morning at 2½ o'clock after a sickness of six days of cholera. On Friday last she was well & so also in the evening – went to church with me – as lively & cheerful & buoyant as in her brightest times. Sunday morning she complained of heaviness at pit of the chest, great oppression there & at some time a slight Diahrea manifested itself. On my way to the store thot it best to consult my physician & he advised me to procure medicine to have at hand to be taken in advance.

"I returned with the Medicine & had her take some of it. At noon when I returned she still had the oppression & advised her to use every care. I returned early that evening but she was no better. I then went for the doctor to see her, which he did and told her that she must take care of herself, go to bed and be quiet. About 7½ o'clock she had an attack of vomiting & ####. Called in the Doctor again who prescribed for her. Mrs. #### sat up with her that night with me, she sunk so rapidly that at 3 o'clock Sunday morning I had to go for the Doctor. He was so alarmed at her condition that he deemed it best to inform me that she had cholera and advised procuring a consulting physician. Before they came, however, she had rallied so effectively that they were led to pronounce her condition exceedingly promising.

"Cousin Nell was with us most of Sunday. Continuing to improve we were led to hope that she would soon be well & the Dr. advised on Monday the preparation of suitable nourishment to be given Tuesday morning. Monday night, however, she was more restless & instead of being in the condition to desire food on Tuesday morning she threw up quantities of bile, and expressed a great burning sensation at the pit of her chest & a constant craving for ice, which we gave her of freely as the Dr. suggested. Tuesday night was passed most comfortable, her condition became more & more hopeful and on Wednesday afternoon her symptoms were so favorable that the doctor pronounced her out of danger. I felt very much encouraged but being with her constantly night & day & knowing fully her condition I did not allow myself to take this comfort fully to my heart.

"By night complaining greatly of the compression on her chest I gave her, at the Drs direction Coloroform to induce sleep, it being essential that she should have rest of body. Besides, he expected the coloroform to act in place of Morphine, the effects of which he desired to avoid & she also. Instead of being relieved, however, I thot she grew worse & sent for the Doctor at 3 o'clock & he did not discover anything unfavorable. Towards 6 o'clock I sent to him to get a consulting physician again. Before their arrival she threw up, a black substance, after which she sank rapidly. They pronounced her case hopeless, as the character of what she threw up indicated dissolution. Her pastor was sent for but she but barely knew him. The stupor of the coloroform deadened her intellect so completely at the same time her uneasiness was so great that we were obliged to give it to her to keep her out of suffering. She knew us all at times & plainly desired to speak but could not.

"Mr. Brooks sang for her a hymn, which she desired him to repeat and from occasional expressions dropped, her mind was evidently engaged on #### matters. She very distinctly said at one time, tell John to be a good boy, meaning her brother John. She continued thus to gradually pass away, having all the time an extraordinarily strong pulse, remarkable vigor & strength. I believe tho' that had we not continued the use of coloroform she would have died sooner. We deemed it best to follow the Doctors instructions to keep her quiet with the coloroform and save her any suffering thus.

"Her suffering I was unable to bear. The dear sweet thing had been & was too great a suffer to allow of its continuance even if thereby she would have been more conscious and I could have conversed freely with her. I could have wished that it could have been so, but the stupor was so great. I have this satisfaction, however, in knowing that she was safe. She is now in heaven, yet doubtless looking down upon us in our terrible distress & desolation. She is with Jesus & happy. Oh! How happy! So happy that it were sin to desire her back again. Still, for all this notwithstanding the great consolation this affords we cannot stifle the emotion we are endowed with. We must miss, dreadfully miss, those dear to us, only so dear to me as she. I am desolate, terribly so and besides the nervous excitement through which I have pas't day & night for six days I may not as fully realize now, still I have a foretaste of that sickness & desolation of heart that I will experience when I come home to my silent house, to meet my little orphan children, without dear constant affectionate & devoted Carrie to meet me. Oh! It is terrible & I could almost pray if it were not for my little one, Lord take me away too.

"Dear sister you are more to me now than ever. You are her only living representative & loving her so devotedly as I did it is but natural that I should cling to and love those nearest to her. Write me often & frequently & thereby afford some alleviation of my horrible distress.

"She died calmly & gently at 2½ o'clock this morning, as dear and devoted a wife as ever lived. How strange seems the ways of Providence but we must not murmur. He doeth all things well & does not affect His children but for their ultimate good. I suppose I'll see that good after awhile. I know this will be a terrible shock to you. God grant you will be able to bear it and in your distress remember me; remember that mine is greater. Let me have your sympathy & your prayers. I have written for my Sister Nannie to come out & take care of the children. If she can come they will be well cared for. Carrie often said if anything should happen to her she would like her to take charge of them. Carrie will be buried tomorrow morning. God grant me strength to bear up under my load of trial. Your affectionate Brother T. G. Russell."

He wrote, again, on September 15, 1866:

"Your last was received yesterday and was read with great satisfaction, for I love to have letters coming from any one who loved my dear Carrie. How I do miss her! She had a place for everything & even almost to the day of her death she gave directions how to dress the children, what dress to put on each [boys wore dresses then] & where it might be found, and above all this her devotion to me was unbounded. I can vividly remember the Saturday morning she felt unwell, when I unsuspectedly returned with some precautionary medicines, how she almost chided me for too great anxiety about her & yet how loving she was about it and how sweetly she kissed me. Alas, I little thot that in one short week those lips would be forever sealed cold in the grave.

"I am so glad I did not leave her in her sickness. I would have regretted it so much. She could not bear me to leave her, thot no body could nurse her but myself and said so. She longed so much for you, wanted so much to have you with her. You were very, very dear to her. I felt so sorry that you were so far away, but as she appeared to be recovering it appeared hardly necessary to write for you & when the relapse did come on she was comparatively unconscious and you could not have got here in time. Besides, it would have been unsafe for that week, over 2000 died of the disease.

"It is however the greatest satisfaction & pleasure to me to know that she saw you all & you her, so recently. Poor Carrie! No, she's not poor but rich, radiant in her glorified body. But she appears poor, viewing her in her grave; she has gone & her like will be but rarely met with in this world. Hers was an unsullied life, to be looked back upon by her friends with the most pleasurable emotions and by me with pangs of sorrow that so rare a jewel, so companionable and loving a spirit should be snatched from my side, in the very bloom of her loveliness and the most critical period of her usefulness, whilst her little ones were but clambering about her knees, and so constantly needed her so apt and ready guidance and instructions.

"But God's will be done. I think I love him & feel what I say for, after all, this worlds experiences are but a dream. We will soon pass through our course of discipline & trials & troubles & then pass away to enter upon eternal joys, compared with which this worlds brightest hours, most pleasurable associations are but the dim shadow of Heavens brightest glories, & from whose dazzling brilliance mortal eyes read it in blindness.

"Dear Sister she is now the occupant of that eternal mansion that her Saviour had prepared for her. She is espoused to another husband, the Lord himself, free from all the heart burnings & sorrows & trials, and disappointments that we mortals are subjected to. We know that this is her condition & knowing it we cannot wish her back. In due time, it may be a short time, we shall be her guest. It is an unutterable pleasure to think of her thus and serves wonderfully to reconcile me to her absence.

"Sister has not come out yet but will come soon as the cholera has pretty nearly left us. I need some one greatly, to arrange the children's clothing for winter. I am very fortunate in having very good girls who are kind to the children & take good care of them I will feel, however, so much better satisfied & settled when sister comes. You are very kind to offer to take some of the little ones. I am sure you have cares enough on you. I can't bear tho' to part with any of them. [Dora is five, Hector two–and–a–half and Eliza is two.]

"I will send on your package of Carrie's things in a short time. I cant bear to part with them but I know she would have wished just such a distribution of them. It will be a sad task to look over them. I cant bear to think of it. Remember me warmly to Hector, John and Mr. Fendall, not forgetting the younger folks. Yr affectionate brother T G Russell."

Carrie's "things" evidently did not include letters she received for correspondence from Hector, Eliza or John were not in the collection, whereas her letters to others are present. Perhaps her husband kept them. There are no more letters from T.G. Russell so there is no information as to what happened to the children. After the above two letters there is a gap of four years until a letter from Hector appeared on July 31, 1870. He had moved to New York and opened a studio.

"I'm still having a hard time to get along. Not much to do tho the usual amount of promises and prospects. For the last few months, however, I've managed to make expenses, but that's about all. If I could get enough of porcelain work I could do well. It pays much better than large portraits, which are so uncertain & take so long to paint. Fredericks' artist is anxious that he & I should start a photograph gallery, making a specialty of colored pictures. I think it would be a success, as we could both command a good deal of patronage among the best people, both here & from the south, but I'm afraid we can't work it for want of <u>capital</u> - can't do anything without that.

"I am painting a portrait of quite a handsome lady at present (a Mrs. McAnerny), an old Richmond friend. It's slow work as she can't get a chance to sit, on account of children, hot weather &c. I have to paint entirely from photographs & I'm having an awful time with the drapery. This is the only order I have on hand now but the lady's husband expects to have his sometime soon, <u>he says</u>. I hope some of my prospects at least will be realized for I'm fearfully 'hard up' & consequently very blue.

"The expected portrait of the deceased individual turned out to be 'perhaps' one of the most <u>complete, decided & cold–blooded practical jokes</u> ever perpetuated upon a confiding & enthusiastic artist. After having made a number of drawings & finally succeeding in getting a likeness, the brother of the deceased desired that I should commence the picture at once & agreed to pay $50 down, for which he made <u>several dozen</u> appointments but on each occasion, something <u>extraordinary occurred</u> to prevent the fulfillment of his promise & my hopes until finally both the picture & the money resolved themselves into one of those pleasant little dreams which so often beguile the waking fancy of struggling artists.

"I'm sorry to hear you suffer so with your eyes, but hope it is nothing serious. I can fully sympathize for mine are about as bad as ever. I can't write or read half an hour without suffering with them & can't write a letter without losing half my lashes, which accounts partly for my having (like yourself) taken several days to accomplish this letter. Had to wait for my lashes to grow. Would like to say more but eyes most out & my papers given out too. Will try & get home in fall or winter, if circumstances permit, for I am crazy to see you all again."

There is only one more letter from Hector, written on October 5, 1874, to Townie. Hec is living at 65 Irving Place in New York. He said he was well and had good prospects, but that is what he usually said. He also expressed "my extreme regret for my long neglect, which I hear has made you all very uneasy. I hope you & Sister will try & forgive me. I have strong hopes of seeing you all Xmas if not sooner." He died on July 2, 1875; he was 35. Eliza was with him. His obituary in the *Alexandria Gazette* on July 10th is the longest of any of the Eaches and is typical of the eulogizing of the day.

"Died, in New York city, on July 2nd, 1875, HECTOR EACHES, aged 35 years, formerly of Alexandria, but of late years an artist of the former place.

"It is not often that an announcement among the sad list of the dead, which we perforce read day by day only to learn but too vividly how friend after friend can drop away from our lives forever – 'face no more, voice no more' – chronicles a loss so pregnant with all grief and deep regret as this is.

"Who that knew him but a few years ago dwelling in our midst but does not recall the handsome face, the lithe and graceful form and the ringing tones of a voice so sweet in word and song that memory will never let the mellow cadence die away. Aye! And how much more we must recall! The charming geniality of manner, winning him so many friends; the generous nature so ready to help any whom it was in his power to help; the gentle heart, tender and loving as a woman's – the kindness that never prompted one word or act to wound another – these we may never forget.

"Yes, we who were shoulder to shoulder with him in the long years of conflict, while we attest the bravery and intrepid daring and all the qualities that made the born soldier, will bear each other witness that at all times and in all scenes, whether amid the roar of battle, the winter's bivouac, the summer's noontide march, he never was other to us than the unselfish, sympathizing friend – the cheerful companion – our gifted comrade, whose thousand acts of daily kindness found record in our hearts and Heaven.

"And we think, too, of his voice, of wondrous sweetness and power, that cheered us on many a weary march, and whiled the laggard hours away in camp – that voice that rang out grandly in the gorges of the Blue Ridge in the 'Marsaillaise,' or changed a jovial glee in the lowlands of the James. He was the most faithful friend in all the meaning of the word, and was that rare type of manhood – a gallant gentleman.

"Therefore with sorrow we gathered around his grave and tearfully and tenderly lowered therein all that was mortal of our friend – taken away from us in all the rich promise of his talent, the last of his name; heaping the clods of his own mother State upon her gifted child."

Hector may not have been the last of his name. Though it is not known whether Daniel was still around, there was still the son of Hector's brother, Thomas, Ewing Eaches, who was 12-years-old and in Kentucky. Still, there is no doubt the Eaches did not enjoy long and prosperous lives, except for Eliza. She died in 1907, midway between her 84th and 85th birthday, but she had become a Fendall. All her brothers and sisters had either died or disappeared from the history books.

The Fendalls

osias Fendall (spelled Ffendall originally), the first of the many Fendalls to arrive in America, landed in Maryland in January 1655. He was 27-years-old. By the time he was in his mid–fifties he had: fought in the Battle of Severn; been taken prisoner and sentenced to death – twice; been granted – and lost – 2,000 acres of land; been appointed governor of Maryland; attempted to overthrow the government; found guilty of attempting to raise a mutiny and banished from the province – twice; moved to Virginia, in 1682, and in 1684 he disappeared, according to some records.

His progeny did not disappear, though. Fendalls people the history books but it is the great–great–great–great grandson of Josias, Townshend Dade Fendall, whose story is told here. Beginning with Josias' son, John, each generation begat a Benjamin, necessitating numbering them for clarity. Townshend (always called Towny) had a father, a brother, a son and a grandson named Benjamin. According to his daughter, Nancy Lee, Towny was born in Charles County, Maryland (though his obituary and other records indicate Prince George's County, MD) on May 25, 1813. Towny's mother, Elizabeth Dade Fendall, penned the earliest letter, on November 13, 1817, as described in the Prologue. The family had moved to Alexandria by that time. For some reason, Towny's father, Benjamin Fendall III, brought the letter home and Elizabeth kept it but it would be three decades before another letter was added.

Unlike his adventurous ancestor, Towny was a staid Episcopalian who preached piety to his children and wrote passionate letters to his wife. While he was wooing Eliza Eaches he was working in Washington, D.C., though his occupation at that time is not known. Towny's first saved letter was written August 24, 1848, to Eliza.

> "Dear Miss Liza, I hope you will not consider it too great a liberty, my writing you a little Note – as it is only to bid you good bye. I shall leave town in about an hour for Maryland to spend a few days and as you might think I had taken my departure for parts unknown, I thought I would just apprise you of my whereabouts. Take care of yourself whilst I am gone, and I pray & beseech you, suspend any action, in a certain matter, that may or might, in the course of human events, take place, until my return. My salutations to romantic Miss Mary – and best wishes for your health & happiness – I remain very truly Sincerely yr friend and Very humble Gent Townshend D. Fendall"

Towny and Eliza were married January 15, 1849. She was born July 7, 1822. Their first child, Benjamin Truman (he would be Benjamin V) was born January 5, 1851. In June, 1852, Eliza was at "Wyoming," the farm of William Luke Marbury near Clinton, Maryland. He was married to Towny's sister, Susan. It was the refuge Eliza sought to escape the oppressive heat of Alexandria's summers. The long petticoats, shirt sleeves and skirts did nothing to dissipate the heat, of course, and all those clothes had to be packed in trunks. Then she had to take a ferry across the Potomac, where she was probably met by a carriage of the Marburys, so it was a major undertaking. She took Ben with her while Towny stayed in Alexandria. It was these summer sojourns of Eliza's that inspired most of the correspondence.

On June 10th, he wrote:

"I have just finished a letter to Fendall [Marbury] and must trespass a little longer upon 'Uncle Sam's' time to write a few lines to my darling little wife & son, to hold sweet converse with the dear objects of my affection & solicitude. I have missed you much, very much my own dear one and my sweet little prattling babe, truly.

"I feel like one who treads alone, but fortunate indeed that Aunt M & Jenney are with me. The empty house would have been hateful to me, my lonely room is bad enough, but sweet slumber soon quiets the aching void & I dream of joys that I have tasted, soon to return. If I could just peep in upon you both and hear the voice of my darling boy hollowing for Pa I should feel very happy.

"My love to my precious little Benj, kiss him & tell him not to forget Pa and that he will bring him an orange. It is now after 3 o.c. & I must close to reach the Boat in time. I hope to get a letter from you tomorrow. Hoping that you & my dear boy are enjoying good health, with all the love I have, I remain Yr devoted Husband Townshend D. Fendall."

On October 21, 1852, five weeks after Eliza lost a daughter at two days old, he penned this sensitive letter to "My Darling Liz."

One of the pumps that provided water to the citizens until the late 1800s.

66

She and Ben were in Piscataway, MD, at "Liberty," the home of John and Elizabeth Marbury. She was another sister of Towny's.

"Napoleon I believe wrote to Josephine daily and so illustrious an example of affection may well be followed and although I have not the vanity to suppose that my letters will be as interesting as his, yet I will claim that they are the result of as pure & devoted love as ever inspired the bosom of any man.

"A heart overburdened with sorrow finds relief in unbosoming to a friend, but a heart full of love has not language to convey the emotions & pulsations that animate, consequently it is only in the presence of the beloved object that a faint outline can be given of the workings within. Your beloved image and our darling boy is ever before me cheering my loneliness, with your sweet smile, ever delightful to the heart of a husband & father, would that I had language to convey to you the love that warms my bosom. Words are inadequate. Ere this reaches you, I trust, I shall have embraced my precious wife & boy.

"I duly rec'd your precious letter yesterday & joyous were the glad tidings of health of yourself and darling boy. It was like balm to the sick heart. I feel greatful (sic) to the protecting hand of a Kind Providence that watches over & guards my beloved ones, may it ever be near them.

"Cloe has got everything very nice at home. [Although some Fendalls and Marburys had slaves, Cloe was a servant.] I engaged a carpenter to cut the doors & put carpet strips & also around the fire place. My love & a kiss to my precious Liz & Boy, in haste, Yr devoted Husband, Townshend."

By this time at least five of Towny's letters (one has not been included here) had been brought home and added to the trunk, box or whatever receptacle contained them but there were none from Eliza, so who was the custodian? It will be another ten years before one appears from her, written one year after the war begins. In the meantime Towny continued his devoted letters during the summers, this one on June 2, 1853.

"How are you, to day, my precious little Wife & darling boy. I hope this charming day finds you both enjoying good health, with greatful hearts, to the great Author of events that we are so highly blessed by his divining favor. May his protecting providence ever be near, to watch over & guide & direct us in the right path, to his honour & glory. I see you smile, my sweet pet, at your unsanctified husband's seriousness. I know the earnest wish & prayer of your heart is to see him sanctified unto him, who is all wisdom & goodness. May we not indulge the hope that this obdurate heart will some day yield to the influence of the holy spirit and become an humble follower in the only safe & true path, that leads to life eternal. Oh, what a glorious thing it must be, to be a sincere Christian. O, most gracious father let thy divine influence soften this hard heart & give me a clear sense of my utter dependence upon they divine grace.

"I miss you & my darling little boy very much indeed. I peep in upon you occasionally. I see my little precious paddling about & talking as busy as a bee. I do want to see you both so much, pray take good care of yourself & Benny. Don't over eat yourself or let Benny, with strawberries & ice cream. I hope to get a letter from you tomorrow, I feel very anxious to hear how you all are.

"Give my love to Aunt Mary & all at Wyoming & Liberty. Give my love & kiss my precious boy and tell him not to forget Papa. I am going to bring him a pair of garters. I hope to be with you on Saturday, in the mean time I pray a Kind providence to guard & protect you & my Benny."

There was a gap of two years between the above letter and the next one, possibly because Eliza had another daughter, Nancy Lee, born November 9, 1853. Towny was now an officer at the Farmers Bank in Alexandria. On May 16, 1855, Towny described his loneliness to Eliza, who was at Wyoming again, with the two children.

"I have just returned from the bank after a pretty fatiguing days work & feel much jaded. I am sitting all alone in the dining room, the very loneliness of which seems to #### at my solitaryness. But fond memory, ever faithful to the lonely heart, treasures upon his green tablet, the image of three dear absent ones and recalls in imagination every smile, every sound that is so delightful to the sight & to the ear. But alas, like all the pleasures of life, they are but momentary and when I look around I find nothing but an aching void. Is not this enough to sicken & sadden the heart? But hope brightens & cheers the future & however deceitful, gives comfort & pleasure under all circumstances. Hope, what would life be without it, is it not the polar Star, that guides & governs our destiny."

During the six years between this letter and the next, Eliza experienced several tragedies. On February 26, 1856, her brother, William Eaches, died at the age of 30. Nine months later, on November 16, 1856, Eliza named her second son William. The following year her father, Joseph, died on December 19, 1857 and within two weeks her older sister, Mary, succumbed to consumption on January 2, 1858. Her other sister, Carrie, brought better news as she married Thomas Russell on August 30, 1860, in St. Louis, Missouri. The next letter, dated April 2, 1861, is from him to "Mr. Townshend Fendall, My dear bro…

"…We can fully sympathize with you in the troubles that are now upon the country and tho we are not so smartly situated to the vicinity of the difficulty as you are, still we have serious difficulties before us to encounter. Your community is unanimous in feeling – having but one purpose – to defend the house of your state and institutions of the south – while with us we have a divided sentiment – part for sustaining the old government and part for resisting all encroachments upon the right of the south. When these opposing forces will clash we know not but clash they well and we fear battles soon. It is dreadful to contemplate the result following such an uprising, as this entire extermination of the Germans & government sympathizers will be thinly accomplished.

"Our state is now becoming strongly in favor of 'secession' and of following the course adopted by the border slave states. [Seven Southern states have seceded.] The people up to the present time are strong for Union but Lincoln's policy of aggression has forced them the other way. #### is a strong secessionist, so also is the legislature and divided action will soon be taken. We will follow the course of Virginia.

"In your last you expressed regret at my secession tendencies. I must confide they have been that way from the first. I loved the old government. I loved the 'Stars & Stripes' so long as they represented a government rendering justice to all, but since that glorious and makeshift ensign has been prostituted to represent Black Republicanism, over despotism, I retire from beneath its folding with the greatest regret.

"For the shape of things we are in a great measure indebted to the white crooked gentry of the North who have been instilling into the minds of their children from the moment they could lisp the word 'slave,' of its abominable sinfulness until prejudice has become so strong amongst them that the duty of exterminating it, regardless of all justice & right in the mobbed has been enforced upon them as a moral soul–saving obligation. This growing sentiment has culminated in the election of one who represented the government – whose avowed principle is that 'this country must be all slave or all free' this together with the disposition of their legislatures to ignore the constitutional duty of remanding slaves to their owners.

"The denial of the territories to the south whose blood & treasure helped in their acquisition and which yielded to – would place the South ultimately at the mercy of the North. In the increase of power of the lobby by the addition of new states, whose influence would be cast to their account and which in time would reach to a constitutional majority is added the constitution and abolish slavery. It is mainly this latter contingency – and which considerancy of spirit of the North is an inevitable one – that has aroused the South to take a firm stand for proper guarantees and which refused has rendered their cause a just one before all the world. There are my reasons for advocating a separation, believing that this result is only a question of time and that it could be better borne now than ever. I must ask pardon for imposing so lengthy a writing upon you, hoping that the desire to justify my course will excuse it.

"Please remember me very kindly to all your household. With best wishes I am yours very truly, T G Russell."

Carrie Eaches, his wife, was a devout Quaker and they were opposed to slavery. Her sisters, Eliza and Mary, had manumitted a slave but, unfortunately, Carrie's feelings about slavery or secession are not found here. Thomas Russell would get his wish shortly, though Missouri did not secede as he hoped (even though St. Louis had the largest slave market in the state.) When the South fired on Fort Sumter April 12, 1861, five days later Virginia became the eighth state to secede from the Union. Three more states would join in a couple of months. On May 24th, thousands of Federal troops and their accoutrements took over Alexandria, confiscating, dismantling or destroying property as they saw fit. Close behind came the brothels, bars, speculators and runaway slaves. Alexandria would remain occupied throughout the war. This meant no Southern mail or newspapers, a curfew and you needed a pass to leave the city but that was only granted to those swearing allegiance to the U. S. Government.

The first battle of the Civil War took place at Manassas, or Bull Run. (Manassas is a town; Bull Run a stream.) It was only 25 miles from Towny's front door and it began Sunday, July 21st. Green Union troops had marched there from Washington a few days earlier. Citizens of D.C. packed picnic lunches and rode their carriages to the arena to watch the spectacle, much as Romans crowded the Coliseum to see the Gladiators kill each other. The day began with eager anticipation; it ended with devastation as the spectators sped back to D.C. alongside the fleeing Federal troops.

Throughout the war Towny wrote to "My dear Aunt," his mother's sister, Mary Dade. She usually lived with Towny but was in Maryland now with her niece, Susan Fitzhugh.

On October 29, 1861, he wrote:

"We have felt very much disappointed and uneasy at not receiving a line from any of you since we parted. Eliza wrote you a day or two after our return, which I hope you rec'd. It is needless to say how anxious we are to hear from you all. We are aware of the movement of troops in MD and feel more than ever anxious about F____

["F" stands for Fannie Bomerey, a slave of Mary's. In 1859 Mary received a letter, not included here, from a suitor, A.G. Conway, requesting her permission that they might marry. The suitor stated the marriage would not interfere with the duties she owed Mary. Comments in later letters will clarify Towny's concern about Fannie.]

"I sent your trunk of winter clothes (with a box to Sister S) a day or two after our return & feel anxious to know if they have yet come to hand. Liz has been very busy house cleaning &c since her return and we have now pretty much everything straightened up. She concluded not to put her new carpets down yet. We have put the best of the old carpets in the back parlor. We have put the carpet in the dining room, it is very comfortable and cousey. We have concluded to put the two boys in the room over the kitchen, which will be very comfortable this winter.

"We have at last purchased a cooking stove & so far it answers admirably, turning out eatables first rate. I think it will be a saving in the way of fuel, at least twenty five dollars, which will pay for the stove the first year. Our hireling, so far, gives satisfaction. She is a good washer & ironer. Her cooking we have not yet tested. I have no doubt of equal capability in that department. I have laid in my fuel for the winter and a supply of provisions. Benny (10) commenced school with Mr. Bitting yesterday & I trust will benefit by his instruction. The charge is six dollars per quarter.

"We are still in a state of State Two, everything perfectly quiet, the monotony only relieved by martial music & tramp of the soldiers. Rumors are abundant, it is impossible to tell which is or will be the next act in the grand drama. A grand battle, it is supposed, will soon take place. There has been a terrible fight near Leesburg, in which the Federals met with terrible slaughter, from 12 to 15 hundred, killed, wounded & taken prisoners. Confederate loss abt 300. [This would be the Battle of Ball's Bluff, 35 miles west of Washington, where many Union soldiers drowned in the Potomac, unable to scale the bluff. The casualties were 921 for the U.S., 149 for the CSA. Towny's casualty figures were invariably overstated for the Union and usually understated for the Confederate forces.]

"Oh how awful the loss of human life, when will this iniquitous war end. Peace; peace, how desirable. The Potomac is & has been for some time completely blockaded & I fear the cutting off of supplies will produce great suffering. I do not think it yet prudent for you to return, for the same reason stated when I saw you. I will let you know when you can return with impunity.

"Our little city continues very healthy, which is a great blessing these troublesome times with great suffering with the poor, everything very high & no work, business of all kinds completely paralyzed. Liz & our dear children enjoy good health & write in warmest love to you all. Willie hurrahs for the Stars & Stripes, he says to fool the soldiers, but is for secess when they are not present. He is as wild and unmanageable as a deer. [It appears Willie, now five, is well on his way to becoming the con artist he will become as an adult.]

In Towny's next letter, December 28th, he trusts…

"…kind providence will not much longer separate us but we must submit, in humble resignation to his divine will, that orders all things for the best. Everything is at present quiet, but no one can tell what a day will bring forth, rumors are rife of the intended movements of the Army, but nothing reliable. God grant that something may occur to relieve us from the painful state of bondage, and we may be free to go & come when we please, secure in life and property.

"The joyous festival of Christmas has passed, not as formerly, fraught with happiness & glee. It was a dull quiet day and but for the firing of powder crackers & pistols, would have scarce been noticed. It rested like a mighty incubus, paralyzing, as it were, the elasticity of the spirits, that in gone by days were so buoyant & happy. How sad & painful the change from my boyish days. Then the occasion was all excitement & preparation, for days before, followed by social parties, Egg–nogg & the varied innocent amusements, incident to the season. Now, what have we, long faces & anxiety, depicted in every linament, startling rumors on every side, dark & lowering clouds overshadowing the future, with scarce a ray of hope to cheer the sad heart of the gloomy surroundings; oh, is not this a sad sad change from olden times. Did our forefathers ever dream of this, when they bequeathed to us that glorious blood bought inheritance, Civil and Religious Liberty. Oh, mysterious fate, has ever Sinful man brought this calamity upon us. War, Civil relentless War, has been lighted & the fratricidal arm, hurling death & direction, father against son, brother against brother, how awful to contemplate. Oh my Country, once the land of the free & the home of the brave, thy once glorious fabric, reeling tottering to the dust, can it be, that we are no longer to rank among the nations of the earth. Must our nationality be blotted out? No, no, forbid it kind heaven, fanaticism cannot, must not prevail, two republics may grow up, but never can be blotted out from existence. We will be freeman, if we cannot agree as brothers, with our nationality, let us separate & stop this suicidal carnage & let the land flowing with milk & honey be at peace. May God in his mercy grant this.

"On Xmas day we attended service at our Lecture Room & had a very fine sermon from Mr. Steward, suitable to the season. The

Sacrament was not administered. We had a plain dinner, Turkeys ever so high we could not indulge but we had oysters & Plumb pudding & a pitcher of Apple Toddy which was fine. The children have been to two parties & enjoyed themselves very much. Willie thinks himself quite a man. Benny is out skating today & seemed to anticipate a happy time.

"We are again without a servant, but hope to get one soon again. Margaret manages to cook for us, so far, but you know she is uncertain. Indeed, she does wonderful, considering all things. Liz has a right tough time, which I very much regret as she is not very strong, more willing than strength to accomplish. I hope you are not in want of any things as it is difficult to get any thing to you. Should you want any money, for Ben, will advance whatever you may require. With best wishes for your health & happiness & a happy <u>New Year</u> to you and all our friends, with much love I am Your affect nephew Townshend D F"

On February 11, 1862, Towny wrote about the arrest of the Reverend Kenzie John Steward, the rector at St. Paul's Church, for refusing to pray for Lincoln: "I hope I shall never witness such a thing again, it beggars language to describe my feelings on the occasion. I send the Local News containing the account which I hope will reach you." He then rambled on about how the city was full with the Military but generally they were orderly. He also assured her he will look out for her, then closed with word of the family.

"…Our darling babes, with the exception of slight colds, keeping well, they are fine noble children, tho I say it myself. Benny for his years is intelligent & is a great comfort to us both, is attentive & studious, progressing admirably. Our little Nannie, as gentle & kind as ever & seems exceedingly anxious to read, frequently takes her book to read to me & is coming on very well. Willie as wild & mischievous as a monkey, he has unquestionably a very sprightly mind & I think will be quick to learn. He is very acute to sound, impulsive but warm hearted."

A letter from Eliza finally appears, March 2, 1862, also addressed to "My Dear Aunt."

"We have been getting on very comfortably; if it were not the constant state of excitement we are kept in, by these arrests, searching house, raising flags on private dwellings etc. So far we have escaped such annoyance but I know not how long we may remain unmolested. You may imagine how uneasy I felt when I saw the soldiers going to Mr B_____ to arrest him, and heard of so many sharing the same fate that evening. No one knew the cause of the arrest of any one."

73

[Some of the notable citizens of Alexandria were forced to ride on the front of troop trains to prevent confederates from firing on the trains. As his next letter attests, this practice was stopped due to outrage expressed by the townspeople.]

The rest of the letter was news of mutual friends. Towny wrote on March 25th:

"You have doubtless seen by the papers the release of all our citizens that were arrested, except four. They are still held as prisoners, upon what charges no one can tell. It is thought by some they may be released today. I shall not however believe it until I see them.

"I have never witnessed so grand a sight as our little city has presented for the last ten days. The wharves have been literally lined up with Steam Boats & Vessels – to transport Troops to some point unknown. I suppose upward of thirty thousand troops have been sent down the river. I can scarcely realize what I have seen. It sickens the heart to think of this fraternal War – & when it will end, heaven only knows & what is to become of us none can tell. I hold my situation now, only from month to month & I think it more than possible that the Bank will close up about the middle of April & what I am to do then, I cannot forsee, but I rely with confidence upon an overruling Providence, with faith & hope, feeling assured that some way of relief will be afforded. I have been reading lately of the escape of the Israelites from Egypt bondage, which gives much consolation.

"Our streets have been crowded with soldiers for the last ten days & to one unaccustomed to such immense bodys of men it is a grand sight, bayonets glittering in the sun. We have had no more fires since the one on King St, of which you have had an account. Liz & the children & myself attended Mr. Bitting's church on Sunday & listened to a very fine sermon. The house was crowded.

"My little household keeps very well. Benny still continues very studious & I think has very much improved under his present tutor & I hope I shall be able to continue hiring him. Nan begins to read very well & as sweet & gentle as ever. Willie is wild & mischievous as ever, very smart, learns his letters, has a very keen ear to sound & I think will soon learn to read."

Towny and Eliza were now prisoners of war, though they were living in their own house, cooking their own food and free to walk about. Their chains were not made of metal but of rules and regulations. The military presence was pervasive, limiting their activities, but they were not exposed to the main killers of the war – dysentery, typhoid and pneumonia. Nor were they confronted with the sight of dead or wounded soldiers in their front yard, as so many were after each battle. In April, 1862, Eliza wrote: "We have had thousands and thousands of troops passing through town for three weeks past. No one seems to know where they are going. The river has been filled with steamers as far down as eye can reach." On April 12th, Towny again advised Aunt Mary:

"I do not think it safe for you to return yet with F_____ for the reason that the influence that would be brought to bear upon her would, I truly believe, induce her to leave you, which she is comparatively free from where she is. Servants are constantly leaving here. Mrs. Snowden's cook left her last Sunday which leaves her with but one, the old nurse. The Bill freeing the slaves in the District has passed. Consequently, the inducement to move off is stronger now than it was prior to the passage of that bill. [The Emancipation Proclamation is passed in January of next year.] It is utterly impossible when they once get to Washington to recover them again. Hence my advice is for you to remain where you now are awhile longer. Possibly in sixty days more a great change may take place.

"The late news is encouraging. I believe we have defeated them at Corinth & Yourk Town. [He is referring to the Battle of Shiloh, in Tennessee, in which the Confederates claimed victory the first day, then were routed on the second.] There seems very little doubt but what McCl [McClellan] has sent for reinforcements, 30,000. I get this from a private source.

"My official duties at the Bank closed on the 10th and the bank has closed for the present. They were very liberal. The Board gave us, in consideration of being removed from office, three months pay from the 10th, which I think will keep me going until things are settled or I can get something to do. So you see I am a Gentleman at Leisure for the present, which I trust may not be long. [It will be five years.] Altho I am at liberty to cross to the other side [citizens can now cross the Potomac] I do not like to leave my house for fear it may be taken possession of by the Feds. If I can get anyone to stay with Liz, I shall certainly be down to see you shortly.

"We have plenty of VA money but cannot use it except at Twenty five percent discount, so we shall have to be as economical as possible. Give our best love to all at Liberty and may God bless and protect you prays your affect nephew Townshend."

Towny's "private source" for news of the war was, at the very least, unreliable. Wherever his information came from, it led Towny to believe the South was winning and the war would be over soon, as evidenced by the following letter from May 17, 1862.

"The news for our side for the last two days is quite encouraging – letters from Richmond under date the 14th, state that Beauregard has completely defeated Wallach at Corinthe, cut him all to pieces. Jackson [meaning Stonewall], it is reported, has driven Banks back to Winchester, certainly to Strausberg. Jackson has been reinforced & has now an army of forty two thousand, no further news from McClellan, since the Battle of Williamsburg. The Federals were badly whipped on that occasion, the loss was awful, we had several of our Townsmen killed & wounded, among the latter was our little Hector, slightly in the hand – he went on with the army. The Feds have stopped all telegraph communication & the papers of course are bearers of lies, which I think is conclusive evidence that they have been worsted.

"I have perfect confidence in our ability to defend Richmond, indeed I believe we shall give the Feds a tremendous whipping. McDowell has not yet crossed the Rappahannock. I have heard from outside sources that the federal loss at the Battle of Williamsburg was thirty thousand – a large number of wounded have been sent to Washington & among them some 250 of the Confederates, wounded & prisoners. I think the indications are favorable for <u>Foreign</u> interference."

The "Battle of Williamsburg" was more a siege than battle. McClellan delayed any action for weeks while he built up for a siege, then Johnston pulled out the night before the siege was to begin. Both Presidents, Lincoln and Davis, were dismayed by the results. As for Towny's claim of the loss of 30,000 Union soldiers, the bloodiest one–day battle of the war, at Antietam, totaled 23,000, yet Towny rattles off the exaggerated numbers as if reciting attendance at a church revival meeting. The totals at Williamsburg were approximately 1700 Confederates and 2000 Union killed. Later that month, in his letter to Eliza, he continued his optimistic outlook, stating, "I feel satisfied that we shall have <u>Foreign</u> interference in our affairs which, from the tone of the papers, is decidedly for the South. I feel sanguine that in a few days we shall hear of McClellan's defeat. The news from the west is encouraging." Three days later, on May 23, 1862, he sent another letter to Eliza.

"I have been disappointed for the last three days at not receiving a little note from you, giving favorable accounts of our darling little daughter. I take it for granted she continues to improve & is probably moving about. [Nan has had measles.] I get on well with the boys. Willie has been soliciting to go over to Mr. Burke's to play with Julian & is quite ingenious & prolific in reasons why he should go. One is that he will prevent Julian from disturbing the baby whilst asleep. I told him he would interrupt Julian in his lessons but his reply was that they had been attended, before breakfast. Dear little heart, I find I have not patience sufficient to humor his innocent caprices. [His "dear little heart" will become larcenous as he grows older.]

"Benny is getting on very well with his school & carrys around the Paper in the eves. He has a Capital of 75 cts which he is very anxious to invest in an axe, but I persuaded not. He says he is certain he saw Cousin Ben's woman Kitty in the street the other day & I think it more than probable that it was her. A rumor of negroes have come from Washington, fearing they would be delivered up to their masters. I do not know that Ben could recover her here, if he were to find her, but I think it would be worth the effort. Say to him if he will come over I will aid him all I can.

"I have no news to write you. We feel satisfied they have been fighting near Richmond and the report is that Beauregard had defeated Halleck at Corinth. I think before many days something decisive will be done."

Once again Towny's information was backwards. Beauregard pulled out before Halleck could engage him, much like Williamsburg, but he did it with great skill. He then pronounced the evacuation "equivalent to a great victory," which may be how Towny got his information. His next letter, May 27th, told Eliza:

"Yesterday was a day of glorious <u>News</u> – we have been eminently successful, the indications are a speedy settlement of our difficulty. Banks has been defeated by Jackson & driven in to MD. McDowell has evacuated Fredksburg & his troops have been sent up to reinforce Banks. Two Regiments passed through here night before last & one last night. The Confederates have captured another train of cars on the Manassas line. I have no doubt McClellan has had a fight & been repulsed, his orders were to give fight at all hazards and the absence of news convinces me that Hallack has met with reverse so you see the day of deliverance draws nigh & that we shall ere long once more enjoy freedom & religious Liberty under our own vine & fig tree in the Sunny South – free from Vandalism.

"Yesterday I am informed of the great excitement in Washington & by the papers I send you, extended north – do not be surprised to hear that Jackson has crossed over the Potomac, in pursuit of Banks. There was a report yesterday evening that Fort McHenry [in Baltimore, MD] had been taken.

"The cook is churning today, the second time since you left, the first was rather a poor yield tho nice butter milk. The boys unite in love to you & Nannie. God bless & protect you both. Your affc husband Townsh D F_____"

Perhaps it was just as well Towny believed the war was about to end. Had he known it would continue for another three years he might have despaired and had great difficulty going on. Convinced the end was at hand, he could always look forward to tomorrow. On July 15, 1862 he told his aunt of hearing from Eliza's brother, Hector.

"Liz received a letter from Hector. He was slightly wounded in the foot & not the shoulder as reported. He writes in good spirits. I also recd a letter from your nephew, Thos Fitzhugh, he was taken prisoner in the same Battle with Hector at White Oak Swamp. He is well & writes for clothes, which I shall send him immediately. They are confined at Fort Delaware. Hector seems to think that they may be removed from that place."

Towny apparently was receiving monetary assistance, for he added:

"My friends are kind, very kind, especially Wyoming. How can I make returns, am almost <u>Bank Rupt</u>. I have the will, the ability is deficient. Fendall [Marbury] is a noble boy, he meets my views particularly, he is generous & high toned, he bestows where there is no expectation of return, there is the nobleman. I may or I may not have the power to reciprocate."

The next letter from Towny, dated August 10, 1862, was to his son, Ben, who was with Aunt Mary Dade Fendall in Maryland. Ben is now 12½-years-old. He wrote:

"I have been intending writing to you from day to day for the last week but with the extreme hot weather and not feeling well I have felt very little like writing. I was very much relieved the day I came home to find the report we heard at Cousin Ben's was entirely unfounded, tho I do not think we are entirely free from something of the sort, ere long, as this Drafting they seem determined to make, may induce them to stop all intercourse, beyond the limits of the city. I am past the age & know, therefore, no fear of being Drafted so you all may be easy on that score.

"I suppose you heard of the arrest of three of our citizens this day week. W. A. Taylor, B. Wheat & Doct Johnson, they now are esteemed hostages for a man said to have been arrested in Richmond by the name of "Close" brother to our "Close." They were confined in the old Capitol building until yesterday. They returned home on payrole last evening, not much worst off. Our old Porter Gavins, at the Bank, was arrested one day last week & put in the slave pen a night & day. He also has been released.

"They have taken the two lower rooms of the Bank, for Gen'l

78

Taylor of N.Y. staff. They say they may not require this more than thirty days. Every thing is very quiet & orderly so far, but no one can tell what may be the next Military manifest. Notice has been given that they will require all the warehouses, the Wharf, for Military purposes. It seems a number of dwelling houses are also required. You have all the War news through the papers I can give.

"Your Mama & myself feel daily anxious about you & pray our Heavenly father to keep his protecting hand near you... His is the only sure dependence, here & hereafter. I hope you are a good boy, obedient & respectful to your elders & especially to your Aunts. I hope you will not neglect your books. You may require no great deal, an hour or two each day to study. It is all important to have your mind stored with useful knowledge, not forgetting that religion should be the basis of all your actions. I rec'd your letter & was very gratified & hope you will continue to write at least once a week.

"I have had your shoes repaired & a new pair made. I will send them to you by the first opportunity that may offer. The pair I bought you in Piscataway & the old ones will last you for some time to come, I hope. Give my best love to dear Aunt Mary & tell her this letter is as much for her as you. She must keep up her spirits & believe all things will yet work right. Give our united love to dear Aunt Susan, Cousin F. Kate & the children. I feel under many, many obligations for their uniform & continued kindness. They are truly friends in mind. I shall be ever grateful for their warm affectionate kindness. May a kind providence guard them & theirs from every danger.

"Your Mama & Sister & Brother write with me in love to you & all friends. Write soon to your affect father, Townshend D. F_____"

By August 28th, Eliza and the other children were also in Maryland.

"I have just rec'd your affectionate letter of the 26th and am truly delighted to hear you are all well. It is a source of great pleasure, in my loneliness, to hear from my absent loved ones.

"We are in the midst of excitement & rumor. The streets are crowded with soldiers, en route to reinforce Pope. The river is dotted with Steamers & transports, presenting the same appearance it did at their embarkation. The sight is grand, but sickening to a southern heart. I think the soldiers are much demoralized & judging from the talk, they are not for more fights. The news we have is of the most cheering character. The report is this morning that Pope is surrounded, that we have possession of Manassas & that Jackson is in his rear. It is also said we have taken an immense amount of commissary stores. [For once Towny's information is correct. The starving boys in gray had captured the supplies at Manassas, whereupon they either ate it or blew it up.]

"An other report is that our pickets have been as low as Burke Station, about 14 miles. A sutler states this morning that the Confeds were within 10 miles of this place. A whole regiment of Cavalry returned here last night, this is fact. The immense number of troops are being forwarded. McC is said to be strengthening the fortifications about Alex. I do not believe that it is the intention of our troops to advance on this place but they may force the Federals back, in which event it will be uncomfortable perhaps to us.

"I have been debating the prospects of leaving home even for a day. My friends all advise me not to go as it would leave my property too much exposed. I have concluded, therefore, to forgo the pleasure of my visit on Saturday as I intended, but will, if nothing occurs to present, meet you at Ben's Saturday & spend the day. They might establish the pass system again. However, sufficient unto the day is the evil thereof. The Bank has not yet been taken. The present Governor says no private family shall be interfered with, whilst this is an occupied house. McVeigh's house was not taken, as we heard when Fendall [Marbury] was here.

"I found on Monday, when I got home, there has been a great flare up. Kitty had got possession of the Wallett & abstracted $3.00 of its contents. John tied her up Sunday night, to make her confess what she had done with it & he says M_____ kicked up a tremendous fuss & would not let him whip her, so he is minus money. Kitty cleared out & has not since been seen by me. John has also vacated for good. I have much to say on this subject but will defer until we meet.

"Rachel was here Tuesday, Wednesday, evidently with the intention of domiciling herself permanently. I asked her what she proposed doing. She said she did not know. I advised her to go home & behave herself. She left, so M_____ states, with good intentions but never reached Mr. W so she is now at large. I ordered her positively not to return here.

"The city, I believe, keeps pretty healthy, except some cases of diphtheria with children. I have not seen or heard any thing of Fanny or Alfred – did you remove that linen shift that was in the garrett. I cannot find it. I suspected that F_____ probably had been here. The cook declares she has not. I do not miss anything about the house but that.

"Give my best love to dear Aunt Mary. I hope she is getting reconciled at the loss of Fanny. Poor old lady, I do feel very much for her. Give my love to all at Wyoming & Liberty. I must now close with best love to you & our dear children. Praying a Kind providence to guard & protect you all I remain, as ever, your own devoted & affect husband, Townsh'd D. F_____ "

Between the above letter of Towny's and his next, two of the most famous battles took place. The Battle of Antietam, near Sharpsburg, MD, on September 17, 1862 was the bloodiest one–day battle of the entire war. The Union lost 12,410 and the Confederates 10,700. Though neither side could proclaim a decisive victory, it may have cost the South the recognition and help it so desperately sought from Great Britain. Less than a year later, on July 1–3, 1863, Lee was defeated at Gettysburg, PA and driven out of northern territory for the rest of the war. The slaughter there, over three days, totaled 51,000. In Towny's next correspondence to Eliza, at Wyoming, he was still lamenting the war in his usual florid style, on September 16, 1864.

"This is a bright & beautiful morning, the sun shining as serenely as if no horrid intestine war was raging & desolating by vandal acts this fair & beautiful land, once the home of the free, the Despot tyrants oppression & persecution. Why is it that a once so glorious Nation should be torn & tattered in fragments and chaos take the place of peace, greatness and plenty. It must be the vengeance of offended deity, for the sins of this once favored people. May he, in his wisdom, soon avert this sore calamity & stop this cruel war of blood & carnage. The sunny South must & will be free, which God grant in his mercy.

"I am sorry to say all our chickens are dead, except two, which I cannot account for, the other two look drooping. I think they have proved unprofitable stock to us. Ben lost, the evening I arrived, his most valuable cow. She fell in a ditch in the pasture & broke her neck. Josie was very much distressed, as it was her pet cow. Indeed she is a very great loss to them, was giving four gallons of milk per day. Our old cow still keeps up her milk & the tomatoes are coming on finely." He concludes with his usual love to all.

On September 21st he was relieved to hear from Eliza that she was well. He added:

"Our dear little boy relieves the monotonous loneliness very much. Occasional sadness will come over me, more the result of the State of Affairs than any seated disease. I hope the return of my dear absent ones will soon put me right.

"The news of yesterday from the valley is rather depressing, if true. It is said that Sheridan has defeated Early with great loss of prisoners, etc. My own opinion is that the account is very much exaggerated and that when we hear the true State of the case, the boot may be slightly on the other leg. There is no doubt a heavy battle has been fought. Our loss is said to be thirty five hundred prisoners [actually, only about 1800 boys in gray were captured], several stands of colors & etc., doubtless

81

it is out to counteract their loss on the Peninsula. In the way of cattle their loss is said to be from twentyfive h'd to five thousand, a glorious haul in the way of beef for the poor starving Confeds. [He is referring to the infamous Beefsteak Raid by Major Gen'l Wade Hampton, JEB Stuart's replacement when he was killed. They came away with 2486 steers of the Union, as romanticized by William Holden and Richard Widmark in the movie *Alvarez Kelly*.]

"We have no news from the West. No one can tell what Grant is about or what he intends to do next, perhaps endeavoring to re–elect Lincoln. Who is to be the next President is in great doubt, and in my opinion of very little account. Nothing but the success of the Army will give the South independence. It will then be sure & permanent.

"Bennie & I are getting on pretty well. The old cow keeps up pretty well. Our tomatoes ripen slowly, just get enough to eat, no more loss in chickens. Maria is toasting coffee, washing to day – no perceptible improvement tho we get on very well. Bennie keeps very well and seems interested in his school. I have had to purchase new books, which is quite a dear item these hard times, but I suppose it will all pay out in the end. I have sold the little Stove for six dollars."

He then signs off with his usual hope all are well, etc.

Before the next correspondence from Towny there was a lot of news. General Phil Sheridan had taken Atlanta and stripped the Shenandoah Valley of anything and everything which would have provided the Confederates any sustenance. News of either of these would have distressed Towny but what followed was even more depressing. On March 4, 1865, Abe Lincoln gave his second inaugural address. Then on April 9th, General Robert E. Lee surrendered the Army of Virginia, though that did not include all the men in gray. The last sizeable force to surrender finally did so on June 23rd. In the meantime, Lincoln was assassinated April 15th, six days after the surrender at Appomattox. Surely Towny wrote about these to his wife or son but no letters remain. Even more curiously, only three letters from Eliza are included so far, yet Towny frequently proclaimed delight at receiving her letters. His letters had to be brought back from Maryland and added to the collection. Did he discard those of Eliza and Ben? August 25, 1865 was the date of his next correspondence and it was to his daughter, Nancy. She was almost twelve and was with Aunt Mary in Maryland.

"My darling little Daughter! I received your sweet letter by Benny, when he came up before & felt very much pleased that you thought of me & to find, also, that my little daughter could write so well & I hope she will write to me often as it will always give me so much pleasure to receive & read your letters.

"Benny told you that I was laid up with a sore foot. I am still unable to walk, tho my foot is better & I hope in a few days to get about again. I am getting very tired of sitting so much. It will be a fortnight tomorrow since I was out of the house, except in the yard, & you may imagine how restless I am getting. Mama has had a great deal to do & I have been unable to assist her, which worries me very much. We have missed our dear little daughter very much indeed. I think you would have been such a nice hand to dress Pa's foot & have relieved Ma of some of her numerous duties.

"It has been the pleasure of our merciful Father to take from us our dear good old Aunt Morgan. She died last night about three O'C. Mr. Beach came for Ma a little before four O'C. It was not an unexpected event, yet it was sudden, she was something better yesterday evening. Sat up & eat her supper & retired without any change to create alarm. Our loss is doubtless her eternal gain but still we cannot help missing her cheerful, happy smile. Dear Old lady, she is relieved of much care & anxiety and no doubt much suffering. God's will be done, may we all be prepared to meet the summons, for the young as well as the old have to die."

"I have no news to write you. In haste, your own devoted Pa Townshend D. Fendall," signing with his usual full name signature.

His next letter to Nancy was written September 4th and was the first of many telling her it was time to come home:

"We have missed our dear little daughter very much & think it is now time for her to be returning home, as the schools are all commencing & we are anxious that you should commence your studys. You are now eleven or twelve years old & you have no time to loose. You have already been too much neglected & you will have to work hard to make up for lost time & I want my little daughter to be equal to other girls of her age.

"I am still confined to the house with my foot. It is something better but I cannot yet walk & I fear it will be some time before I shall be able to do so. Doct Murphy is attending me, he has directed a wash, which allays the swelling but does not seem to benefit me in any other way & to make matters worse Benny has been laid up for the last week or ten days with his foot. He rubbed the skin of his heel off with a new pair of shoes & has been unable to move about until the last two or three days.

"We have been very much worried with servants, the girl we had was taken sick more than a week ago & is still sick. We are now without a servant but have the promise of one next week, but I suppose as usual shall be disappointed. Mama has a very laborious time. I am unable to render but little assistance, so you see we are in

83

a rather bad fix; & what is worse than all, have no money, & I can't move about to get any. Hope things will be better after awhile.

"Benny & Willie went to the Circus & Managerie yesterday, the latter was perfectly delighted. We all wished very much that you had been here to have gone with them. It is one of the grandest affairs that has ever been exhibited here before, amongst the animals was an "Hipopotamus." Willie gives a wonderful account of that. He will have another to relate when you return home. Your brother B proposes going on a moonlight excursion to Glymont [in Charles Co, MD] this eve, if his foot is well enough. He anticipated of course much pleasure."

He closed, once again proclaiming he had no news to write to her and asked her to get her Aunt Mary to revise and correct her letter, admonishing her to be "very particular in your <u>spelling</u>," advice he might follow. Eliza also scolded her about her spelling in her addition:

"I have just read your letter which we were very glad to receive, it was remarkably well worded, but you are very careless in spelling; make a great many mistakes, which is owing to the great hurry that you always write in; and for which there is no necessity. You must not attempt to write to Lucy or any of your little companions without writing first on a slate, and getting cousin Jimmie or 'little Nanny' to correct it for you. I think of sending you to school to Miss Fanny Gwinn, which will be very near for you in the winter and she is said to be an excellent teacher. You have been from home nearly four weeks. I have missed you dreadfully and have had a very hard time but it is not worth while to complain of that as it is so often the case these times. I want you to come home the first opportunity as I will have to fix you up a little. Your affect ma E E Fendall."

By August of 1867 Towny was finally employed, by the Alexandria Water Company, as secretary and treasurer. Ironically, when the company moved to the old bank building, he would end up working in the same room he had worked in as an officer of the bank, according to his obituary. He wrote Eliza: "I met with several friends on the cars & the ride would have been pleasant but for the intolerable heat & the negro element. The cars were filled with passengers & I had no alternative but to ride with them. O glorious reconstruction, equality & the Yankeys." Streetcars did not begin operating in Alexandria until 1892 so he was referring to a train.

On September 11, 1867 he admonished Nancy to...

"...be a little more particular, not leave out letters in your words & a little more attention to your spelling. I am not finding fault dear child but it is for your good that I call attention to these things. Your brother will be up on Saturday. Say to Mama to have the waggon to meet him at the station. I shall send her & you some peaches, the box they go in will answer to put the chicken in if she gets away. I shall also send a Tin buckett for the butter, which I hope she has succeeded in getting. It is very scarce & high here. I hope nothing may occur to prevent Bennie on Saturday."

His letter to his "darling Liz" two days later was more amorous:

"I am delighted at the prospect of soon seeing you. Our dear boy Benny goes up tomorrow for you & I write you a line of remembrance & a token of affection. An absence of four weeks seems like an age of seperation. I will not deny that I have often wished for your dear presence, to cheer my lonely hours, & to put in tune the quiet chords of the heart, which ever vibrate with delight when you are near. What a dreary wilderness this world would be if it were not for the anticipation & hopes & presence of some dear object. Truly the greatest boon that the Creator bestowed upon man was the creation & bestowing of a partner, to council & solace the pilgrimage of life. Existence to me would be a painful blank & I do rejoice that my own precious loved one will soon be within my warm embrace, to cheer with her sweet voice & touch my desolate home. I say desolate because home is desolate & has been in the absence of the dear object that makes it joyous & happy. I verily believe if left alone I should go back to a state of semi barbarism. I trust you may have a pleasant ride & arrive in safety."

By May, 1868, Ben was 17 and, judging by his address, at the Charlotte Hall Military Academy, now the Maryland Veterans Home for disabled vets. He asked Towny to look for *Wells Familiar Science or Comstock Chemistry* in the garret, adding he was "still enjoying first rate health & spirits." In a longer letter to his "Ma," on January 2, 1869, he asked for more practical items. He had evidently graduated and was now working for a railroad in Lynchburg, Virginia.

"I wrote to you some days since for a pair of pants which I suppose you have gotten before this. Please send them as soon as you can to Lynchburg. I spent my xmas at Mrs. Aprille's (?) had a very nice time. There were several young ladies there but I did not have much to do with them as they are things I have done with. One has fooled me and if another one does I want some friend of mine to knock me in the head.

"I don't know exactly what pay I draw but think about $45, board about $30. We have crossed Staunton River and are in Pittsylvania, hope to reach Danville by March. Mr. Norvill, one of our party, expects to go to Louisiana soon says if I want to go he'll take me & insure me from $100 to $150 per month and board, but if I can get on the levees I'll go there as I'd have more spare time. Mr. Wharton, who has charge of the party, has told me I am capable of taking charge at a level when ever I can get a place. I don't know what else to say, you accuse me of being laconic, but can only add that very well is your hopeful son, B T Fendall."

On August 19 Towny wrote Liz and Nancy he was sending them some watermelon, cantalope and peaches, then mentions "many outrages committed by the negroes. Do not allow Nannie to go off the streets of the town. If you wish to visit out of town, hire a hack. You can get one for a dollar or two. You saw that account of the rape on Miss Thompson near Front Royal."

One week later he expanded on his loneliness:

"I can't realize how any one can be happy in this world without some object to incite to action, and drive away the morbid thoughts of ennui, which will affect both mind & body, unless we have something tangible to look forward to. 'Man should not be alone' is clearly proven, by the bestowal of the Great Creator, of Eve to Adam, therefore the high precedent sustains me in the opinion that our moral & physical natures require that we should have some one to unburden our cares & pleasures, & who so appropriate as a loving wife whose smiles will always lighten our burdens & add to our joys."

In August of 1870 Nancy was almost 17 and visiting Dr. Ward and his family in Warrenton, Virginia. On the 6th, Towny wrote his…

"…darling little daughter, I am all alone, Mother & children are gone and only the bare wall & an empty solitary house with one, old occupant, and that terrible.

"Your dear Mama left this mg at 11 o'c a.m.train for Rawley Springs, in care of your Cousin Sam, to spend a week or two. [Rawley was one of many springs throughout Virginia that was very popular. People would go there for the mineral water, professed to cure every ailment. The Fendalls and Tacketts all spent many weeks at several of the springs.] She was quite well, but had to get ready in a great flurry and I fear on her arrival will find that she has forgotten sundry little fixings. I trust she may have a pleasant and safe ride and the Springs prove a benefit. Bennie left yesterday for Md to spend a couple of weeks, he was very well. Will left today, in company with his cousin Jennie.

"Your Mama rec'd your letter and we were truly delighted to hear you are well and enjoying yourself so much. I do not know how we shall return the kind hospitality of Doct & Mrs Ward, express our greatful acknowledgements. I am afraid my dear daughter you may wear out your friends by staying too long – of that you must judge. I am glad that Mrs W. disapproved of the buggy ride, it fully coincides with my sense of propriety. You are young and inexperienced and must be very careful of what you do or say. Be advised by Mrs. W. and I feel sure she will advise wisely.

"Before I close my dear child I must give you a few words of advise. I hope you will be prudent & not expose your self & keep late hours and not be familiar with young men – dignity of character commands much more respect than too much freedom. I do not mean that you shall be prudish, but that you shall so act as to command the love & respect of all – and never my dear child forget your first duty is to your heavenly father upon his mercy & protection rely, asking at all times his advise & protection, by prayer and read the sacred volume daily with a prayerful heart.

"Write to me often, it will be a great comfort to me in my loneliness – don't hesitate to let me know, should you want any thing. Your Mama will write you from the Springs. God bless & protect you my precious daughter – prays your ever devoted father Townshend D. Fendall."

August 10, 1870, Towny wrote Nancy:

"Your sweet affectionate letter of the 8th I rec'd last evening & I was truly delighted to hear you were well and still enjoying yourself so much. It is delightful to my feeling to know that you are so bright & happy. It belongs to youth to be thus, but in youth we should lay up stores for old age, which if we live will come, therefore my precious child do not wed yourself too much to the pleasures of this world, they are transitory & fleeting – all is bright now, but a cloud may over shadow your bright path way – be prepared to meet the change by laying up those more endearing stores that prepare you for eternity. This world with all its pleasures is but an abiding place soon passeth away. I do not wish to allay one of your pleasures but to admonish you, that all that glitters is not gold, therefore do not give your self too much to pleasure but be rational & reasonable, be not wedded to earthly idols, let your heart look with reverence to the great Author of all pleasure (the only true source of all the earthly pleasures we enjoy). I hope my little daughter will not think I am preaching a sermon or that my remarks are applicable to any thing that has occurred. I am admonishing her to guard against that which

might estrange her young heart from good thoughts & her heavenly father.

"Your ink is so pale that my old eyes could hardly decipher the writing & then you write in too great a hurry and are not sufficiently particular in spelling. I say this in no spirit of scolding or complaint but I wish to call your attention, for the future. I find several words improperly spelt, for instance, needed, you spell with a 'K', <u>kneeded</u>. I am sure you know better, it is owing to a careless thoughtless habit you have fallen into." (The reader is well aware of his misspelled words but doesn't know how tough it was at times to translate his writing, especially when he wrote both ways on the paper, as he did in several letters to Nancy. It was started as a way to save paper during the war, writing over one page in the opposite direction of the first writing. As his letters were very long, perhaps he also did it to save paper then. Whatever the reason, it was difficult to decipher, perhaps as much for Nancy as it was for the author.)

He went on to relate seven more pages of news about her brothers, friends and various relatives, adding, as usual, he had "no news to write." The phrase appears in almost all his letters hereafter. He described his loneliness and was surprised she had no fruit, as he had peaches and milk every day. Closing with his customary wish God protect her, he added a postscript: "You must let me know if you want anything. I think you had better have your washing all done in Warrenton, even if you have to pay a little extra. Does your money hold out, if it does not, let me know."

August 16th brought forth the following to Nancy:

"I rec'd your sweet letter last eve and was truly delighted to hear you were well & still enjoying yourself so much. I am afraid you will become so attached to Warrenton you will not be satisfied with home again. You have been from home now four or five weeks & I am afraid you will wear your friends welcome out. When do you propose returning. I hope shortly. It seems an age since you left me. I want to see you dreadfully bad. I am spending a very lonely time. Well I suppose when you all get back you will make it up to me, in the pleasant accounts of your visits.

"Cousin Sam Beach returned yesterday from the Springs and brought me a very sweet letter from Mama. She is very well and enjoying herself. She has improved in health and I hope will return to us rosy and as fat as a partridge. I think they will all return first of next week. I think of going up on Saturday to stay a few days. I had a letter from Bennie yesterday. He and all friends were well. He was at your Cousin Fendalls where he wrote, says the little stranger is a fine little fellow & that mother & child getting on finely. It is now dinner time & I must go to my lonely meal (nice peaches today) & finish this when I come back.

"Well I ret'd from dinner a little while ago – took a little nap & feel a little stupid. I heard from your uncle Hector yesterday through Ned Ashly. He was very #### & gone to work in Carnell with a prospect of success, plenty of work. I hope all this may be true and that he may get to the upper round of the ladder of fame in his profession. I saw little Alice at the door this mg as I was passing. Miss Kitty & Mrs. MacPherson are well.

Will Fendall

"My kind regards to Doct & Mrs. Ward & Mrs. Hamilton. Love to Mamie. You must hold yourself in readiness to return at a moments warning. I keep very well & am getting on pretty well house keeping. God bless you my precious child. May you soon return renewed in health & strength to your devoted father Townshend D. Fendall"

In this huge collection of letters there are many oddities, ranging from the presence of some letters to the absence of others. This was particularly true with the Fendalls. Dozens of letters from Townshend to Eliza or Nancy are included, indicating they brought the letters home from wherever they had been. But where are the letters they wrote back? He invariably lamented his loneliness when they were gone; why didn't he keep the letters that he claimed delighted him? There are many fascinating letters from Ben, describing his snobbery, ethics, moral fiber, and affection for his sister, as well as a detailed description of his literally "working on the railroad" in his struggle for success as an engineer – which he achieved. Much of Will's correspondence is also present. His pen was dipped in honey as he lavished loving thoughts on his mother and sister. Both of them became stuck in that honey, believing it sweet, but it was a trap. While he was declaring love he was lining his pockets with funds they entrusted to him. Funds that they would learn, too late, had disappeared. Will also liked to brag about his way with the ladies.

Nancy's letters, on the other hand, are missing, until she married in 1883, except for several letters she received and sent to a suitor she rejected, named C. L. Clagett. These were written in March 1876 and, strangely, both her and his correspondence are present. Her letters do not appear to be copied so how did she acquire them? And where are all the letters she wrote to her parents, requesting she be allowed to stay "just one more week" wherever she was visiting? Every summer she sent such letters and every summer Towny and Eliza wrote back, telling her she should come home. Their letters are included; only one of hers remains. Letters from Ben or Will to Nancy, still living at home, were also saved. Why weren't hers? There is a slim, if seemingly farfetched, explanation. She could have destroyed them when she lived at home. After she married, her letters to her absent husband accumulated, along with his to her, until August 17, 1896. Her letter on that date implored Jack to burn her letters. Fortunately for us he does not burn all, but their daughters did, at her request. Whatever the reason, we must wait until she marries to derive any sense of who she is from her correspondence, except to note her inclination to ignore all instructions she return home when she didn't wish to do so.

Benjamin Fendall, from the Baltimore Sun, September 25, 1907.

One of Ben's letters was sent to Nancy on May 28, 1871. He was in Pittsylvania, one of the southernmost counties of Virginia and wrote:

"I am going to try and be more punctual and answer letters from home more promptly than I have done heretofore. The delegation from Chalk Level has been in town for some days, staying with their brother & the Engineers have been having a fine large time. It would have done you good to have seen Wilkins & myself get in the C L carriage & drive off with the young ladies, much to the amazement of the villagers, who look upon the aforesaid damsels as something far above the ordinary run of #### & how a rough Engineer should presume to speak, much more ride in their carriage was something far above their comprehension.

"Chalk Level does not admire the villagers & vice versa because they consider the former to be too much of the patrician order. Expect to go down to see the young ladies quite frequently while I am here. Mrs. Martin (the widow) has very kindly offered to lend me her buggy & horse when ever I want it & my opinion is that she is quite an able woman.

"I wrote to Ma some days since with various little commissions for her to attend to. I told all about myself that I know except about my pay. Well now on this subject I know nothing with absolute certainty but from what I can gather from reliable sources it will be about $1,000 pr annum [over $17,000 today], which is better perhaps than Mr. H. could do for me, notwithstanding his views to the contrary. I don't consider Mr. B to be a very able prophet as he predicted that I'd never do anything at engineering. I hardly think you would know your brother if you were to see him, so rough & sunburned he looks with out coat or collar; all that is left of his former care for his beloved person is the tenderness where with he watches over his hands, making the most strenuous efforts to preserve their former whiteness & softness.

"By the way if you can crowd in a pair of white pants & a white vest or two among those things I wrote for they would be thankfully rec'd. If however, the bundle has left it makes no difference. The things ordered are intended solely for Chalk Level & now as I have destroyed all the paper I can tonight I'll quit. With much love I am yr devoted Bro B T Fendall."

On August 23, 1871, Towny informed Nancy he was on his way to see his dying sister, Susan Marbury, at "Wyoming," where Eliza and the children have spent many a summer. Eliza had just left for Rawley Springs. The following day he wrote Eliza:

"An all wise providence in his wisdom, has taken from us our cherished and beloved eldest sister Susan. Ben [Fendall] came for me yesterday mg abt 11 o'clock. She was then alive but I felt satisfied, from what he told me, she could not survive. I hastened as soon as I could, but ere I reached Wyoming her pure spirit had winged its flight to the mansions of the blessed, whom doubtless she is with her beloved ones that have preceded her, enjoying the blessed happiness of a reunion.

"She was taken on Monday with a dizziness and oppression in her head. Yesterday mg she turned better, but in a short time became worse & finally insensible & never spoke after and died abt 3 o'clock P.M. She retained her faculties up to her insensibility & did not dread the result, her only care Sister Mary told me, seemed to be the little boys, an irreparable loss to them.

"It has been a terrible shock to me as I was totally unprepared, but what a consolation to believe that she was prepared, with her 'lamps trimmed and burning,' for the summons. I feel that our loss tho sudden & unexpected is her eternal gain. No more care, no more suffering, but with angels, enjoying the promised reward of the righteous. She was a dear & loving Sister & has ever manifested the warmest & deepest affection for me & mine. Her kind and generous heart ever ready & willing to serve. Gods will be done. Her mortal remains will be deposited in their last resting place tomorrow afternoon at 3 o'clock. God willing I shall attend. I deeply regret you are not here, to accompany me. I know I have the sympathy of your kind heart, under this heavy bereavement and I know, too, you loved my dear dear Sister.

"I wrote to Nannie yesterday a few lines just before I left, informing her of the illness of her Aunt & expressing fears of the result & I have written this eve the sad intelligence. As you could not possibly reach in time for the funeral I prefer your remaining where you are, until such time as you may desire to return. Our dear little Willie & friends are well, but in great distress. Bennie will return I presume this eve & I should like, if he can, for him to accompany me tomorrow. Yr devoted & affect husband, Townshend D. Fendall."

August 29, 1871, to Eliza:

"I truly regret to hear your eyes continue so painful. I had hoped the Rawley water would have relieved. [Eliza may suffer blepharitis, the same condition as her brother, Hector, which is an inflammation of the eyelash follicle. If so, Rawley's iron springs would not have alleviated that in the least.]

"Having already conveyed to you the sad inteligence of my beloved Sister I have but little more to add on this painful subject. Bennie & I paid the last sad duties of respect to her dear memory, on Friday, & we saw the last of the mortal remains deposited in their earthly sepulcher. It was a sad & painful scene. When I looked around those narrow grounds & saw the evidences of the dear departed ones, Father, Mother, Sisters, brother & nieces & I had accompayned them all to their last resting places on this earth, it was solemn & harrowing. But O – how consoling to believe that our loss is their eternal gain – and doubtless they are reaping the reward of a well spent life. What a happy reunion in heaven, where all is glory. No more suffering & cares no more parting – may their bright example induce us to be prepared to meet them in that glorious, happy Spirit land.

"The funeral was attended by a number of sorrowing friends – a very appropriate & touching address by Dr. Marbury of her life & character and of her great loss to the church, the Revd Mr. Tolls gave a very good address. Truly a bright & shining & noble character has gone, leaving an aching void, to relations & friends. She was no ordinary person endowed by Nature, with a superior mind, with a will & energy to pursue & accomplish – and will, all gentle & sweet, child like in her sweet gentle manners, with a force of character, commanding & dignified, tempered with a pure Christian spirit – all ways prompt & ready charitable duties and unwavering in her devotion to her Church, she then will be a great loss.

"She was a devoted Mother, Sister & friend. Sainted beloved Sister fare well. Oh that the pure Mantle could rest upon thy sorrowing relatives, that they too might meet the joyful words. 'Well done good & faithful servant' enter then on the right hand. I feel & believe she is happy. It is human to feel – deeply feel – this terrible bereavement, but the #### hope is a consolation. May her memory ever rest with us, the bright examples guide & direct our sojourn.

"Bennie & I retd to Mrs. Beyers & spent the night, too late to get over the ferry. Next mg (Saturday) we came over to breakfast &

92

Bennie took the Cars at 8 o'c for Warrenton & was to leave Monday for Lynchburg, en route for Pittsylvania C. H. Robb came down Sunday eve, left Ben & Nan very well. I recd a very kind affect letter from Nan Saturday. She was much distressed at her Aunt's death. Our dear little Willie & friends were all well when I left them. Dear Sister Mary very much cast down. It has been a terrible blow to her. Do write to her when you can."

On April 21, 1872, Ben – still at Chalk Level – wrote his sister:

"It is almost bed time & I am quite sleepy but I will try and make a small 'naration' before retiring. The weather is getting delightful at last, the fruit trees have been in flower for some time and the woods are getting quite green, and the Whip–poor–wills are at their works, which is one of the surest indications of warm weather that is. The probabilities are that we shall have a very fine fruit year which is a 'consummation devoutly to be wished.'

"I should like so much to see Miss Jennie Davidge, she certainly would not want for a beau if I were at home. She is just as sweet as she can be. I am afraid tho Alexandria men are losing what little taste they ever had. Give my kindest regards to her tell her I am very sorry that I am away from home, can't see her &c&c. How long will she stay?

"I wish you would purchase the 'Chosee Informal Galop' for me and send it by mail. I promised a young female a piece of music. If there is any newer Galop which is prettier than the above you may send that in its stead. With much love to all – As ever, Yr affect Bro B. T. Fendall."

In his next letter, written September 19th, Ben described his work:

"I must really beg pardon for not having written to you sooner but the fact is I am as busy as I can be. I have two or three bridges to inspect several times a week and there is a large quantity of work being finished off or dressed up as we term it and it takes all my time during the day and at night I am too sleepy to be able to write.

"Everything is exceedingly dull here. The young ladies & gentlemen amuse themselves with croquet, hunting &c. Croquet as you know is my pet abomination. We have had court here all this week and as usual everything has been worse than the itch at the hotel with the crowd of country people that are always on hand upon such occasions. I frequently have my lunch sent to my office court week to keep from eating with or near them, they are so insufferably hoggish.

"If I can get a buggy & horse I want to take Katie driving this afternoon as the weather is perfectly delightful. I have no news whatever. [Like father, like son?] Am as well as ever. I must close and go see about my team. With kind regards I am as ever yr affect bro B. T. Fendall."

Nancy, now almost 19 and therefore no longer in school, was obviously visiting somewhere and, as usual, had overstayed her visit. Eliza had recently returned from Maryland and, after bringing her up to date on the cousins, chastised her on September 27th:

"I received a letter from Mamie Ward yesterday, she wanted me to have some black velvet cleaned and pressed for her. I wrote to her today and told her I thought it would be impossible for you to visit Warrenton [where Mrs. Ward lives], you have been from home nearly all the Summer and I <u>cannot</u> spare you any longer. I have been feeling very badly ever since my return from Md, and your pa and cousin Lizzie seem to be very fearful I may have typhoid fever, but I think it is only from loss of rest, and hard work since I came home. I always feel languid and a great want of energy as evening comes on but I have no fever and think it is owing to fatigue. I have no house servant yet which I find very inconvenient when I have company. Nace does very well as far as waiting on the table goes but he is a trial in other respects.

"Sunday evening – I commenced this letter on Friday, but was interrupted before I could finish it; yesterday I was preserving all day and when I got through was so completely broken down I had to retire directly after tea. I have a sore throat, and as usual have taken cold from being overheated, you know I never can stand cooking. Your pa and I were very much disappointed as well as surprised to find from your last letter you wanted to stay longer when we were expecting you home daily. I wrote to you before I left Md telling you I thought you had staid long enough. I think you are trespassing too long on Mrs. Corse's hospitality. I never dreamed of you staying more than two weeks and you have extended your visit to four and still wanting to stay longer. Now you <u>must</u> come home this week. I have a great deal to do and want your assistance as well as your society.

"Give my love to Mrs. Corse and tell her I am exceedingly obliged to her for not allowing you to go to Warrenton, particularly, as you would have to stay at Manissa all night. Love to Fannie and Mary tell the latter I am fearful you will make her twice glad. I hope she will come down and make you a visit this winter when Mamie Ward comes. Hoping to see you in a <u>few</u> days, I am as ever your devoted Mother."

Six days later Nancy had still not returned home. She repeatedly ignored her parent's pleas for her return, wherever and whenever she went visiting. Now Towny wrote:

"I believe I owe you a letter, but expecting you home last week, I thought it hardly worth while to write. Little did I think when you left how five long weary weeks would roll around before I saw you again, if I had dreamed you were going to stay so long, I never would have consented to your going – it seems as if I had no daughter at all, you have been so constantly absent from me all the Summer. It is a severe trial to me and then I fear you will wear out your welcome. I am sure your friends have been kind from your staying so long but I fear you have imposed too long upon their hospitality. I hope you will not prolong your visit beyond Monday at farthest. [This was written on a Thursday.]

"Your Ma & myself are very uneasy about Bennie, we have not had a letter from him for nearly three weeks – a very unusual circumstance, as he has never failed to write once a week. I have written to him this eve to enquire the cause. I hope he is not sick. Your Ma is well again, but has been very busy preserving & pickling the last several days & I fear the fatigue will lay her up again. Will is very well & quite studious. We all write with the fond hope of soon seeing you. Your devoted father Townshend D. Fendall."

Ben, though slightly less than three years older than Nancy, nevertheless chastised her whenever he felt she strayed from his ideas of propriety. On January 5, 1873, he was glad to hear she was "having so pleasant a time" visiting again, but he thought her trip "with Mr. Berry was rather an imprudent one as it turned out but as he is a Mason and I suppose he knows me as such I feel no fear. So long as you are with a Mason who knows your brother is one too, you are safe from all danger save 'the acts of God or the King's.'"

Nancy was visiting in Baltimore, at the home of Dr. Albert W. Grey, at 195 N. Howard Street, but that didn't save her from admonishments from her mother, regarding her behavior, or from her father, regarding what he considered the "duties of life." Eliza's letter came first, on February 14, 1873.

"I tell you what a lonely week I have had. What do you think of my being shut up in a house since Monday [it's Friday] without seeing a single white face but pa and Will's. Not a soul to speek to all day, except at meals; it has been raining or snowing nearly the whole week, until this morning. When the sun came out I could stand it no longer, determined to go up and dine with cousin Lizzie. Whilst I was there Con received your letter, which has caused me some little anxiety, hearing you are not well, I fear you have taken cold. I am sure your shoes are too thin, go out and get a heavy pair with thick soles, suitable for walking in this damp weather; do be careful my dear child, your health is of more importance than any thing else.

"Pace has just returned from the office and I am again disappointed, you <u>must</u> try and write to us twice a week and than you can keep me posted in regard to all your movements. My dear child I hope you are particular in keeping your room in order, and do not through your clothes 'around loose' as you and Mamie have been doing. Do <u>always</u> be prompt at meals; by neglecting these little things you may greatly annoy systematic persons.

"Look out when you are shopping for some little present for aunt Mary, goods are much higher on Baltimore St than some of the more retired streets; get Miss #### to show you where you can find the cheep, try and get a pair of nice fitting corsets long waisted. I <u>must</u> hear from you often. Do you play and sing much? In your walks you might go into some of those piano establishments and inquire the price of good second handed Knabe. Will & bro sent me a circular the other day they are agents for Steffs which they greatly praise. Have you been to the theatre opera?

"Pa and Will send much love, the former says if you get sick you will see him very soon. Mr. B. is complaining just as you are, I am sure you have taken cold and I am always fearful of inflammation of the bowel if suffered to run on. Do let me hear from you at once. Your devoted Mother."

Next, Eliza advised Nancy on her attire, on the 19th:

"I think it is very sweet and kind in Mrs. Gray to go to the trouble of having company for you, with all she has to attend to. Give a great deal of love to her and tell her to make you obey her in all things, and be a <u>good child</u>. I do not want you to trespass too long upon her kindness. I think it will soon be time for you to be turning your face homewards. I think if Mrs. Gray has a small company you had better wear your black silk as you may have a chance of going to some large party where you will need the pink. Why don't you tell me something about how you dress in the evenings and what you walk out in. I hope you do not wear your black silk except on special occasions, the black cashmier will not be so easily injured and will better stand the wear and tare and was not so costly a dress as the silk. You ought to wear your blue in the house for a change." [And she chastised Nancy for her spelling!]

One letter from Nancy, pleading her case, has survived and is quoted exactly as written. This one is dated March 13, 1873 and was to:

"My dearest Mother. Mrs. Herbert called to see me yesterday and wanted me to go & spend this evening with her but we are going to have company to Tea with us this evening so she is coming tomorrow evening and take me to Christ Church and from church I am going to spend the evening with her she says Mr. Herbert is very anxious to see me and to hear me sing as Willie has been telling them what a charming voice I have Will was here Tuesday night showed me a long letter from Ben in which he complimented his sister highly – dear sweet boy I do love him (Ben I mean) I like Willie Herbert very much he has been exceedingly polite to me he took me to St Pauls church yesterday evening We just have lots of beaux every night & I am enjoying myself beyond expression I go to church every day now – There is an 'English Opera' coming here next week and Willie H has asked me to go he says I must stay to it & he will write and ask you himself to let me stay – The Dr & Mrs G say there is no earthly necessity of your making me come home I told them you did not make me but only told me you thought it was time for me to come home so if you and Pa dont seriously object – I will stay over and go to the Opera as I have never been to one in my life but if you think it best that I should come home Monday write by the next mail & let me know Dr G says he wont let me come home unless Pa comes for me that he does want to see him so much – I have been out all the morning walking with Carry Smith – I expect you will say I am playing the 'Mommie game' but I would love so much to see an Opera if I stay I dont yet know what night Willie Herbert will take me therefore I dont know yet what day I would come home – I do want to see you all so much I have so much to talk about – I am going out to see Miss Kittie tomorrow morning – I wish you were here to shop with me – I will now have to close with very much love to all – Mrs G the Dr Miss S & Nettie all send much love and say do let me stay – I am your devoted daughter Nan."

On Saturday, March 15th, Towny wrote in his usual "it's for your own good" manner:

"Ma & myself are very much disappointed to find you will not be with us on Monday, which we looked forward to with great pleasure but as you seem to think a little longer stay would add to your pleasure, we yield to your wishes as her letter expresses my only objection is 1st, that you have trespassed long enough upon the hospitality of the kind friends & 2ndly, I fear the bad effects upon your youthful mind. It may distract you from the more important & serious duties of life.

A little pleasure is well enough, but to become entirely engrossed with worldly pleasure may have a tendency to make us indifferent to those more important & sacred duties we owe to him whom we are proud to serve. I would not & do not wish to mar one pleasure of your youthful life, but I think & fear you may think too much of this world & your own pleasures. I hope you will not forget that we are only sojourning here, to prepare for blessed immortality."

Eliza added to the above letter:

"...I suppose, as pa finds he cannot go on for you to–day as he thought of doing, we will <u>have</u> to permit you to stay a few days longer. You must certainly come the day after the opera, you have now been from home a great deal longer than we ever dreamed of your staying. Let us know what evening the opera will take place and your pa or Will can meet you or go the next day. I have not been well for several days, have taken cold, and it is a hard matter for me to get through the house keeping."

In case you're wondering if Nancy dutifully came home right after the opera, a couple of sentences from Eliza, on the 18th, answers that:

"When you wrote to know if you might prolong your visit to attend the opera I supposed it would take place about Tuesday or Wednesday and you would certainly return on the last mentioned or Thursday at any rate, but I find if we 'give an <u>inch</u> you take a <u>mile</u>.' Now you fix on Saturday, calculating on getting a <u>second</u> chance to the opera and Mrs. Gray helping you on." Nan never did come home after the first letter requesting she do so."

In July, Eliza and Nancy went visiting relatives. Towny wrote this to Eliza:

"As I sit alone in my office, love alone sustains me in the absence of the lone star, of the hearts affection, and makes me long to embrace the dear object, that is entwined so endearingly, for nearly a quarter of a century. [They married January 15, 1849.] My youthful love is as ardent and unalloyed as the day I plighted. I feel now, as I did then and I am fully persuaded that age cannot abate the ardency of sincere youthful affection, such thoughts have entered spontaneous in my mind at this moment & may he rule & direct – even keep alive to the end of our lives – without a cloud to over shadow our declining years." Along with miscellaneous news, he adds "The servants are well & attentive."

By November 1873 Ben was two months shy of being 23 and still laying track for the Baltimore & Ohio Railroad. On the 16th he was in Strasburg, VA, delayed by weather:

"I suffered a great deal Friday with my hands, having to use them so much about the brass on the instrument. We had it very fine to day however. Did not go to church to day as there were services only at the Presbyterian church and I pray to be delivered from 'all false doctrine heresy and schism.' I concluded it was best to stay away. I am trying to quit tobacco. I have only chewed two twists since I left home and hope to be able to quit altogether before I return."

On November 30th Ben told Nancy he…

"…went to church this mg, to the Lutheran Church and heard a man make an ass of himself. There are no Episcopal churches in this country. While I was in Winchester I went to the Masonic Lodge. They have one of the prettiest lodge rooms I ever saw. It is finely frescoed and furnished with very handsome seats &c.

"The country here is very beautiful. We are almost entirely surrounded by high mountains. The village is the deadest place of its size I ever saw, as soon as you leave the R.R. depot everything like business is over. I am boarding at a most interesting place called the Kirster [?] House, one of the #### in my opinion has been maudlin for ten years. He is one of those men who know everything, it makes no difference what you talk about he proceeds at once to elucidate and as might be expected makes some of the most ridiculous blunders. For instance, I asked one of the RR conductors what majority the conservatives had in Alex & this fool put in his mouth and said 20,000 which was a great many more than the whole population amounts to. The other partner is deaf as a post and makes some very absurd answers. I asked last night if Mr. Thompson had been to supper and he answered that 'he did not think we would have any rain before Monday.' They feed pretty well however and if idiot No. 1 would just not talk so continually I would get along quite well.

"I have not shaved since I left home and my beard is about a ¼ inch long all over my face and looks very nasty. I don't intend to shave or put on a white shirt until I come home, which will be about Xmas. The way we work is this, Mr. Thompson goes ahead and superintends the chaining and I follow behind him and take the elevation with the level. This we will do from here to Harrisonburg, then I will take the transit and make the survey back to this place and he will run the levels back to check me in case I should make any mistake. The whole distance there & back is 102 miles and as we make about 3 miles per diem I think allowing for Sundays and bad weather we will get through about the time I said, Xmas. We come across sulfur and iron springs quite often in our travels and I always drink the water as it is antibillious and keeps the system in good order.

"The wind is blowing very hard this afternoon and out of doors it is quite cold but in the cave here I am sitting in my shirt sleeves and slippers and am perfectly comfortable. Whenever I put them on I think of my dear 'little' sister and Miss Sallie, give my kind regards to her and tell her not to teach you to say naughty things like she did me. How comes on the German? Swimmingly I hope. With much love to all I am as ever Yr affectionate bro B.T. Fendall."

On March 25, 1874, Ben wrote Nancy from Burton, W.V., about six miles from PA:

"Your last epistle, illustrated edition, came duly to hand last night also the funds and the package by express. Those garters of mine are very short and broad in comparison with the boots I have been wearing. My instruments came to hand to day they are all right. The bill for them should be $26.44, to which the freight is to be added. Tell pa so he may know whether he has paid too much and ask him to let me know what the frt from Troy to Alex was & also from Alex to Burton.

"Please write to uncle Hec and ask him to look in some of the second hand bookstores in N.Y. and see if he can find a book entitled 'Encyclopedia of Civil Engineering' by Edward Cresy. It is an English work and although somewhat out of date contains a vast amount of valuable information. The price in England is 2£ 2s. or about $10.50 in our currency. If he can find it tell him to let me know the price and if it is not too much I will order it. You might look some time when you are in Washington. I never had time in passing through myself but looked in Balto & could not find it. I have made up my mind to make a first class Engineer of myself.

"This is a most beastly place, nasty fried meat and soda biscuits, my pet abominations, am I never to be delivered from such horrors? The people around live in hollows along the mountains where they don't see the sun more than three hours in the day and have never been out of the county. Perfectly ignorant, ergo, perfectly happy. I call them 'snakes' which I consider a happy thought." He manages to send his love to four women in the last page of his letter.

On April 1st he answered Will's letter:

"We did no work yesterday, nor will we do any to day on acc of the snow, which is quite deep and still falling. Bolling has not sent me my money yet, I am entitled to it the 15th of every mo and it is only on account of his infernal negligence that I don't get it regularly. All he has to do is ask the Treas for it and it will be forth coming at once. I owe pa nearly $50 and in the present state of his finances it is not convenient for him to loan me the money and I know it. If I had not fully expected the check I should not have ordered the instruments. Bolling promised to send me the money at Cumberland & it is all the fault of his forgetfulness. During the height of the panic the Co was only about a week behind hand in paying off their employees. The Co don't promise much but always pay what they do promise.

"I think I will be with the Co some six mo's yet as they have a lot of real estate of which they have no plats &c and we will most probably survey the land and fix things up. I think we will be here at least a week longer. We have had much trouble in establishing lines and that kind of thing, think the man who made the original survey was drunk. Hoping you will soon get something to do I am as ever Your affect Bro B.T. Fendall"

Will would be 18 in November but apparently had no particular job, other than helping out his father. Whether that was at home or at the Alexandria Water Company, where Towny was still employed, is not clear. He said he had nothing to do, then related all the news of others and his own activities and plans. The letter is dated July 30, 1874, to "My dear Nan,...

"...Dug Gray called to see us on his way home, he has been spending a week or so in Leesburg, said he was invited to a party every night whilst he was there but did not go to any of them, as he went there for rest and not for parties; I don't admire his taste although it may be logical. There is to be an Excursion to Marshall Hall [an amusement park] to–night, it will leave at 8 o'clock and return at twelve with the old folks; and go back after the young ones about four. I don't know wheather I will go or not as I have been invited to join a party at Mt. Vernon they start from Fort Foot to–morrow morning at eight and of course if I go on the Excursion I won't be in a condition to go to Mt. V.

"Pa had a letter from Ben yesterday he will be home on Saturday, he has been appointed first assistant of the Co in Thompson's place, as he has left. Aunt Mary and coz Jennie will be up to day and will stay over until next week. I shall make ma go back with them, and pa too if he will, but I know neither would go this week as they would not miss seeing Ben.

"I wish when you write you would give me the Little Womans

(R. Webb) direction as I owe her a letter. I have the peace called Farewell and I shall copy it and send it up to you, it is the prettiest thing you ever heard. Give my love to Nancy and tell her she need not be uneasy about beaus as there are plenty of them comming up the last of this week or first of next, some from Washington and from this place. Several of the fellows here are in love, but my heart is unoccupied as usual. Sometimes I think I haven't got any or very little as I don't fall in love with any of these beauties around me, can't love them to save my life. I expect it is the last thing for me too as I expect to or rather am bent on going to Alab in the Fall. But then you know we can't always tell for perhaps I might take a trip to some where else. Speaking of love, just give mine to any of the fair sex that look like they wanted it (they <u>will</u> be <u>numerous</u>).

"Coz Lizzie & Con will be home to–day and then it will not be so lonesome for me. I will have John Marbury with me next week and I wrote to Will to get his father to let him come up too; told him to give my love to M### and tell her that my separation from her had made me a mere shadow of my former self. We went on a serenade the other night, the ladies say it was the best one they had ever heard, we sang Little foot steps, Row the boat lightly & other new and very sweet songs. I went to see Lillie Massey Sunday night, talked a little love to her; <u>swore</u> I was coming up to Washington to see her before she left for the North; she goes on Saturday, going to make a visit to her sister.

"Pa has something for me to do so I must close; my love to all I remain your devoted bro Wm E. Fendall."

By August 5, 1874, Ben was in Cranberry Summit, about 50 miles southeast of Charleston, WV, as the proverbial crow flies, and wrote to Nancy:

A trolley

"I have nothing in the world of interest to write but suppose I will have to let you know I am alive. When I left Alexandria I got orders to have the line chained from Balto to Cumberland, the moderate distance of 178 miles, every inch of which I walked through some of the hottest weather we have had this summer, averaged about thirteen miles per day. Since then I have laid out two water stations and now have orders to get up maps of all stations, sidings etc between this and Grafton inclusive. I shall be at home Saturday and Sunday. Wish you could be there.

"When you write you had best direct your letters to Alex as they are better posted as to my movements & think I will move from here to Newburg about Wednesday. I am going to try and get ma to go to the springs when I go home, hear she is unwell. In that case you will have to come home and look after pa. Kind regards to aunt Grace grandma and the rest. Hoping that you are having a pleasant time and will be able to spare enough to write soon to your vagabond brother B T Fendall."

On August 31st he wrote:

"So far as funds are concerned, Nancy, I have no greater pleasure than seeing you with nice rigging on. Pleases me more than playing billiards. So let me have my way where I don't do any harm. Apropos to billiards, there is an intense satisfaction in seeing the pretty red & white balls glide so smoothly & evenly over the green cloth and then when they crack it is so jolly. I beat old Will 'plum out of his boots' when I was home. Calls himself a crack shot and I can discount him.

"Dined with Courtland when in Alex & she gave me some flowers which I told her I was going to press, and have kept my word, have them in my field book, one of the few times in my life I did not lie about a thing of that sort. I'll miss Courtland so much maybe we will never see each other again. Well, Well such is life. Will had some striped socks when I was at home and he used to punch his feet up in every body's face to show them."

The rest of his letter is rambling commentary, not worth repeating.

Nancy was still in Warrenton, staying with Dr. and Mrs. Ward. Eliza wrote on September 3, 1874 and, for once, did not urge her to come home. Nancy was almost 21, yet Eliza still checked up on her, questioning if she had sent her "black and white calico to be washed?" Also wondered why she sent her hoops home in the warm weather, suggesting hoops had a cooling effect. At half–past six o'clock she had to stop and dress for tea. In a postscript she agreed to get Nancy the gloves she wanted but asked why she

hadn't bought them in Warrenton with her own money, then adds Nancy "must be as economical as possible for there is a great deal to do this winter and very little to do it with." Nevertheless, she is still "anxious to have the parlor papered."

On that same day Ben also penned a note to Nancy, in which he was…

"…so glad you are enjoying yourself so much. Dance and play while you can, Nancy darling, and may Heaven grant that the day is far off when you will not care for such things, when they will bore you. Oh youth! Youth! Why did mine pass before it began? I am happy enough in the woods if I can see or hear from home folks occasionally but put me in a ball room and I am wretched. And then my accursed poverty prevents my indulging in any thing I have a taste for. I'd be as happy as a King could I afford to read and travel but I'm too poor to buy books, much less travel. Nothing but work, work, howsoever far I look in to the future, until death brings rest.

"Poor people don't go to the devil. Their place of torment is here on earth. Then again I could be happy if I were to marry some girl that I loved &c but the same ####, poverty, comes in again. I am alone and have been for sometime and all my leisure moments are spent in scheming & thinking how I can get gold, bright beautiful, yellow gold but I am no nearer my mark than I was ten years ago. Girls don't have all these troubles so don't think about what I've been saying but as I said before Dance and sing while you can until real old age puts an end to it by deadening the sense. When heart and body grow old together old age is not painful.

"Write soon to your old leather skinned brother. How funny he'd look with his copper colored face beside your pretty white skinned beaux. How they'd examine him through their eye glasses and wonder how any creature could be so vulgar as to pride himself on having an eye whose sight was as clear as a hawk's, glory in forty inches of chest instead of being romantic and consumptive.

"Love to Aunt Grace & the rest. I suppose you delivered my message to Marnie. Don't suppose she intends to write to me. Can't blame her. I am neither pretty nor rich and can't Dance the Boston or lead the German and 'as sich' have no right to expect a belle to devote any of her time to me. I'm going to Grafton Wednesday and will be there for a week I expect. Fondly yours, B T F."

Letters unrelated to immediate family members were also found in the collection, including the following, on September 28, 1874, to Towny:

"My dear Uncle, Sally requests me to ask you to see your cook & her husband about coming to us. Please enquire about her husband. If of good character & capable of attending to horses, driving & gardening, we will be glad to get them with us soon as aunt Lizzie [Eliza] can spare the cook. We will give the man twelve dollars a month [$225 today] and his wife $6.00 per month & give them a very comfortable house & furnish them wood. Your sincerely attached nephew Fendall Marbury." No further information about whether this transaction took place or not.

Ben was in Pennsboro, WV in November, 1874. He told Nancy it was a "cussed" place. He would have enjoyed it more in 2008, when it listed bull riding, boxing, ice skating, soccer, tennis, wrestling, golf and the usual sports of today. He wrote:

"I am stopping with a Methodist preacher, who has all the cant and hypocrisy common to his class. Makes a lousy 'no–ration' before each meal about 'sanctifying' the beastly fried bacon. It may be sanctified but it is not good. While he is sanctifying I am inwardly praying to be delivered from the ill–omened old man and that I may not be poisoned by the 'vile interventions of the enemy' that he has set before me. Some poor devil came and asked for something to eat yesterday and as might be expected the old wretch lied, said he had none. I would not have done thus and I don't even call myself a christian, much less do I set myself up to teach others. 'Woe unto you Scribes, Pharisees, hypocrites.'

"I leave here to–morrow, have some little work to do at West Union which I will finish some time during the day and then I'll start for Rowlesburg, at which I hope to find letters from home awaiting me. We are going to lay another track up Cheat River grade and want to see what can be done in the matter of changing the line. See if we can't save money and distance. Can't say how long I will be at Rowlesburg. Some time I expect.

"I met an old friend of mine in Wheeling, Col Frank Armistead. Said he had met you at the Corse's. I was very much afraid he would want to borrow a check but he did not and I was happy. Lots of things in Wheeling calculated to interest an Engineer but very few that young women would care about. Awful dirty place, smoke and cinders everywhere. Hard population, knock people down, 'toated' my little pistol about with me, walked around like a little man. When I get through at Cheat River I may be moved east in which event I'll try and get home. Love to all, Affec yrs, B.T. Fendall."

Will's letter to Nancy, written May 9, 1875, displays a sharp contrast to those of Ben. Will wrote:

"Yours of the past came to hand and I hardly have the face to ask you to forgive me for not writting before, but as you see I have. I hope my impudence being exceeded only by my good intentions for the future will pacify my dear little sis [Nan is three years older] & make her once more willing to receive her hopeful young bro (who has still an 'open and contrite heart') within those sweet bonds of love & peace which a sisters soft words & smile alone can give & like the softest zephyrs are the exquisite breath of a tropical clime it will palliate all pain. While the low murmured tones, which come tremblingly through, sadly trouble the heart, and yet sweeten it, too."

It sounds like Will has already begun his phony proclamations of love and devotion to his sister and he's only 18½. These will continue in the same vein through the years and be basically duplicated to their mother. For now they seem innocent enough, though a bit ostentatious, but when he begins receiving Nancy's and their mother's funds to invest, they become a cover for his stealing those funds.

On May 29th, Eliza wrote Nancy about the visit she and Towny made to see his sister, Mary, who had fallen. She adds:

"Your pa and I did not return last eve, he concluded to remain all night and take an early start. This morning we had a most delightful drive as I took the reins for once in my life and your pa admitted that I handled them finely. Tell this to the Dr.

"We just missed seeing Will, he was at Liberty the day before. On our way home we called at Wyoming, the family living there gathered me some beautiful flowers, which I have arranged <u>artistically</u>, I wish you could enjoy them, they perfume the whole parlor and look so lovely under the gaslight. Your pa admonishes me it is bed time. I will finish tomorrow.

"Sunday afternoon. My dear child you can't imagine how I miss you, your pa is asleep, as usual on Sunday eve, the servants gone and I seated alone in my room, every thing is still as death. My thoughts are with my absent children and poor aunt Mary. I should like to hear from her and know she slept last night for she suffered dreadfully the night before. Just to think, she will have to lay in one position for weeks to come, her foot has to be kept fastened down to the bed–post, to prevent the moving. They have one of those air pillows made of India–rubber which they gently press under her back that is some relief to her, though she cannot turn a particle. It is nearly 5 o'clock.

I must get ready for church. Mr. Norton's sermon this morning was a eulogy on Dr Andrews character. Tell me about your hat in your next letter. Your devoted Mother."

By June 5th Eliza and Towny had, "at last finished painting and I have been very busy yesterday and to day house cleaning, my servants are both so slow I had to hire an extra one. I am glad to hear you are enjoying yourself [in Baltimore], hope you will be ready to come home next week." After a couple pages of chitchat she adds, "Mamie was certain she saw you at the races, but she could not get through the crowd to speak to you." Sounds like Nan was highly entertained during her visits. No wonder she didn't want to come home.

On June 6th, Ben was in Wheeling, WV. Professing he had "little or nothing to say," he proceeded to say a lot:

"We are trying to get another location for our Hunsfield line and my instructions are to survey all lines which from the looks of the ground I think practicable. We propose to build a line from a point on our P. W. & B. line to Little Washington, PA, [about 30 miles east of Wheeling] the road from there here is already constructed but goes over about three miles of city where we have to run with great caution which necessitates the loosing of much time. To avoid that and get a line outside of the city or to tunnel under the city is the affair I have in hand at present. The line when complete will save about seventy miles between Balto, Columbus, Chicago and points in the northwest and our line #### Piedmont, Grafton & Parkersburg will be used for our Western and Southwestern connections, Cincinnati, St. Louis etc. If you will look at the map you will find that after the B & O leaves Cumberland it is going away from Wheeling instead of to it. We were forced around the way we go by the PA Legislature who would not grant us a Charter but by whipping the devil around we have finally succeeded in getting through on our new line. Instead of using grades of 116 ft per mile we will have #### over 50 ft. This no doubt is very interesting (?) to you but I have little else to write about."

Less than a month later Eliza's brother, Hector Eaches, died on July 2nd. She was with him but there are no letters regarding the event, possibly because everyone came back to Alexandria for his funeral. A letter from Will appears, on October 5, 1875, to his "beloved sister":

"I will not tax you with a description of the contracted – though saddened brow of your maternal relative, all caused by your ungovernable passion for singing. Just think we are deprived of your beaming countenance for two more days. O! would that you were not a bird.

"I expect you think me a hard case, not having rec'd a line from me since your departure and that I have forgotten my beloved and only sister but you must not think so for although whirled on by outrageous fortune, only broken in its monotony by the occasional smile or frown of the loved ones at home, I will ever retain in this breast the purest love for you. What ever lands and seas divide, my soul will cling to thine etc.

"I met Mary Ann, my now mortgaged cousin, and the ethereal 'Grace' last week on the train for W_____ and by the by you must apologize to the former for my improprieties; attempting to kiss her on the train (I mean on the cheek). Circumstances alter cases. 'Doubtful things are very uncertain.' So much time had alapsed since I had seen the <u>dear one</u>, that I was quite frantic, therefore I was not accountable for my misdemeanor but in this my cooler reflection I see I was wrong and time with the apology must blot out the sin. I think if I had to go over it again I should most likely act in the same way (for she looked 'Heavenly' her face was as radient as the morning sun.)

"There is a great to–do about Lottery in town, it has been found out to be a fraud, and consequently thousands of people are swindled out of their money, for of course they did not expect to be swindled, when such a man as Jas Barber was President & Judge Williams Vice Pres't. I will send you the Alex Gazette which gives an account of the whole thing. Give my pious to all the family and believe me your devoted bro Wm. E. Fendall."

It is difficult to determine whether Ben's next letter is facetious or serious. He's in Wheeling; Nancy is at 403 Druid Hill Ave, Baltimore. It is now January 11, 1876. "At present we are having some beastly cold weather, fortunately for me however 'I don't got any' field work to do. I have been in hopes that I could get to Balt while you were there but don't see much chance at present.

"Would advise you to cultivate the Bowie girls as they may be of use to you. My plan is the true one, viz' cultivate no body but people that can be of service to you. People who are exalted by birth, brains or money (especially the latter) I pay particular court to. The young ladies in question combine all three. Avoid people after the manner of Maddox. It is well to have the reputation of being #### and remarks like 'who are they' 'never heard of them before' go far to establish such a reputation."

1876 marked the Centennial year. It had been 100 years since the Declaration of Independence had been signed. Nancy was 22 and had definitely declared her independence some years ago. Young ladies were not expected to seek employment after high school and college was not a prerequisite for the title of "Mrs" so what was there for her but to become a lady of leisure. There is no indication in any of the correspondence she attended any institute of higher learning but, judging by her frequent absences from Alexandria, if she had it must have been a charm school. How else to account for her long visits to Dr. and Mrs. Ward, Mr. and Mrs. Corse, Dr. and Mrs. Albert Gray and others?

It was not a case of visiting her grandmothers for she had none. Nor were they aunts or uncles. In spite of the Fendalls tendency to call everyone "cousin," few who went by that title were actually related. All of Eliza's siblings were gone. One sister of Towny, Mary Trueman Fendall, was still living but she was a spinster. The Wards probably had a daughter about Nancy's age, Mamie, for Eliza mentioned her visiting them in the winter. Still it does seem an imposition for Nan to spend five and six weeks at a time, depending on the hospitality of others to feed and entertain her.

Then there was the matter of clothes. In 1876 the bustle was in vogue and dresses were made of yards and yards of material, sometimes a combination of different fabrics. The skirts were not only floor length, they had trains, even for day wear. As a result brooms were seldom needed, as ladies sashayed down stairs, across floors and even down the sidewalk, sweeping up everything in their path. Her hosts may have had servants to do the washing and ironing but that was hard labor. The only other option would have been to take her dresses and numerous petticoats to a professional establishment. Did Nancy pay for that or did she coyly accept their benefaction?

Eliza's next letter, June 19, 1876, also indicated Nancy was not a very caring daughter. She wrote she had…

"…little to write about, except my ailments and I know you don't want to hear me complain of neuralgia, besides having so much to do, awful loneliness &c. I think the latter increases the burden of every thing else; I have had to throw down the work two or three times to–day and go to bed, feeling so weak and nervous; besides a dreadful pain in my back. I think this damp weather has something to do with it but I am at work to–night, in the parlor with 'pa' and Will, the latter for a wonder, staid in, one thing kept him was a heavy storm of wind & rain which came on just after he sat down to tea, & another thing, he was up very late last night, having attended a large ball in Georgetown, to which you also had an invitation.

"You are missing all the fun & frolic here but I expect you are enjoying yourself more in Baltimore. Mrs. De Lewis gives the next dance, she called to see me last week, invited Will and said she was so sorry you were away. Will says they had a delightful time last night, met a great many acquaintances, passed himself off as a married man to one young lady, who seemed to be greatly surprised, ain't he too bad.

"Your cat is growing finely, is very affectionate, I just now put her out of my lap. Well! Now something about your movements. I think you have been with Cassie quite long enough, I am afraid you will wear out your welcome and if you have made a favorable impression it may wear out by seeing too much of you. Give my love to Mrs T – and Cassie and thank them for their kindness and attention to you; ask Cassie if she cannot return with you, perhaps the parties will not be entirely over, and if they are, we will try and find something to interest her; you can go often to Washington to see Mamie which I know will give her pleasure.

"If you see any strong edgings or trimmings for under garments get me a few yds and I will refund in my next. Write soon to your lonely Mother."

In his next letter, July 21, 1876, Will wrote Nancy:

"Pa, ma and aunt Mary left for coz J – on Wednesday; so you see I am alone. I hope pa will remain for some time as I think the country air will be of service to him and there is really nothing for him to do here, as I can attend to every thing as well as he can.

"Lee Holcomb, Ashley Minor and myself drove out in the country yesterday evening to see the Misses Ross they are staying about two miles from town; they you know are the young ladies who were staying at the Andersons last Winter. We had a very pleasant time and arrived in Alex about eleven o'clock; they gave us a cordial invitation to come out again which we will do as we have a driver, carriage & two fine horses at our disposal. I am glad you and Constance are having such a nice time and so many beaux, horseback rides &c. They say it is very lively in Warrenton this year, no end to Balls and parties. I hope I will be able to get down to the country before you all leave; it would be so nice for us to be together. Believe me as ever your devoted bro Wm. E. Fendall" which he signs with great flourish.

A letter from Towny on August 4, 1876, tells Nancy:

"Don't let pleasure absorb too much of your time – to ignore the more important duties of life – they should be combined & the latter predominate." He then relates news about every acquaintance, adding his usual, "I have nothing in the way of news to send you."

Will, still nine months shy of his 21st birthday, was not the least bit shy about bragging of what he considered to be his accomplishments and his conquests of the fair sex. He felt no compunction about lying to gain his goals, whether to seduce a young woman into believing he was enamored or to seduce his sister into believing he was trustworthy. He was neither. In his letter of February 13, 1877, after going on at great length about taking a walk, he proudly boasted to Nancy about his latest conquest. It happened at a wedding, where he "had the best time at the wedding that I have ever had in my life." He then embellished the statement:

"In the first place I never before saw so many beautiful girls together, and there were <u>two</u> who were <u>surpassingly beautiful</u> the which (but don't blame me my dear sister, because I could not resist) I took on the steps and ——— [his dashes] the same old story. After much persuasion I convinced one that I loved her better than all else on earth or ——— &c &c and consequently was accepted, the other was a little more difficult however. She said she would like to have time to consider the serious matter, however would let me know this week. I have found out since that she was engaged; and that she discarded the poor wretch; if it be so ——— so much the more. I once came very near making a vow, to myself, that I would never get into such a scrap again; but then you know the music and the ——— and the ——— was too much for one so unstable as your humble servant. But what is the use of repining. For where there is a "Will" there's a way &c. [Will will not marry for another 25 years. One can only guess how many hearts he broke in that time. He will then marry two widows with children but not sire any of his own.]

"Griff and Frank want me to come out to Dallas, Tex and I have a half mind to do so after I am admitted. There is to be a Miss Fletcher staying at the Snowdens this week. She is the daughter of Gov Fletcher of Mo; she lives in St. Louis so Maud writes for me to call on her, which I had already promised the Snowdens to do. Pa & Ma send love. I must close as I am at the end of my fourth page. My regards to all with you and lots of love for yourself. I am ever your devoted Will."

One week later Eliza wrote Nancy her regular...

"Your pa and I think it is time you were coming home, you have already been away <u>four</u> weeks and <u>here</u> you will have fewer temptations during Lent, certainly no <u>theatre</u> to attend." [She is in Baltimore.] She then added:

"Your pa has been talking every day this week about writing to you and Will said this morning he would write, but that was the last of it. He is all devotion to a young lady from St. Louis, a Miss Fletcher,

Con knows her, and called to see her to–day; she is staying with Mrs. Hal Snowden. This morning I was at work in my room when I heard a great laughing and talking down in the parlor, followed by music on the piano. I came down thinking it was Con, but instead, found Mrs. Snowden & Miss Fletcher. Will had called them in; she is a very pretty & sprightly girl, will be here for two or three weeks.

"I don't know when I shall write again, I am very busy, have just cut out my wrapper and have some work to do for Ben, besides lots of other things. I am suffering very much with my eyes, intend to get Dr. Lewis to examine them. Ben insists that he sees something like a film over the ball. Will says it is <u>not so</u>. I hope the latter assertion is right. Good night, you shall be remembered in the prayers of your ever devoted Mother."

Towny's letters were full of flowery expressions, but he couldn't hold a candle to Will's flummery, as evidenced by his letter to Ben on September 11, 1878:

"Your letter came, my dear Ben, like a sun tram in a winter's day for I have had many little trials & vexations such as wear out the human frame – as drops of water will the hoary rock. Yet most likely I should have let them pass as the idle wind – which I respect not had I not been affected by the blackning clouds never changing save where distiled into sprinkling showers – true representations indeed of gloom & sorrow. I know I should not give way to such things – but try to cheer those around me instead of holding – as it were – dark communion with the clouds; but I am of that peculiar temperament 'That I can not hide (always) what I am; I must be sad when I have cause and smile at no man's jests – laugh when I am merry &c.'

"Words are inadequate to express the high appreciation of your thoughtfulness in sending the different articles unreminded & my deep love and gratitude for the presents & loan of dress suit; I feel that when you hear this you will be half repaid [sounds like Will believes flattery will get him everywhere], for as Milton says – A grateful mind by owing owes not, but still pays, at once indebted and discharged. We shall both think of you and wish for you to–morrow night. Ma & pa both send much love. Nan joins with the same accompanied by a chorus of messages which are too numerous to pen.

"We sold our calf to–day rec'd $5, notwithstanding the man insisted on its not being worth but $4. I would attribute the increase to ma's <u>financering</u> (excuse my coining words). Children get drunk – as they say – from going round & round – now I should be so if whirling the head could produce it for at every stroke of the pen I have to dodge a mosquitoe which imparts but a small ease to style.

"Jake Bhorous – the fellow who keeps the bar room next to our

Office – came in to show me a new gun he had just purchased. I to devil him, said I should like to borrow it. Said he 'Nar sir, nar sir, mine gun & my wife I lends to no man.' Hurrah for the #### & eagle & the gay young monkey on high, I know I am not drunk nor dry, but that I have sand in my eye: And so I will say good by; for Morpheus waits me on high when the net bars the 'skites' to fly and <u>William</u> your brother am I."

While Will disguised his real character in letters professing fake love, Ben realistically described his life working on the railroad. On September 7, 1879 he wrote:

"All my letters have come to hand my dear Nancy but through the stupidity of the mail boy I had begun to think you had all deserted me. Among other letters I got one from Miss Ruth telling me she intended going to Fendall Marbury's Friday. I wanted to go down with her but could not quite make my arrangements. I wish I could be with you today.

"Our party is out in the country boarding with an old Dutchman. We have to wash on the front porch in the morning, have to get our own water from the spring &c. There are only two of us who have been out before. I have a young man at the transit who has only the theory of the thing but he does very well and will do better. If I leave him long he gets nervous. Of course I have to be ahead looking out the line and I leave instructions as to what shall be done in the mean time and being inexperienced the youngster gets a little off but he does quite well and will soon do better.

"You can continue directing my letters to Johnstown [PA, 60 miles SE of Pittsburgh] for the present. I will be very well satisfied if we get through by December. We are not going to have a good time either. There are absolutely no genteel people in Somerset Co: nothing but Penn Dutch most of them being 'Dunkards.' As ever your affect Bro BTF."

From Davidsville, a wide place in the road about five miles southwest of Johnstown, on September 28:

"Your sweet and welcome letter reached me all safe last week and I am going to try my best to answer it, but in what way I am entirely at a loss. The fact is I have nothing to say further than that I am perfectly well and comparatively happy. The prospect of seeing you all seems to get further off each day.

"Where the party is at work now is about as bad a place as I ever saw. The laurel is so thick that a black snake would have great difficulty in getting thru and so steep that the axemen have to hold on with one hand while they chop with the other. I push the men all day and do what I will some days we only go a quarter of a mile. In fair ground I could go five miles. So far things get worse. We are following a little creek that seems to have cut a bed for itself through solid rock and enormous boulders have fallen in and tend to stop it up again. Skinned knees and torn 'unmentionables' are quite the order of the day in the party.

"I am sorry to say I won't be able to get you any pretty ferns as the frost has nipped them. If I had any way of getting them to you I would send you some lovely leaves but I will have to pass. Tell pa please to send me about $10 – I need a little money for washing mending & tobacco. Send it in a letter I should think would be safe. Tell him I will send him a check before long.

Mr. Randolph the Chief Eng'r comes out every two or three weeks and stays about a day. As he does not say anything I suppose he is satisfied. He is a nice old man and lets me have my own way and we get on elegantly together. With much love to all."

On October 5th, still in Davidsville, Ben told Nancy:

"To day being Sunday I devote it as usual to epistolary correspondence. I have the same startling announcement to make that I have so often made before, viz: that I am well and progressing slowly. I got in one–half mile of work last week, with a prospect of doing about one mile more next week if I have good luck. I have my usual stipend in the shape of a check for eighty one dollars which I enclose endorsed payable to pa's order.

"One of our men got a very nice pair of Napoleon top boots in Martinsburg for ten dollars. They are sewed, tongue book with seams up the back of the leg, regular hand made, double soles and uppers and first class work in every respect. If Caff will make me a pair like them in every respect for the same money he can send me a pair, to this place by way of Somerset, care of the Agent B & O Express. Caff has my measure. I don't want them quite so tight as he makes gaiters but not much larger as they are quite comfortable. The main thing is to have them high in the instep so as they will go on easy. I don't want very high legs. Having devoted a page to the subject of Boots and having given I hope directions sufficiently specific I hope to get my boots all right. If Caff can't like the price I will get them in Martinsburg. Let me know if he will make them.

"I certainly do want to see you all at home. I miss pa's nice toddies Sunday. I'd as soon think of drinking poison as the liquor they have out here. With much love to all the dear ones at home and a large share for yourself I am as ever Your affectionate B.T. Fendall."

From Stoystown, 10 miles south of Davidsville, November 16th:

"Sunday, again, my darling Nancy, and with its rest comes the opportunity of having a little talk with you sister mine. I am all alone in my office, where, don't be shocked, I have been at work all morning studying over maps and profiles and making plans for next week's work. The boys have all gone to church and I am glad of it. I can think better and, little girl, I want to think all I can for I am in a 'mighty tight fix.' Bridges on one side, tunnels on the other. Can I get between and avoid both? If so, how? Those are the questions that are up for solution. Baylor, who is in charge of the other party, and myself are about to 'jain up.' We are not more than a mile apart. We consult, we propose, we throw things around, use profane language, drive rodmen out of the room, take a smoke, and go at it again. He is as bad off as I am. We both want to see Mr. Randolph, fifteen miles of line have I located that he had never seen. He seems to have confidence in me. Flattering but disagreeable. I am under a strain all the time. I can't sit still. I can't write quietly to you. I almost believe I am nervous.

"The only thing that keeps me up is the weather, which is charming but cold enough to make the cheeks of the healthy country girls a shade redder than usual. Lots of them have passed the window this morning on their way to church and I am afraid that 'the boys' of whom I spoke just now have gone to church more to flirt with the aforesaid red cheeks than to worship. 'Well! Well! Gather ye roses while ye may.' I do want to see you all so badly and I hope it will not be long before I do. I am ever yours BTF."

By December 21st he had made it another 10 miles to Somerset, PA and wrote:

"I was induced to pay a visit a few nights since. Called on some of the town of Somerset. The way I came to call was in this way. I have a young fellow with me who comes originally from this place, and by the way he is a very nice fellow. He knows every body and goes around a good deal. So the other night he came and insisted I should go with him to make up a whist party. I refused at first but he importuned to such an extent that for fear of wounding him I went. And as I expected I found the girls ignorant, 'green' and coarse in face, figure and manner. But at the same time their airs and graces were intensely amusing and their conversation more so. Just enough education to display their ignorance and just enough taste for literature to make them read the most dreadful of the dreadful 'yellow backs.'

"As a specimen one of them said she had rather swear than use slang. Three minutes before I heard her playfully remark she would snatch her lady friend 'bald headed' and three minutes after I heard her ask a gentleman 'not to go back on her and give her away.' I did not inquire of her what she considered slang, only agreed with the admirable sentiments to which she had given utterance against it. What I say first I say last there are no nice people in PA west of the mountains except possibly a few in Washington Co and one or two Pittsburg families who came originally from the east. They disgust and amuse me. These people are a great stickler about social position &c and the height of their ambition with the girls is to stand in a shop and with the young men to teach a country school. Hoping to see you this week I am as ever Your affectionate brother BTF."

On May 1, 1880 Ben wrote on stationery of the "Engineering Department, Somerset and Cambria Rail Road" from Davidsville, PA to Nancy at 352 N. Eutaw St. Baltimore, MD…"

"…You will be surprised no doubt to see from the heading that I am down here but the Chief Eng'r was sick last Sunday and sent me down here to help Manning out. He has some very rough work and as I located the line thro here, I know all about how to change and improve it. I would have put all in good shape before I left had I not been instructed by the chief to push ahead and not dress up any.

"I came very near losing a man to day. He was very near falling over a perpendicular cliff sixty feet high but thanks to his stout arms and a tough laurel he saved himself. I thought I was going to have a little rest, last week. I got all of my residency in good shape and had nothing to do, but the Chief waltzed me off. I did hate it too. It was all right for some of us to help Manning out but did not think I was the man to do it. I get more extra jobs than any of them. I can take my party and do more work than any of the rest and get ahead and then have to help about something else.

"I am so glad you are having a good time in Balt; wish I was there. I am trying to get back to Somerset to a swell reception Thursday. Sent for my dress suit; expect to be very gay. Went to a dance there and waltzed all the evening with my little Mary Beth. Took her out on the porch and made love to her. She had a while silk shawl thrown over her head and looked too lovely. She just dances like a fairy.

"Write to me as often as you can. You don't know how I love to hear from you and how often I think of you as I sit munching my lunch or smoking after it under some big hemlock. Good night sweet heart and believe me as ever Your affectionate Brother B. T Fendall."

By July 1880 Ben was in Mannington, WV, southwest of Morgantown. He was now five months shy of his 30th birthday and had been "working on the railroad" since he was 17 and the toll was beginning to tell on him. In spite of his lamentations to his sister, however, he does not quit but goes on to reach his goal of becoming a great engineer, settling down in Baltimore and eventually designing bridges. Will chose the less rigorous life of a lawyer.

"...The heat is ever before me. My dear little girl an Engineer's lot is not a happy one. I am often tempted to pull and give up and let things go bad and I go along with them. This ever lasting grind worries the spirit right out of a fellow. No let up, no prospect for any other life than the one I have had for twelve long weary tiresome years. Work until I am too old to work any longer then drop out of ranks and make room for someone else never be missed or thought of any more. Life is not worth the living. Who of us in looking back would live our lives over? I would not for one. Some few little bright spots. Some few oases but most blank desert or ugly rocks and sharp thorns that stick us even now when we think about them. No, no Nancy dear, it is not worth the living.

"I hope it is cooler with you than it is here but I fear it is not. When I come in at night I have to change all of my clothing. My clothes are as wet with perspiration as though I had been over board. I assure you I do not exaggerate when I tell you I can wring water out of them. The sun would be bad enough but I have the heat from the rails besides which is as bad as the sun.

"There is a company here boring for oil. They have their well down seven hundred feet and have fair indications of striking soon. They will go fifteen hundred feet and if they get no oil they'll give it up. It is quite interesting to me. I hope they will make a good strike as it will benefit this God forgotten country very much and bring in some civilized men. It will also be a good thing for our road.

"Don't let my gloomy thoughts effect you my dear. You know I get that way sometimes and have to go to someone and usually select you as my victim. I dare say in a week it will be all over. Good night and a kiss from your loving Ben."

In August Nancy and Eliza were at Cape May and Nancy received this from Towny:

"My darling Nancy Lee, it is raining delightfully and has been since 6 P.M. and has cooled the air very much – the day has been excessively Hot almost unbearable. The dry earth is drinking in like a thirsty man – how good and generous is our

Kind Heavenly Father to send us, poor unworthy creatures, such refreshing blessings.

"Well here I am, Will on one side & I the other of the table in the dining room writing, he I suppose to one of his many <u>Victims</u> & I to my darling little Nancy L – to say that I sent her a handsome Hammock – to slumber under the cool shade of the mountain trees – to dream of her old <u>Dad</u> – & of 'joys that have departed, never more to return' not with you I trust. The hammock went by Express the 31st. I hope you have rec'd & like it. Good bye my own precious darling little daughter – and believe me ever your own devoted Old Dad." [Note: This is the <u>only</u> letter in the collection where he signs "Dad" and not his full name. Perhaps it is also worth noting both Towny and Eliza seemed to find Will's cavalier behavior toward women amusing.]

By March of 1881 Ben was in Grafton, WV, about 20 miles south of Morgantown. He…

Wilkes Street RR Tunnel, next to Fendall's house.

"...had a push job on hand and got sixty five men at work on it and fifty of them deserted me. It just snowed for about three days and nights last week and at some places the snow is a foot deep. Have been compelled to discharge some of my men for disobedience and neglect and can not get good men in there places and I am just discouraged. Every man's hand has been against me for some time and I intend to fill the bill and let my hand be against every man. I am going to be Richard III and hate every body.

"Florence [his future wife] sent me such a lovely little present the other day. When I saw her in Philadelphia I told her I expected to get a room and furnish it very nicely. So she went to work and made me something awfully pretty to put in it. It is a little thing to hold a whisk. Made out of red satin and embroidered in the nicest possible style. She sent a whisk covered with the same material on top. The whole business is just as pretty as can be.

"Tell pa & ma that just as soon as I can get the time I will send some money home. I am away from town from seven A.M. until nine P.M. and don't have a chance to get the postal order or a draft. With much love to all I am as ever Your affectionate Ben."

A few weeks later, on March 20th, Ben hit a new low and wrote Nancy:

"Your sweet letter has been rec'd my dear Nancy and I of course was charmed to hear from you all. I have had the blues awfully here lately and Col Johnston came out and evidently did not like the way things were being managed by me. He did not say much and I don't think he made allowances he should have made. I have learned something tho; and I am going to act on it.

"It is a mean thing, but I am going to do it. You know I like to do things thoroughly. That I have been doing here. You may make a show for less money and in less time than you can make a complete job. Now I am going to make a show and no more and Johnston will think I am the biggest man in the world. I am getting his measure. I will gain ground and lose respect. The true secret in life is to study people's weaknesses and play on them. Be utterly selfish. I know you think this is awful and because I love you dearly and would not be so to you, you think I would not be so at all but you are mistaken. If I were rich I should be different. Poor people can't do all they wish. High moral principles are luxuries that only the rich can indulge in. You and your friend start up the hill, your friend gets in your way, pitch him over and go on. Our 'Esse quam Videri' [to be, rather than to seem to be] does well to fool people but we are too poor to follow it out. I'd like to be like pa, but that don't pay. His mistake was that he was too high toned. He would rather break than cringe.

"I was so much obliged for the cards you sent me it was so

119

thoughtful and sweet in you only you could have used the money to a greater advantage for your self in something pretty to wear. Don't construe this into disinterested magnanimous generosity on my part, for it is not. One of the greatest pleasures I have in life is to see you have nice things. It affords me more pleasure than to have them myself. So it is selfishness at last. I may fool the world but I'll tell you the truth. I wish you would send on the Gazette [Alexandria newspaper] once in a while. With much love I am as ever Your affectionate Ben."

Letters from Will are few and far between in the collection but they do present such a clear measure of the man it seems worthwhile to include them when they appear. The following was to his sister, this time in Oak Grove, MD, written June 28, 1881. It will be a dozen years before another letter is found from Will. It is riddled with misspelled words, which are copied as written, rather than adding "sics" to every one. He was now 25 years old and, if practicing law, let's hope he wasn't charging by the word.

"Doubtless you will think me a hard hearted wretch and as such remember me in your orisons when I inform you that for the past two or three days I have led an ideal life, notwithstanding the absence of those most near & dear. Perhaps the reason I do not feel the pangs of what people are want to term 'missing one' is owing to my intence love for you all which plays upon my imagination to such an extent that the sweetest memories of you are I may say omnipresent and I am with you in spirit if not in substance. However I am sure I should have enjoyed as keenly the sight of you in reality – as I have for several days in my minds eye – But to the point. How have I passed my time? in idleness? not at all!

"On Saturday evening after pa & ma left I closed his Office & returned to the deserted mansion; I was soon lost in my work, which was to set to rights every thing which was a chaos in my room particularly – well this was accomplished with a master strok or probably 'twould be better to say a mistress – I locked every room except my own [this seems to have been a normal procedure for Nan will instruct her husband to lock not only doors but drawers when she is away], which in point of neetness I can assure you would do credit to a spinster of 40 or 50 summers – my task finished I sat down to a somewhat wholesome meal as well as uninviting – perhaps to your fastidious palate, #### & ice coffee being a part. However I enjoyed it. I then closed the house and strolled up town where I met Joe Addison who returned with me and we spred ourselves around in bachelor stile and read. We retired about twelve after imbibing ice milk in the neighborhood of a quart – then a little short smoke & the days work was over and we soon fell into that dreamless sleep which is most perfect rest. I had given out breakfast which was a good one – & orders for the same to be served at 10 a.m. promptly. Also that we were not to be disturbed from our slumbers before 9:30.

"It is useless to say the orders were carried out to the letter & after a bath & etc we sat down to breakfast as the clock struck ten. Are you not lost in admiration at the perfect system. It would put you ladys to the blush were you here. Joe said he could not stay to dinner as he had promised Mrs. Waller to stay there but would come down Monday night & spend the rest of his time with me. I told Sara & Chas they could go for the day only for one of them to come in time for the cow etc. I was then of cours thrown on the cold charity of the world for a dinner but at that time – after such a breakfast it was dreadful to think of dinner.

"I had a strong desire – if I had any, for spiritual food so I strolled towards St Pauls Church – but either the desire was exhausted by the walk or the fact that a young sprout by the name of Duggy H### was to hold forth in that good old address I like so much I don't know which – but tis well at times to leave something to the imagination & so I will do here.

"I had several invitations to dine out. I accepted the Beaches. After dinner I went into the library & droped ma a short letter. By the by I have not heard from either of them since they left – however I hope they arrived O.K. About half after 3 I came home to swing my hamock & read 'Matrimony' while I swung. By the by it is a very clever book. I mailed it to you in care of J. Berry Esq Brick Church P.O. but now I see from Mrs. B's postal the P.O. is Oak Grove so you had better send to the station for it. I swang & smoked & read until about 7 P.M. then I took Net to church (Grace) where I heard that poor old sermon I used to like so much, this time it was lunged out by the eloquent gifted wonderous 'Birch Sprout.'

"I presume you are all looking at the Comet. We had a severe storm last night it was nearly grand to behold. Con expects her friends on Thursday. I shall call on Mrs. Lee (Carrie Wattles) to–night as she is in town. Ben of course was not with me on Sunday. I enclose a note for Mrs. Berry which you will be so good as to deliver. I am sorry I can not be with you all – she is very nice indeed to write for me. Don't forget to send to Brick Church P.O. if you have not rec'd the book 'Matrimony.' Excuse every thing. Remember me to all. Yours devotedly, WmE. F."

In between the above epistle and the next letter found in the collection, Nancy was married, on October 17, 1883, to John (called Jack) Ford Tackett. All correspondence relating to this long but separated union is found in the Tackett chapter. Mail, which continued to be sent to Nancy or her parents by her brothers, but not directly related to her marriage, are included here.

The first of these is what today would be considered old-fashioned: formal permission to marry. It was written by the sister of Ben's intended, Florence Phillips Mason, on October 14, 1886.

"My dear Mr. Fendall, Mother has been an invalid so many years that I have acted as her amanuensis under many & varied circumstances. She now bids me give you her blessing; and say, that, though her acquaintance with you is very limited, she feels safe in committing the happiness of her child to your keeping – yet it is not without a pang that she surrenders her to any one, however worthy of the trust.

"Floy has been so long the best beloved of my heart, that you will forgive me for saying there is a depth and tenderness in her nature which few can penetrate – you found the key to the secret door – in taking this dearest treasure from us, guard well the prize, and let us find in her happiness our rest! With every kind wish, Very truly, Gertrude Mason."

Ben relays this news to:

"My Dear Ma, Miss Florence Mason and I are engaged. I have asked her mother's consent to our marriage which will be in the winter or next spring. I enclose Miss Gertrude's letter. I would like to have Nannie call on her and if you are well enough I would like you to call also. Her address is 1833 G St. Washington D.C. Take the Ave cars to 18th st and then one square south to G. With dear love to all believe me Your devoted son B.T.F. Thank Will for the poetry he so kindly copied for me."

In July 1893 there was a sudden spate of letters, from Will, absolutely dripping with sweet words, loving thoughts and seemingly generous offers to Nancy and to Towny, who was very ill and would die this month. Nancy was with their father in Culpeper County, VA. Will was staying at the home Jack Tackett had bought, at 211 South St. Asaph Street in Alexandria. The house will be turned into a boarding house, as described in the correspondence between Jack and Nancy. Based on later letters, Will, nearing his thirty-seventh birthday, was paying Nancy rent. The first of Will's letters is dated July 3rd, at 7:30 a.m. All the letters have been condensed.

"My precious darling sister because you have not rec'd the many–many letters I have written you in my mind [this is a favorite ploy of his] is no reason that you think I have forgotten you for there is not a day or hour or moment that you and those dear old people & sweet little children are away from me in thought – but to tell the truth when I have had the opportunity when the hurry of days work was over the letters went out to you in dreams – & longings to see – to kiss & to embrace each of you in turn & I was physically too lazy to write. You have been so sweet writing to me too – that I am writing to you now and it will do for the dear darling little mother & precious old father for the 4th of July – next I will write them both a letter – tell ma I would have sent her satin pieces but having put her letter away so carefully I could not find it – until now – I did not have the opportunity to send by Florence as I did not know until I heard she was with you all. I am so busy all day & night too for that matter that I have no time for play – in fact my play days are over – I have had my share so don't mind.

"Tell dear father I rec'd the checks enclosed in his dear letter – and will attend to all his requests. His letter was a great comfort to me & showed great strength and far from any thing like a ill man – though he did have to get out of bed to write it I am sure he is stronger than he has been for a long time. I sent him some senna leaves to use (by taking a pinch & chewing & swallowing every night before retiring) instead of Lemons did he receive them. I have never heard. I enclosed them in a letter to mother I think. I think twould be much better to let up on the Lemons as it evidently is no good to him precious old darling. I wish & hope he will grow better each day.

"I am so glad my sweet Nancy you keep me before those dear children of yrs – precious Nancy Lee my idol – Sophy 'Tacks' my little one – it would break my heart if they forgot me for the love I feel for them is like that for you my precious sister – too deep – almost for words – and so sometimes in looking back I fear I have seemed indifferent – when I felt most – but then I always thot you understand – you know – for we are one and always will be – as no others are one."

On July 4th at 1:40 a.m.: "My beloved father, I know I ought to be in bed – but I must – before I seek natures sweet restorer drop you a few lines in answer to the greatest pleasure (yr letter) I have rec'd for many days. When I read it I could have leaped for joy – for there was nothing of the sick man in it – but full of strength & right to the point in not alone news but business, just as though you had never been sick at all. All of your orders shall be attended to – some have already been done.

"I enclose two papers of U.S. Gov' for you to sign & return at your earliest convenience – together with the check which you desired for Paying Nancy board &c – Hope to hear dear little mother rec'd the paper & silk pieces sent her this a.m. I took them to the train also a letter to dear Nancy. I am so glad you have all yr grand children with you – that alone will make you feel young & strong again – notwithstanding this beastly weather. I do trust the weather will clear up – for then you can go out – and the fresh country mountain air is what you need more than all the medicine. Well I must close my darling father with kisses for you and the precious little mother – Nancy – Nancy Lee, Sophy, Mason & the rest – Ever yr devoted son Wm E. Fendall."

On July 5th Will wrote: "I am so thankful you are free from that dreadful nausea – and also that the Dr has put you on a milk diet – there is nothing like it. Everything runs smoothly at the Office and if nothing prevents I want to run up Saturday to see you all – for I am homesick for the sight of my dear ones. I did not used to miss people but as the years roll by I become more & more dependent on my dear peoples love and affection & don't want them away from me for long.

"I am keeping up the books at the Office & have been quite interested in it – you my darling father are so systematic that it is very little trouble. [Will is also practicing law.] I just follow what you have done – Would that I could follow in yr foot steps in many other ways. Maybe I will learn by & by. I am sorry to hear the dear little mother is under the weather – & dear Nancy too – I trust they and all of you will be improving when this reaches you.

"Lily & Algernon are very sweet in asking for you and send their love when ever I write. Little Marion is still away but expects to return to–morrow. [Lily was Lily Twiggs Myers–Chalmers; Algernon and Marion were her children. She and Will will marry but not for nine more years.] Let me hope the next news will be that your diet agrees with you & that you are still improving. P.S. Please sign & mail enclosed ck."

Will's next two letters are very lengthy, then his correspondence disappears for three years. As these are written just before and after Towny dies, most of his comments are included here. The first was dated July 12, 1893:

"<u>Courage</u> my dearest Nancy for all days can not be bright – I too have been depressed – though your sweet note of yesterday was so full of encouragement still I could not sleep and now I feel I was conscious – though I did not know it – that father was not so well. The one thing that I wish is that I could be there and help you – little baby & dear little mother to keep up – but my thoughts are there and my soul too to encourage & brace you up.

124

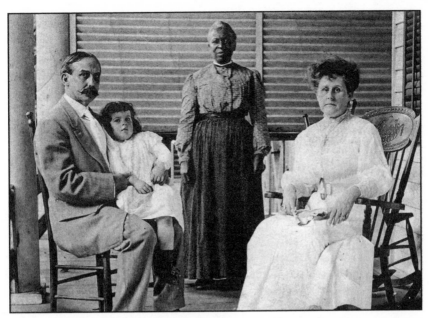

Will Fendall with his first wife, Lily Chalmers and her daughter, Marian.

"The pills the Dr gave pa were to move his bowels – it may be best – in fact I think right – that he should not take any more while his bowels are loose – poor old gentleman he has not much flesh to loose. Oh my dear darling sister when I look about & see the trouble others have had so much more worthy of kindness from the hands of the Creator than I – I feel crushed even when I feel sad at the troubles that seem to be gathering – but who can tell it may be there are still many days left me to make amends to my dear old people who have been so much to me – and for whom I feel now I have done nothing for.

"Pour out your heart & burdens to me sweet sister. Keep smiling & pleasant happy words for the weak & needy – I will hold you up – my strength is masculine I expect to be leaned upon and I am too glad for the happy days not to expect to meet some time dark ones like these seem to be now – yea & darker if I must.

"Sophy still keeps house – she and the old gentleman are going down on the Elect car this Eve to River side park so Jack & Charlie & I will run the house." [Sophie is Jack Tackett's sister, Charlie is his brother and the old gentleman is their father.]

No spider ever wove a web more deadly, yet invisible, than Will was weaving now. He would entangle his entire family in it, even Ben, though not as completely as the others. Perhaps they all presumed he, as an attorney, would know how to invest and avoid taxes as much as possible. He would

125

know what was legal and what was not. What they didn't know and didn't find out until it was too late, was he also knew how to hide how and where he was stashing the funds with which he was being entrusted. Eliza was counting on him to disperse her estate when she died. Jack and Nancy gave him money to invest for them through the years. All thought their money was in safe hands. It was not; it was in greedy hands and Will got away with it until Jack died in 1908, the year after Eliza, and Nancy suddenly discovered no inheritance was coming from either of them. But that was fifteen years off, so Will still had lots of time to draw in his victims and wrap them up in his blandishments. What better time than when all others were in genuine mourning over Towny's death July 23, 1893 (Towny was 80). Will's letter to Nancy was dated July 28th and he poured it on thick:

> "…does a good man – a genuine good man – ever die – I think not – I know not – yes we can not turn to right or left – in front – or look back that He is not there – let the tears rise to the heart and gather in the eye – 'tis natural and must be – we can not live forever and how much better a sweet good by – without pain or oblivion – than the lingering decay – the body without the mind – the heart without the power to feel – I think of such scenes, for I have witnessed them and then I think of my precious and sainted father's end – and I repeat over & over again –

> "Mark the upright man – behold the perfect man – for his end is peace & rest – & can we doubt for one moment that this is exemplified in our father – in leaving us 'tis but a passing into the pleasant drowsy shade a little before us – we will go there by & by & rest for has he not left a great heritage to us, a monument of Truth Honesty purety of mind – Ah! Darling I know it is hard to feel that we can not feel his touch & hear his voice as we used to but how much better – rest so from Suffering – then sweet sleep.

> "Dont bother about me my sweet heart – I am too much a philosopher to sink under a burden and if from your standpoint a dear Providence brought us here for a good & wise purpose – should we instruct him when he takes one away – grieve we must – 'twould not be human if we did not – but not such grief as will make us forget – even when alone with that grief – that there are others very dear – others that were most dear to Him and to forget for a moment would grieve the dear father deeply – for he knows (if as I think some times his sweet life is near me) that we love him now and always –

> "I enclose a letter from Water Co – you will see by the Gazette they passed Resolutions and ordered the Treas to send mother check for four hundred dollars (which she can send back, endorsed by Jack & have it deposited to her credit until I can find a safe investment for her) the amount that dear father would have rec'd for the time he was elected to 1st November 1893 – you also see they did not elect me as

his successor – but 'tis for the best though they know it not – indeed I would not have it – my plans are a little uncertain but I know I want rest & before I open an office any where I will take a little rest – somewhere. I have been very busy getting dear fathers effects from the Office & have about finished.

"Love to the precious mother and many Kisses for you both & the children – Love to Jack – kindest remembrances to the household – & Mother ever devotedly yr Affectionate bro Wm F. Fendall."

The $400 mentioned above would not be deposited into a "safe investment" for Eliza but into Will's private cache. As for Will not being appointed Towny's "successor," perhaps others in Alexandria were not as easily conned by Will as was his family. When Towny died he had six grandchildren. Ben and Florence had three: Benjamin Mason VI, born February 29, 1888, Mary Gertrude, born December 29, 1889, and Florence Mason, born July 5, 1891. Nancy and Jack Tackett also had three, though their second daughter, Eliza Fendall, born May 5, 1890, had died of cholera on July 1, 1891. Their two remaining daughters were Nancy Lee Fendall (yes, she had the same full name as her mother), born May 17, 1887, and Sophie Ford, born June 3, 1892.

Will and Lily were not married, yet were at least living in the same house in various locations around the state. Lily's husband, Algernon Coleman Chambers, was still living, so Lily was either divorced or at least separated from him. Her father had been A. C. Myers, U.S. Army and later quartermaster general of the Confederate States Army. She and Will would not marry until 1902, two years after Algernon died. As they did a lot of traveling, with her three children in tow, Will could not have been practicing law in Alexandria much, so we can only guess who was paying the bills.

On August 29, 1896, Will wrote to Nan from Edgewood, near Raleigh, VA. Nancy, though long since married, continued to enjoy her summers away from Alexandria. Here she was enjoying the hospitality of the Alonzo Berry family in Williamsport, MD. Will wrote of the drive he and Lily took. Will frequently mentions "the dear little mother's" headaches; perhaps they were migraines. He continues his travelogue:

"Yesterday eve Lily & I in the buggy & Marion & David [her children] in the cart – went to return the visits of some impossible people by the name of Conrads (it used to be, so Mr. Ws says, Kunerads) they called on us, so of course we had to return their visit. They are worth millions – and are as common as they are rich.

The family consists of the mother who looks for all the world like a 'dummy' of the third class – two daughters (in short dresses though 18 & 17) and they are fixed up like the mother – only their eyebrows are more painted. The father is a cross bet' a stable keeper & a Dutch butcher – though perfectly good material – gave us the most pressing invitation to come & see their fete.

"He insisted on taking us through their Palace – for it is all that money can buy. They have Chinese servants, brought with them from the West. The man the son of a boatman & something else – who went to Montanna 30 years ago & in many ways that were dark he made his money. We laughed a great deal over it – and were most happy to return to our own little Cot where we found that sweet air of refinement that God not man gives and money never buys.

"Algy had gone to the Tournament & Ball – we sat up sometime playing whist & then retired for a good nights rest which was enjoyed by all save poor Lily who, being worried to death about Algy less he should take cold, kept awake until the wee hours when he returned from the Ball O. K.

"The days pass very rapidly here and I can not realize that I have been here two weeks. You ask when I shall return that I can hardly say, as much depends on it, certainly not any sooner than I am absolutely obliged to, as I loathe Alexa in Sept. Well good by & God bless you Darlin' Sister. Kiss dear little Mother for me & the little ones. I certainly would love to pop in on you all. Love & kisses many for all, ever yr devoted brother Wm Fendall."

After a decade, a letter from Ben appeared on July 5, 1897. He and Florence were living in Baltimore and he was still with the B & O Railroad, but now behind a desk. In his letter to Eliza, he wrote:

"To day is little Florence's Birthday she's six and will have her cake this evening with the proper number of candles and other accessories; as you may imagine she is most happy. Floy is expected to leave for Culpeper Friday or Saturday. I hope she can get off Friday as Saturday is so bad on account of 'niggers.' Your devoted son B T Fendall."

On July 3, 1898, Will is at the Jordan White Sulphur Springs in Virginia (near Winchester) with Lily and her children. He wrote his...

"Sweet little mother your dear letter written this morning I have just read with so much pleasure. Yes darling my spirit & heart too are always with you & the dear ones at home – time & distance has no power to really separate me from you."

128

After four more pages, relating what they have been doing, he closes with: "I kiss your lips your brows & cheeks. Love & kisses for one and all my dear ones and believe me now and always your own devoted son, WEF" He will continue his proclamations of love to the end of her life.

On May 30, 1899, Ben's letter to "My Dear Mother" was full of heartache:

> "Our little baby [Florence, just eight years old] still breathes, but deaths cold hand is upon her. Her heart is beating but her sweet little voice is hushed forever. It will never say to me again 'You's my sweet daddy.' They are all waiting for her, over there. I can see them all. Little Eliza [Nancy's child] and grand pa and tante all waiting for their little girl. They love her so and they are better than we are. They will take such good care of her in the beautiful country. But it is so hard, so hard. I love her too, mother, so dearly. And Floy, poor thing. But God knows best. It is all best, but so hard, mother, so hard. Such a warm affectionate little heart she had, so full of life and enjoying everything so much. I can never be the same man again. If I can only be a better man and go to her. The end is not far now. I can't write any more. Pray for me mother, pray for your broken hearted son." (There is no signature here.)

The following day Will wrote to Jack about the funeral. Jack is in New York on a buying trip for the Tackett store:

> "Just a line to say that the arrangements for the dear little girls funeral is this – services at the house (128 West Lafayette) tomorrow (Thursday, 1st June) at seven o'clock – her dear little body is to be taken next morning to Front Royal. Florence & Ben will go; and the children (Mason & Mary) will remain here – at home with Miss Timberlake and a cousin of Florence's – until their return Friday night. In other words a short service here Thursday 7 P.M. and they will take the train next morning at 6:22, reach Alex about 8:20 or 8:30 a.m. (at the Southern Ry Sta) reach Front Royal at 11:40 a.m. Leave Front Royal that eve at 5:47 and return here same night.
> "I am very glad I came as I have been of much benefit & comfort – the sweet little child is lying on her bed as though asleep. I trust you all are well. Good night, the mail is about to start. Yrs Will."

In Will's next letter to Eliza, July 12, 1899, he said he was writing in Lily's room while she and Algernon (her son) were talking in the library.

He also mentioned he "sees the old gentleman" (Jack Tackett's father) and Jack daily. Marion (Lily's daughter) has just received a pin of a "crown of pearls from one of her many admirers. It came direct from Tiffany's New York – the young fellow is quite desperate – and very wealthy." (Marion is seventeen.)

Will related other news for several more pages, then closed with:

> "Well darling I will close with the assurance that you are never out of my mind – and my first thought in the morning – & last at night is of my dear little mother – and how I miss you & think & think about you only God knows – if I wrote my real thoughts I could write volumes – but I trust I can run down & see you ere long – I wish you could go away with me this summer…. With love & kisses from all, ever your devoted son Will."

Ben, now the City Engineer in Baltimore, wrote his mother on May 12, 1902:

> "I have just received notice of my election to full membership in 'The American Society of Civil Engineers.' We Engineers consider it a great honor and privilege to put Am. Soc. C.E. after our names, and it certainly is, for the Society ranks second to none, not even the English Institute of Engineers. The Transactions and Papers of the Society are read and studied by Engineers over the whole world and considered authority. The next thing I want is the 'Gold Medal' of the Society which is awarded annually for the best paper presented by any member. We are all well. Your ever loving Ben."

On August 21, 1902, Will wrote his "darling little Mother" from Sweet Chalybeate Springs. In southwest Virginia, on the border with West Virginia, the springs contained the strongest carbonated mineral water and a supposed cure for sterility. Admittedly, it is an unsubstantiated stretch from there to wonder if Will was sterile, but he did frequent several springs and he did not sire any children of his own that are known. He tells Eliza: "I write you so many letters in thought that the material letter escapes me." If that sounds familiar, he wrote much the same to Nancy on July 3, 1893. He continued, describing moonlit nights, Lily reading aloud to him, etc. A few days later, on the 25th, he proclaimed:

> "your boy – ever wayward, wandering Willie – took up the collection at the Offertory. Lily said it filled her soul with joy, that I bore myself as though 'twas always so – it just happened that none of the other men was in possition to act – I prayed for you & the other

130

dear ones – darling mother – or rather I thanked the Good God that he had blessed me so long in spit (sic) of my unworthiness – with the many many blessings – the greatest the living mothers love & thought..."

Two weeks later they were all still at Sweet Chalybeate, though when he wrote another letter of piety and devotion (so similar to his others it is not included here) he wrote from his own room. By today's standards it would be presumed he and Lily were cohabitating. If so, why did they have separate rooms? Was that to fool the children? This was in 1902, long before the days of the flappers or other sexually promiscuous behavior that shocked but also titillated the so-called upper class, yet there was no hint of scandal here, in all the correspondence. Will had always bragged about his way with women and was obviously doing his best to please Lily, but they traveled together for at least nine years before they were married. That event finally took place on November 20, 1902, one day after Lily's daughter Marion was married and four days after Will's forty-sixth birthday. It was a quiet wedding, held at Jack and Nancy's house at 211 South St. Asaph (though the newspaper incorrectly lists it at South Fairfax Street) at 11 a.m. The Rev. P. P. Phillips of St. Paul's Episcopal Church performed the rites.

Two days later, Will wrote the following to Nancy, from Haddon Hall in Atlantic City, NJ:

"...I can never thank you darling sister for the lovely way you arranged every thing for our wedding and my – my darling little wife Lily – appreciated it & I believe so wrote mother or you. There was a very good account of our wedding in Fridays Post. I am anxious to see the account in the *Alexandria Gazette*. I asked Mr. McKnight to save me a dozen or so.

"We both appreciated so much the beautiful gift from you & dear Jack & you must thank him again & again. David is enjoying every moment [so her son joins the honeymooning couple] and this sea air is doing us a great deal of good. Marion & William are at the Brighton – they called on us last night and we called this morning – they too are very comfortably fixed. We are to dine with them this evening – and then we will go to see Kyrle Bellew in a Gentleman of France [a new play by Harriet Ford].

"I have missed much of life in not knowing the perfect side before – but then had I married earlier I would have made a great mistake – though how great I might not have known. William Bryant [Marion's husband] will call Lily Mrs C – & then correct & say mother. Marion says he will speak of her as Mrs. Chalmers – which at times is a little embarrassing.

"Well my dear little sister I will close with kisses from both of us. Lunch is ready & so is Lily – so Willy closes – and is the very happiest of men & always your affectionate brother Wm E Fendall."

In his letter to Eliza on Thanksgiving, November 27th, he wrote: "My darling little wife is dearer to me every moment. God grant we may be spared to each other & to our dear ones & our dear ones to us for many many years." Unfortunately, his wish will not be granted, as Lily dies of scarlet fever in less than eight years.

In April of the following year Ben wrote to Eliza, regarding Will having joined the church:

"I hope some of these days I will follow his example, but you know I have very pronounced views on such matters, a little different from many people. Such a step is a most solemn thing to me, not a sentiment or a superstition but a tremendous fact. I alone can and must decide and I do not feel that the time has come. God has given me far more than I deserve, far more than he has given to better men and some day I hope to be in the church, but I do not, in any sense, feel worthy now.

"I got a very flattering invitation to take hold of a big concern to-day more pay than I get now. I am considering the question but shall go a little slow and not jump until I am good and ready. The children are well and we are fairly well fixed as to servants. Fond love to all. Devotedly Your Boy."

In July of 1903 Will wrote Eliza, who was at Virginia Beach with Nancy and Jack, bringing her up to date on happenings in Alexandria. He told her he dropped in at 211 South St. Asaph every day on his way to his office. What is interesting about this is he added "you know you have never been to my house yet." He also told her he had their porch and cellar door painted and fixed the bell in their kitchen and was trying to arrange for a trip for Lily. His next letter indicates he arranged that for it is written from Yellow Sulphur Springs in Montgomery County on August 7th. In it he wrote Eliza:

"I do long to have you in my arms once more darling little mother & do wish I could get you here on the winds for a little while. Any thing for a change & you would so enjoy sitting under their beautiful oak trees – one can be far above the crowd & see – without hearing – there are all sorts & kinds of nooks over looking the grounds. I think I grow more in love with my dear little wife every day – her physical beauty is but a small part of her charm. There are many agreeable people here but we keep to ourselves – walk & read &c &c."

Perhaps keeping to themselves had more to do with Lily's aloofness than a desire for only each other's company. Will's next two letters mention Lily having trouble coping with the dreadful noises, from the street, of common people. They kept her in a nervous state. After this there was a respite of several years from Will's correspondence, until 1909, but that should not be surprising as he also lived in Alexandria and they may have had a telephone. During this interval, however, Ben's letters still appeared. In February of 1904 there had been a fire in Baltimore which wiped out the business center...

> "...from Liberty St. to the Falls, about twelve squares in length and from Lexington St to Pratt, about five squares in width, then down the Falls through the lumber district beyond Broadway nearly a mile and a half and two or three squares wide is all gone. I have organized a force of a thousand men in the last two days and have been directing their movements tonight I am so tired and sleepy that my mind is simply benumbed."

This was written on the 11th. By the 18th [a Thursday] Ben hoped "to have the principal streets open for safe wagon traffic by Sunday night" but he had no idea when he might be able to see Eliza.

The months of April and May brought forth letters relating Mason had German measles, then the possibility he would get chicken pox, after, which Mary came down with the measles. Both children were disfigured by the disease and Ben could not visit his mother and Nancy lest he carry the disease to them.

Speaking of Nancy, her story has been neglected up until now, primarily because none of her letters to her parents or brothers were kept. In her correspondence to her husband she would frequently ask him to burn her letters (which we are fortunate he did not always do). Whether she burned those she sent to her family is not known but only one letter was found in the collection, written on March 13, 1873 (and quoted earlier), wherein she pleading to stay away longer than her parents wished. To tell her story, however, we must go back to the 1880s when she leaves her parent's home and begins a quarter century of long-distance, but passionate, marriage to John Tackett.

The Tacketts

Nancy Lee Fendall was born November 9, 1853, in Alexandria, Virginia, the only surviving daughter of Townshend (or Towny) Dade and Eliza Eaches Fendall. Another daughter had been born the previous year but died when two days old. Nancy's brother, Ben, was almost three years older than she and another brother, Will, would join the family three years after Nancy. They say the middle child has the hardest time but that didn't apply to Nancy. She was spoiled, not only by the men in the family but by her mother as well. In spite of the scarcity of letters in the collection **from** Nancy, those kept that were written **to** her describe a rather self–centered young lady.

Nancy Fendall Tackett, Mrs. Jack Tackett.

Her parents were continually admonishing her for one thing or another. Her father chastised her for her sloppy spelling and worried she was becoming too enamored of having a good time and accumulating material things, thus neglecting her duties "to the great Author of all pleasure (the only true source of all the earthly pleasures we enjoy)," Towny wrote in a long letter on August 10, 1870, when she was almost 17. It was one of many sermons he preached to her through the years, always professing it was for her own good. There are also numerous letters in the section on the Fendalls wherein both Towny and Eliza repeatedly insisted she come home from wherever she was, to no avail, even though Eliza was ill. Nancy ignored their pleas and continued to impose on others.

Nancy's husband also spoiled her, but they had a most unusual marriage and Nancy may have deserved whatever attention she could get. In all their 24½ years of marriage they never lived together for more than a few weeks at a time. During those years Jack lived in a hotel room, without running water, and ate all his meals out. For many years there weren't even bath facilities down the hall from his room and he had to go to a barbershop and pay to have a bath. Meanwhile Nancy raised the children and ran the household but they proved the old adage, "absence makes the heart grow fonder," for they wrote passionate love letters to each other every day for all those years.

Nancy was an attractive young lady and was not lacking in beaus. One, in particular (C. L. Clagett, from Maryland) was especially ardent in his pursuit when she was 23. At that age and at that time many women would be worried about becoming old maids and would have hesitated before refusing any offer of marriage but Nancy apparently was not concerned and resisted his attention. She would not marry until she was just shy of 30. Her husband was John Ford (always called Jack) Tackett, born April 20, 1857 in Fredericksburg, VA. He had a brother Charles and a sister, Sophie. Their mother had died three days after Sophie's birth.

John (Jack) Ford Tackett

Jack had the best intentions for his wife and family but they came to naught. His road through life was full of potholes and pitfalls. At 16 he enrolled in the Virginia Military Institute and took part with the cadets in 1864 and 1865 in front of Richmond. The corps disbanded after Lee's surrender in April 1865 and he returned to the Institute, graduating with distinction as a civil engineer in 1868. Instead of pursuing that path, however, he tried to help his father in his failing manufacturing business. Later, when his father moved to Alexandria and set up a dry goods business, that was barely more successful and Jack was trapped in a life he would regret, though he was always optimistic circumstances would improve soon.

Like his father-in-law, Towny Fendall, Jack preached the gospel and trusted the Lord knew what was best, even when it came to weather. He believed the trials he faced on earth were preparing him for a better life in heaven and hoped he and Nancy would go together but she outlived him by 32 years. His last years were spent as a drummer (traveling salesman), after selling his interest in a dry goods business in Norfolk, VA, in a desperate attempt to provide for his family. He failed at this, too, and was bankrupt when he died in 1908.

Jack was a bit of a dandy and impressed by the trappings of the well-to-do with whom he sometimes shared dinner in his hotel's dining room. He was also vain and when he was 55 he proclaimed himself 45. He was as fastidious as his circumstances would allow and was well liked. Above all else he was deeply in love with Nancy and his inability to provide her with a comfortable life left him feeling he was a failure. While true Jack was unable to, as they say, bring home the bacon, he made up for it with his unceasing and faithful devotion through almost 25 years of marriage.

On October 17, 1883, the night before Nancy was married, her father, Towny sent her $50 in "pin money" as she was "entering on the voyage of life." The next day Jack wrote a letter to "Dear little Mother" from the

Barnum City Hotel in Baltimore, MD, commenting on the lovely wedding and assuring Eliza her daughter was fine and promising to take care of her. Nancy added a footnote to say how happy she was and that Jack was as gentle, tender and considerate as a woman.

Three days later Nancy expounded on the virtues of her husband to "dearest Papa" in a six–page letter. It was written from The Colonnade at 35 Lafayette Place in New York. She referred to Jack as "Mr. Tackett" and raved about his kind loving care. She also thanked Towny for the wedding and related their activities in New York. After the honeymoon they returned to Alexandria, where Jack took up his role as buyer for his father's business, necessitating regular week–long trips to New York to purchase various dry goods for their store, Tackett & Marshall.

On May 17, 1887 Nancy gave birth to her first daughter and namesake, Nancy Lee Fendall Tackett. Jack heard the news in New York via a letter from Eliza. She wrote:

Nancy Lee Tackett

"She got through most satisfactorily and in a much shorter time than any of us anticipated and bore up most heroically and to day seems bright and inclined to tattle, which I always discourage. She seems to love the dear little one already, and trys to imagine a striking likeness to its father. I know she would have preferred a boy but says now she does not care, she is so thankful to her Heavenly Father that it is all right in form and feature, that she will not trouble about the sex and I tell her it may prove to be as great a comfort to her as my daughter has been to me.

"Your father came down this m–g, said it was very unexpected to him, the old gentleman looked and seemed much better and I could see greatly rejoiced at the arrival. We have had many visits and notes of congratulations and just before dinner Mrs. Ned White sent her card on a silver waiter, with a most exquisite bouquet, which I assure you was highly appreciated. Others sent notes which Nan wanted me to answer and the nurse and servants have constant demands so that my time is entirely taken up.

"Nan had various pains on Monday, which she attributed to other causes, and during the afternoon Con & Carrie Stabler came in and she was sewing and seemed as bright talking and laughing with them as usual, but at supper time she said she felt so badly that she agreed to have a cup of coffee sent up, which I was preparing for her, when she came down and as I was suffering dreadfully with rheumatism in my back I proposed that we should both retire at 8 o'clock, and I would sleep with her, but after undressing and moving around a while she complained more and I began to suspect, and proposed to her to come in my room for a while and I would get pa to go up for Dr. G who came about 9 o'clock & soon discovered the pain was not what she thought. I proposed sending for Will who I knew was at Snowden's as I with the Dr thought it time to send for Mrs. Richards. Will soon found her and she got here before ten o'clock and by that time the pains began to be very severe and more rapid and of course getting worse until the <u>final</u>, which was like being transported from earth to Heaven to the mother and a load of anxiety removed from all of our hearts. I read all your letters to Nan, as it is never <u>allowable</u> for a woman to use her eyes at this time."

Eliza went on at length about how much shorter time it took than usual and Nancy…

"…has been so well and I am determined to try and keep her so by refusing all persons admittance to her room. Con and all her friends think it so wise. I did let Sophy go in for a few minutes this m–g, we both thought Jack's sister was too near not to be admitted, she is delighted with the little niece it weighed seven pounds has dark hair and Nan thinks blue eyes but they always have that cast at first. The nurse has just washed it and it has no symptoms of hydrophobia [an abnormal fear of water] but rather likes the water. The nurse proposed sending a sample of its finger nails which she has just cut and wrapped up for you.

"When Nan was first taken I asked if she would like you telegraphed for she said no, as the Dr thought everything was progressing so well and would be all right, that she would rather wait and give you good news than have you in the dreadful suspense you would undergo if you started home, and as you expected to come so soon she thought it best to wait. She sends a great deal of love and kisses, also a portion from the little daughter. I could write more if I was well and had the time. With love from your devoted little mother."

Within a month Jack was trying to figure out how to bring his two girls to New York. On June 12th he wrote from the St. Denis Hotel on Broadway & 11th:

"All during Old Huntington's service I found myself planning some arrangement how we could be together more. For I don't think I can stand being absent from my life all fall winter and spring so after the fall season is over I think we will make some arrangement to get two rooms & bring baby on with a nurse & go to house–keeping in a small way." This is one of many unfulfilled dreams for Jack.

He went on to tell her he went to a baseball match, then walked down the 5th Avenue side of the park from 11th to 65th Sts, where...

> "...there have been some magnificent houses put up there in the past few years & others are in progress. The wealth & magnificence of New York are becoming almost like a tale of the Arabian nights. Some of the views are lovely on this side of the park. One especially struck me – a miniature lake surrounded by gently rolling hills clad with a verdure that looked like soft velvet. The lake dotted here and there with the sails of tiny ships which belonged to the youngsters. How the children seemed to enjoy themselves & what little things are toddling around everywhere. How glad I will be when little Nancy Lee can go with us. How her little eyes will dilate in wonder at all the things she will see if God spares her & us. We will live over again the delights of our childhood. You can go to dressing dolls again & I to reading fairy tales. Yesterday evening, tho, I had the blues. I was longing with an intense yearning for my girls & would not be comforted because they were not with me. For yourself my hearts treasure all the love & kisses I could express to you are but a faint measure of those I have in my heart that are yours. Your dear Jack."

Jack was impressed with all manifestations of wealth, whether in fancy houses or dress. He would admire the ladies and gentlemen attired in what he considered to be elegant fashion, and discredit those who did not measure up to his idea of good taste and breeding. In other words he, like Will and Lily Fendall, looked down on "common" people. Jack also had an appreciative eye for an attractive woman but it is obvious, from his impassioned letters to Nancy, he never strayed.

It is also obvious Nancy's love for Jack never wavered even though she bore the burden of managing the household and children. For the next ten years we are privy to her personal life and feelings before she asked Jack to burn her letters. Considering that only one of her letters survived, prior to her marriage, this is an unexpected bonus. On Sunday, September 18, 1887, she wrote Jack, who was with Dunham Buckley & Co., 340 Broadway in New York, the following:

> "Yes darling I was indeed just truly disappointed to be deprived of yr dear companionship today but I am striving to be very philosophical & bear with patience all that comes & I even have the sweet comfort of <u>knowing</u> you never willingly stay away from yr Nancy – the hardest trial I have is being so constantly separated from you but there is no help for it & I can only earnestly pray that we may be spared to each other & that the day may not be far distant when we may be able to settle down in our little spot on earth <u>together</u> for

a short rest. My constant fear is that you may over tax yr strength for darling you are not the strongest of men & I do hate to think of yr tiring yr precious self down as you have been doing during this last year or eighteen months, how I wish I cd put my arms about yr dear neck this very minute & try to tell you one half the unspeakable love I have in my heart of hearts for you, my sweet unselfish lover."

After general news she added:

"I have succeeded in getting a very nice looking colored girl as a nurse, hope she may prove to be as nice as she looks. She will nurse & do the house work & the baby's washing for $7 a month. I will give her $5 and Ma will give her $2 & board her which I think a very comfortable arrangement. I feel as if I cd write you a lot more but I am going to church with Pa & it is time to dress – with a heart full of love & lots of kisses & the sincere hope of seeing you soon, Yr devoted Nancy."

On October 16th Jack wrote:

"How I wish I could be face to face and that I could hold you in my arms & to my heart & tell you of all the deep strong love I have for you. When this reaches you we will have been four years married. Four years blessed and hallowed to us by tender and sacred memories. Four years of married life without a harsh word or a hard thought of each other. God grant that as the past has been may the future be.

"I suppose Pa came to day to see his grandchild. I expect she will be a great pet with him but we must not let her be spoiled. A spoiled child always has to suffer in after life. Kiss the dear babe & tell her of her father's great love for her and for you my own darling love & kisses innumerable. Your devoted husband Jack."

One of Nancy's innumerable requests for Jack to send her something was sent November 1st:

"I have a little sample of Berkley Cambric No. 188 I think & I am very anxious to get some like it to make Nancy Lee some short dresses & they haven't any at the store fine enough so if you can without very much trouble get me some like it I wd be ever so much obliged. This sample came from the Boston Store & was 20cts a yard but I knew you cd get it for me much cheaper than that in NY & I wanted about 12 yds if you can find it. I wd like to have it as soon as you cd send it conveniently.

"Mother wants you to get her two pair of worsted draws you got her vests last winter & the draws I don't think she thought quite heavy enough her number I think is 32 – she wants good warm heavy ones to ward off sciatica says she is willing to give $1.50 for them if you cannot get her good ones for less but of course if she can get what <u>you</u> think good for less money she wd be very glad." Both Nancy and Jack rarely used punctuation.

On July 13, 1888, Nancy is in Mattaponi with Nancy Lee, now 14 months old, and fabric wasn't the only thing she asked Jack to bring her. He was in Alexandria but it was summer and that always meant Nancy was elsewhere. In fact, it is probably safe to say Nancy never stayed in Alexandria during the summer months. Here her request may seem odd to anyone today but back then children died from teething. Nancy wrote:

"Dear little Nancy Lee was suffering so with her gums the Doctor was obliged to lance them and she is now going to sleep and seems relieved. Please bring down with you love a small flask of good whiskey & about a half pint or a gill of Sherry wine as he says she has suffered so with her teeth she needs some thing to give her strength – he has also ordered what he calls a 'quinine jacket' which I have made of flannel & cousin Sallie has some quinine but not enough so please bring a <u>half an ounce</u> bottle of quinine with you. Oh! my love how glad I will be to see you tomorrow evening the carriage will meet you at the station, I feel as if it had been a month since last Monday."

Jack and Nancy each wrote letters on May 26, 1889, Nancy describing festivities surrounding the unveiling of the Confederate Statue in Alexandria on May 24th and Jack relating almost every minute of his day in New York, beginning with his going to Grace Church. He then went to the Metropolitan Museum, followed by watching the NY Coaching Club horses but no matter how much news he reported he always expressed his love for Nancy in a unique way. Here he told her:

"…our love is not that of slave & master or lord but of equals friends lovers – tied by silken cords that unite but which we do not feel as bonds. Ah each day you grow deeper into my best part deeper into my respect love & reverence, how I wish I could see you to tell you all this but you feel that it is so, do you not my darling? A heart full of love & kiss for you from your devoted Jack."

Nancy has a second daughter, whom she named after her mother, Eliza Fendall, on May 5, 1890. Jack was again in New York and wrote:

> "My darling wife, Pa's telegram was a great surprise and I am truly & devoutly thankful that you are thru with your troubles and are out of the weary waiting. As usual you fooled us again. How my heart is with you but as long as all is going well I will not change my time coming til Nancy's birth day [May 17] unless you feel that you want me very badly & then I will come to you on Friday of the week. How I will love to see the darling baby. Another sweet little girl a sister & companion for dear Nancy Lee.
>
> "Girls are so much sweeter than boys and they are so much more in our lives. Most men are necessary evils and good women are Gods ministering Angels. Am longing to see the new treasure." Tragically, Eliza died of cholera at 14 months.

In September Jack learned the McVeigh house would be sold at public auction, which meant Nancy had to wait a bit longer for the house she wanted. On December 6, 1891, Jack purchased 211 South St. Asaph for $4,600, equivalent to $108,876 in 2008. It sold for over $4 million in 2005. It was, and still is, a handsome three-story house with two side lots, which were purchased separately for $1,935. Jack would drop dead in the garden in 1908. For now the house would become room-and-board for her mother and their fathers. Will would also room there, as would many unrelated others. In her letter of May 1, 1891, Nancy related "Father Tackett brought me a check for $36, that is his board up to the 1st of May. You know they [meaning him and his daughter, Sophie] came 15th of April." That makes it $72 a month for two rooms and meals. Presumably her father and mother paid the same rate. Nancy paid their gardener $1.25 per day.

On little Eliza's only birthday, May 5th, Nancy wrote what Nancy Lee had said to Eliza: "Papa & Mama hasn't no money to give you nuffin cause theys got this big old new house but yr sisters got money & she will buy you a dolly." Two months later, on July 1st, Eliza succumbed to cholera, the second in the family to do so but not the last. Two days later Floy, Ben Fendall's wife, sent her condolences then gave birth to her namesake, Florence Mason, on the 5th of July. Eight years later she, too, would die of cholera. Eliza was buried in St. Paul's Cemetery in Alexandria but not until October 8th. Nancy pressed some flowers from the gravesite, stitching them to paper, then penned the following:

> "My angel child! How I recall all her sweet gentle ways her loving looks her beautiful deep blue eyes. How like sunshine she was to all & what sweet memories we have of her in our heart of hearts –

211 S. Street Asaph, Nancy's boarding house. White building was the post office and the building beyond that was The Lyceum.

Side view of 211 S. Street Asaph

211 S. Street Asaph after the 1960 renovation.

It wd almost stagger my belief in anything did we not **know** that God calls the sweet & pure to grace His Heavenly throne & that of such as Eliza is the Kingdom of Heaven."

In December Jack wrote he wanted nothing for Xmas and was not buying any presents for Nancy except the lots to the house which he had given her last Christmas. He would give a turkey to William, their handyman, and "something for the poor."

In April of 1892 Jack decided to close his lease for his living quarters in New York. He planned to send a folding bed home, along with books, pictures and two tables, then sell the rest to his landlord, hoping to recoup $100, which he would let Nancy use to buy something for the house. He instructed her to pay the servants, Mattie and George. His next letter, May 4th, provided an inventory of his belongings:

"I had the man pack the things last night – it took til nearly 11 o'clock, they will be shipped today – I sent all Pa's & your crockery in a barrel – Forgot the vases which I will bring home with me got in everything of Pas except a broken carte basket. Have the barrel carefully unpacked as you will frequently find one small article in another as for instance a cup in teakettle & the Cooler is full of China.

144

"The rugs are all well wrapped & inside them you will find the books, sisters shoes – which I think account for her feeling so badly while in NY. In another box are all the pictures which should also be very carefully unpacked. The fur rug is on top of them the two table tops are in with the rugs. The legs of the tables I will send from the store & will wrap with them the table cover and some soiled towels – & also my flannels & jocks which I will get you to have washed for me by the time I come home next week. I will bring the balance of the towels home with me. I will fix with William when I come home abt paying him I shall give him abt 25¢ a week. [Remember, the gardener got $1.25 a day.] Fondly Jack."

On May 8th Jack regretted giving up his room at the Hampshire, after checking out their renovation work but…

"…am more and more convinced that I have acted wisely as I think in the future I shall only be in N York abt two months in the year. [Another unfulfilled dream.] Frankly it seems a farce my being here now for the young man I pay $3.00 a week is doing the work just as well as I do and some days the work is a mere farce. You need not say this but I think gradually I will work this thing my way & save a great deal of my valuable time to be applied where it will do most good besides accomplishing quite a saving in money but I will have to do all this gradually as at first it will meet with considerable opposition. I have all along wanted to get some one to take the books at home so that I could get Johnny's service in the store. He is an excellent salesman & is a good strong worker besides. I can get a bright girl to keep the books for one quarter of what I pay him. Don't mention any of these things to any one til I am ready to act.

"I wish very much I could be with you darling but God willing I will next Sunday be with you to help & comfort you, and soon

the trial will be over & you will have a bright little life to cheer & gladden your heart. [Nancy is pregnant with her third daughter, Sophie Ford, who will be born June 3rd.] Not to fill the lost ones place but still a comfort. I wish if the pain & sorrow of bringing the little ones was not so great that we might always have a baby with us. Yours ever, Jack."

Sophie Tackett Blanton

Nancy was at "North Cliff" in Culpeper, VA, nursing her father, in July, 1893. Floy,

145

Ben's wife, was also there with their three children. Towny would die before the month was over but Nancy thought the doctor "may be mistakened in his diagnosis of the case as Drs often are, still what he says certainly seems to correspond with some of Pa's symptoms." On the third she wrote Jack to have two prescriptions filled in Alexandria as she had a "rather poor opinion of country drugs." The doctor had diagnosed serious stomach trouble and put Towny on a liquid diet. When asked if her pa was in any "immediate danger" the doctor said he might live for years. He died on the 23rd, two months past his 80th birthday.

It was a particularly trying time for Nancy as she watched Floy's children play with Nancy Lee. Nancy's Eliza was just five months younger than Mary Gertrude and she couldn't help but think what a big girl her Eliza would have been, "had it been God's will to have left her here with these earthly flowers." Eliza had been gone two years.

North Cliff appears to be a hotel of some sort as Nancy wrote, on August 8th:

> "There is a house full of gay young invited company here tonight they seem to be having a very lively time with music &c how out of keeping it all seems with our feelings & how very trying such things are when ones heart is smarting under such heavy bereavement as ours.
>
> "I enclose you the no of Sophie Fords little Powders which I will get you to send to Leadbeaters [an apothecary] & have put up and send me in yr next letter as they come more quickly that way – hers are nearly out. She is fast asleep but I will steal some kisses to send you & here are some from Nancy Lee.
>
> "If Ma's shawl has been dyed she says she will get you to send it to her by mail & I was thinking if the mourning writing paper [stationery with a black border] I wrote you about has arrived you might send me about two quires of the paper & a package of the envelopes in the shawl & you can send me a ¼ dozen of these falcon pens from Frenches. I get a ½ doz for 5 cts & they last me a long time.
>
> "Well darling I must say good night it is bed time & my rest has been so much broken for dear little Sophie Ford seems most restless of late – more teeth though she looks so well & bright during the day. I think so much of yr lonely time at home darling & I shall be glad when the time comes for me to return to you. Good night my own Sweet–heart. Love & kisses from yr devoted Nancy."

Jack, on Tackett & Marshall stationery, August 13, related how he fixed his own dinner, after Jane boiled him a chicken:

Leadbetter Apothecary, where Nancy sent Jack to get medicine to send to her when she was away.

"I went to church and when I came out met Ben who said he had come over a little earlier than usual & gone out to the Cemetery so we went home from church and he took dinner with me which he seemed to greatly enjoy and be rather amused at my taking the trouble to clear the table & brush the crumbs off the dessert but I like things decently & in order servant or no servant.

"I have just returned from a visit to the cemetery. I took some of our crepe myrtle to put on the graves of our loved ones who are away from toil strife and care & are at peace & rest while we miss these loved forms from our midst. How happy we shd be to think that with the one she went unsoiled & untouched by any of lifes temptations & cares & that the other was so full of years & honor that he is sure to meet the 'Well done Good & faithful servant enter thou unto the joy of thy Lord.' I cleared away the faded flowers from your fathers resting place & just left the spray of crepe myrtle."

August 29th Jack sent Nancy a check of Tackett & Marshall "as I have no money in bank myself – to pay Mrs. Coons for one months board for you & Nancy & mother & I was up there abt 10 days which makes the additional $7.00."

Nancy's next letter, written August 31, 1893, was very informative regarding her attitude about their situation and what she considered to be her justifiable needs. It may seem presumptuous to analyze her behavior when she can't defend herself but having read all of her kept letters the author defends her interpretation. Nancy took herself, two daughters, mother (and father, who just died) and a servant to Culpeper for a summer sojourn away from sweltering Alexandria, while Jack rattled around in the very large house he bought for her, with Jane, another servant, his only companion. True, electric fans were not yet easily available but that house had a lot of windows, a screened porch and large side yard. More importantly, they were not actually wealthy, only acting as if they were. It was costing Jack the proverbial pretty penny to indulge his wife.

The reality of their lives was Jack had to spend weeks at a time in New York for his father's business. He hated it and constantly lamented their separation. She protested the parting equally but gave up nothing to change it. She still followed her past pattern, permitted by her parents, of indulging herself with whatever she wanted. Here she beseeched Jack for yet another servant, using Sophie's sore gums as the reason. They already had two servants and, though it was a big house, they hadn't turned it into a boarding house yet. So just what did Nancy do all day other than write letters, go calling and dress for tea? Draw your own conclusions; here is the letter:

"Your dear letter came to me at dinner time my darling, I too feel anxious to be at home with you for I feel much there needs my attention & there is so much to be done for the Autumn & Winter – fixing & this is the last day of Summer. I shall feel very glad when the servant question is all settled & fixed. Mattie said today she thought perhaps there was a cousin of hers up here near Brandy Station I might get said she seemed a good strong girl – I only wish it was so we cd get along with two but I don't see very well how it cd be managed for dear Sophie Ford needs such constant attention that Matties time is pretty full with her & the other work she does at home & it wd cost much more to put our washing out than to have a house girl – it is so different with a small & large family. I am glad Jane is doing so well she certainly is a much better servant all alone than she is with any other.

"You said nothing of old Wm today so I do hope he is better I know my love your hands are full & there is so much on yr mind but I do trust things may take a happy turn oh! if I cd only do <u>some thing</u> to really help you, I do love you so so dearly & wd do <u>any thing</u> in my power to help you but there seems nothing I can do.

"I hope we will now soon have some settled cool weather so we can get home but I like you wd rather wait ten days too long away than to return one day too soon on babys account the dear little thing keeps remarkably well when you see how dreadfully inflamed her gums are, she keeps her little fingers in her mouth all the time I have felt so thankful we cd have her here during all this hot weather but you may feel sure home I will come my darling as soon as I feel it is safe.

"Last night there were eleven men & eight girls besides our usual house hold but Mrs. Coons managed to fix them all comfortably. I shall be very glad for a little quiet for I do not feel in a frame of mind to be able to stand much gay young company & noise & confusion but try my best to keep up before others & not let them feel my presence a constraint to their bright young spirits but it is so hard with an aching heart to be any thing but sad.

"Nancy Lee & Sophie Ford have <u>thoroughly</u> enjoyed the company & Mattie has regularly dressed them in their best & taken them out to see all who arrived. Well darling it is time to dress for tea so I must close. The weather looks very much like rain this evening Sophie Ford & Nancy Lee send kisses to Papa dear – With dear love & kisses many from yr ever devoted Nancy."

Jack's response, on September 1, was a bit testy:

"I had a long talk with Dr. Gibson last night he said of course coming home depended on the weather but I said there was no earthly danger of your bringing Soph back by the time your month was up – said that she wd be in no more danger in town than in the Country – that even if we had some warm days the nights & mornings wd be cool and that she wd fare quite well at home as anywhere else, so I think you had best come home by tomorrow week at which time your month is up. You can get Mr. Coons or Rob to check your trunks &c for you & Pa will meet you at the train Saturday night a week or if you prefer coming a few days sooner you can do so. I enclose a check which you can fill in enough to pay Mrs. Coons & for your tickets. Your ticket & Matties will be 1.65 each shd you not have enough of the 5.00 sent to cover make it more & get Mrs. Coons to give you the difference in cash.

"As to the servant question can the girl do the home work & assist Jane in the washing & ironing. I certainly think we ought to be able to get a servant to do this and with three servants & a boy to bring up wood & coal & attend to the fires I certainly think1 we shd be able to get on without employing additional help for the washing & ironing. If this girl will do this & Mattie knows her to be capable I would employ her & let her come home with you. I think Jane will be very glad to have you at home again but she has certainly been a comfort to me during your absence she has not wasted anything & I really think she has taken a pride in seeing how well she could do. There has hardly been a night she has been away before 8 o'clock."

They needed a boy to care for the fires as each room had a fireplace or some sort of wood–burning stove.

"It will be a glad thought to have you meet me at home on my return from NY. Good night love Kisses & love for all, Your devoted Jack. Direct your next letter to Denis Barney at Nth St NY."

Jack intended to leave for NY the next night but realized it was Labor Day weekend so postponed his departure and wrote:

"Wm, while improved, has not yet returned to the store and we still make a shift with Wm Jr who is a character and he has really done fairly well. I pay him 10 cents a day which I think rejoices his heart greatly. This morning Jane got us a delicious breakfast that I am sure you would have enjoyed. Beautiful grapes from the Tackett farm, Peaches & cream, Waffles that melted in your mouth, scrambled eggs & fresh tomatoes that a French chef could not have excelled. I am getting very proud of my marketing qualities. For dinner we had a nice little tenderloin steak, corn pudding, stewed tomatoes, baked sweet & Irish potatoes, an ice cold watermelon. I let Jane off after dinner and I officiated as chief waiter & silver washer. I made some really nice coffee had peaches & cream & cold bread.

"Next Sunday by this time I hope we may all be gathered together again. I fear the coming winter is to be a hard one and it will entail much suffering. So many people are out of employment & so many reductions in salary. The RR here has discharged lots of men and has cut ten per cent from all salary from 100 to 200 Y twenty percent from men like B Thompson & I expect Mr. Marbury. I fear Ben [Nancy's brother] suffers too as I see the B & O cuts all men over $150 ten per cent. I will be very glad if we escape with as little as 10 pr ct in our business. Well we will have to live as cheap & spend as little as possible til the times get better. Give much love to the darlings & many kisses for yourself. Your own Jack."

One year later, on September 9, 1894, Jack was at the St. Denis Hotel on Broadway & 11th Street in New York. He was very homesick:

"My darling wife, I miss you & the dear babes more & more each time I leave you and my heart seems to long especially for you to day my own precious wife. I wish that you were here that I might draw you to me in close embrace feel the touch of your dear hands & the caresses you are always willing to give to me and to kiss you again and again and to tell you the old old story that never loses by repeating and to hear it from you, what a very lover like letter from a husband of nearly 11 years. Thank God we can feel & write this to each other, that age has not dulled any sentiment with us but that our honeymoon is still full & not likely to wane until the great giver of all,

God calls us to the more perfect life with him. When it comes I trust it may come to us at the same time that we may be as united then as we have been in this life."

This is not the first time, nor will it be the last, that Jack divulged his wish they "go together," so to speak. It may seem a bit maudlin in the 21st Century but it was his way of expressing his deep devotion to Nancy and his desire they be united forever. She does not seem upset by these comments but in spite of her bereavement at his death she outlived him by 32 years.

That Christmas Nancy made a list of the china set Jack gave her. It was rather ostentatious, even for today. It consisted of one dozen each of dinner, soup and oyster plates, cups and saucers, butter patts, bone and breakfast plates. Then there was one each of a butter plate, tureen & dish for it, gravy boat, fruit dish and salad dish, plus four covered vegetable dishes and an equal number of meat dishes. There is no indication in the correspondence they were contemplating turning 211 South St. Asaph into a boarding house but when they did the extensive set of china must have come in handy.

In July of 1896 Nancy was in Croom, MD, with her mother but without her children. She sent her love to the girls and Jack, then advised him to: "Please give Jane 45 cts to pay the milk boy who comes every morning I told her to get a ½ gallon from him each day, 9 cts a ½ gallon, so for today, Friday, Sat Sunday & Monday she will need 45 cts, won't she?" She signed off as "yr ever devoted little wife Nancy," then added "Remember me to the servants."

By August Nancy had gone from Croom, east of the Potomac, to Williamsport, southwest of Hagerstown, to a farm called "Rose Hill." This would be a regular retreat in the summer, even after Jack died. For now he suffered in solitude back in Alexandria, with only a servant for company. Meanwhile Nancy enjoyed the company of her mother, daughters and countless friends. Her letters were a combination of desire for him and for something he could do for her. On the 17th she wrote two letters, one in the morning and one in the evening. Both combined the above. In the morning she wrote:

"I had such a sweet dream of you last night felt so distinctly yr dear embrace & kisses & heard so plainly yr sweet loving words & I am hoping to get yr dear written words in a few hours."

Then she added very explicit instructions on where to find a tie she wanted:

151

"I wish you wd please look in the little pink straw basket in my top drawer & see if I left a black silk neck tie (which was once yours) & send it to me. If the tie is not there I think you will find a piece of black ribbon in the basket that will do as a neck tie to wear with my shirt waist as I came off without any. The key to my drawer is on my little bunch of keys which you will find in yr drawer next to my top drawer. Be sure to lock the drawer & put the keys back in yr drawer. I left some of yr shirts in that drawer for you because I thought you needed more room to spread yr self while yr girls are away. I fear I left my top drawer in rather 'a mess' as Soph wd say so don't view it with a critics eye for I left it in such haste. If you don't find it there don't worry about it for I don't know where I cd have mislaid it & you can send me instead one & an eighth yards of some cheap black ribbon from the store which I can use as a tie the width does not matter much. I hate to trouble you about such things but I really need it."

Does anyone wonder why she didn't just go into Hagerstown and buy some ribbon? Well, she's not through. That evening, after receiving his letter she had this to say:

"I wd indeed love to have seen you on Sunday in yr pink shirt & linen suit did you buy the suit ready made too, or did you have it made? I wd certainly try to get some more of the shirts if they are so satisfactory – by the way you sent me yr letter from Will with the address of the man who has his razors that he wanted hollow ground – Ross 9th St East Side between G & F St price for his work 55 cts so if you go up to get yr shirts & it is near the razor place you might get them."

Requesting something from Jack was a regular occurrence but her next request almost stopped this book when Nancy's great–granddaughter was told about it. Nancy wrote Jack:

"It is hard to write all one wishes but when I see you I will tell you some things I cannot very well write by-the-way darling <u>please burn</u> my letters for what I write you I don't care for any one else ever to see & letters will get thrown around no matter how carefully we may value them."

Nancy was certainly right about letters being thrown around. In this case they were collected, by the bushel. Obviously Jack did not always obey this command but when their great-granddaughter learned of Nancy's comment she was distressed she had turned over the letters, until she was reminded Nancy got all the letters back when Jack died and she did not then destroy them herself.

The next day Nancy expressed her desire again:

"I have bathed & adorned our dear little daughters my darling & arrayed my self in my best skirt & checked silk waist with daisys in my hair & at my throat & I wish my own sweet–heart was here to see & love me & that I might give him one of my best & sweetest kisses, oh! Did I ever think a long time ago I wd ever write such a thing to a 'boy' but then I did not know how entirely & devotedly I cd love my <u>own</u> boy bless yr dear heart I only love you more & more each day I live."

Ironically there are several letters from Nancy during August, even after she asked they be burned, but none remaining from Jack, though she mentions his. Besides her passionate proclamations of love for him Nancy also regularly requested yards and yards of fabric from Jack's store, but not always for herself. She would show a group of women, whom she called "the ladies," samples of his merchandise, from which they would order a dozen yards of whatever they liked. Nancy said she was "drumming up trade for this dull season" and the orders were substantial but she still managed to put in a request or two of her own. After four pages of which lady wanted what, she added:

"Thank you so much darling for 'our' cravat you sent in yr dear letter today which I so enjoyed, (the letter I mean) & will enjoy our cravat with my shirt waist – I am sorry too you lost the little sample of lace I sent you it was that little cheap linen lace edge you sell at 4 cts a yard Ma got some like it from Miss Annie, I think it costs 1½ cts a yard & as you lost the piece I will get you please to send me two yards. I have the rest all sewed on or wd send you another sample hope you may yet find the sample I sent as it just fits in a certain place where it was to go, of course if you think it a risk to send the edge without sample I can rip off some & sen d you – I expect you are thinking I am sending for some <u>thing</u> every time I write but I don't think I will send for anything more when you send the white ribbon for Nance & this little lace trimming for Soph."

Her vow didn't last long for two days later she wrote:

"When you send the lawns [fabric] for the ladies please put in the bundle besides Nancy Lee's reefer, some candy for <u>me</u>. Cockey has some nice old fashioned cream candy some is seasoned with vanilla & some with 'pepmint' it is 15 cts a pound & I wd like a ½ lb of each kind in separate bundles it is nice & soft & I have been wanting some ever since I came & thought this is a fine chance to get it as it wd not add to the express on the bundle." Packages

153

were put on a train, picked up in Hagerstown and delivered by horse–drawn wagons.

The next morning she added:

"Before I awoke this a.m. in my room I was sitting with you on a beach in a lovely moon lit garden with yr dear loving arms about me, with yr sweet kisses on my lips & yr tender loving words being whispered to me in yr own dear way & I was so entirely happy that the awakening to find you so far away from me was painful. It seems such a long time since this day two weeks ago – in some ways the days seem to fly but in others they drag."

On August 27, 1896, after her usual report on how the girls were and how much fun they were having, she responded to Jack's request:

"You asked about the key to yr leather trunk. I think it is in the trunk it always stays in the key hole if you don't find it there it might possibly be on the same bunch with my drawer bureau keys – please lock up all my drawers my desk wardrobe &c & put the keys away in my drawer & lock them up. When you go [to New York] & you keep the pantry door into the kitchen locked don't you & please have the refrigerator [actually an ice box] moved from the place where it always stands so the floor there may get perfectly dry & the little tub which stays under to catch the water turned up so that may dry out well too. I have intended to ask you to attend to this every time I write but always forget. I wd lock the door between the kitchen & dining room too can't be too careful."

Imagine locking every door and drawer in your house when you leave. Until Nancy returns, when Jack left there was no one in the house so from whom was he locking it up?

On September 8th Jack informed Nancy about the complicated way he must go to join her, starting from New York:

"I am spending every energy to get home by Thursday evening if possible & if I do will be able to come to you on the late train subway leaving Washington at 5 o'cl arriving Sat Hagerstown at 8 coming to Williamsport on the trolley & Agnes said they wd meet me at Williamsport so if you hear nothing to the contrary you may expect me on Saturday night but I may find I can't in which case I sh telegraph you but I hope & want to see you."

Their anniversary on October 17, 1897, prompted this:

"My darling wife if my pocket was as rich in dollars as my heart is in love for you this box would be full of diamonds, to mark the fourteenth anniversary of the happiest day of my life. But there is the sweet consciousness in my heart that the gift will have more value from the nature that prompts it than any intrinsic worth could give it. May we be spared to each other for many anniversaries is the prayer of your devoted Jack."

From Nancy's few letters, which Jack did not burn but brought home with him, we find she was just as ardent as he. Like her brother, Will Fendall, she could lay it on thick at times but at least she was sincere, whereas Will was not. A good example would be her letter of November 30, 1898, written at 5:15 P.M. Jack had just left for New York and she was in a dither:

"What wd I not give to be in yr dear strong arms this very moment my darling love & you are speeding away mile by mile from me but the miles make no difference in our love for I feel for time & eternity that will be the <u>same</u>. Some how you seemed to go away in such a hurry & I was so dazed & sad & interrupted I did not seem to say all I wished to, I was so worried about yr not having a strap for yr box & sorry I cd not go to W [Washington, to catch the train] with you but darling I felt I cd not controle myself so sad as my heart is."

In January 1899 Jack had moved into The Buckingham at 5th & 50th Street, NY and in his next four letters he rhapsodized over the hotel and its clientele. January 19th he wrote:

"How I wish you were here with me to enjoy this sweet restful house. It is hard to realize I am in New York. This writing room used in common by the ladies & gentlemen is a lovely place as I look out to 5th Ave from where I am the room must be 150 feet long [half the length of a football field?] filled with easy chairs divans palms here & there scattered. A most musical clock is just chiming 7:30, in the room are the news stands, telegraph &c but there is no noise, polite attendants & guests glide noiselessly about on the softest of carpets & rugs. I am struck by the difference in the office when I came in the clerk handed me my key without my asking for it & made the pleasant little remark of the weather, that ever fruitful & easy topic…"

March 8th:

"How my heart longs for my darling this evening. I seem each year to miss you more & more & to want to have you with me on these little trips – they would then be as much pleasure as business & I know you would so enjoy the quiet rest of this house. This room seems a favorite lounging place for both old & young ladies & gentleman.

"There was standing just before me such a dainty looking young girl in one of the prettiest gowns. It was a soft violet in color, fitting very close to the figure and trimmed quite elaborately with an appliqué of a darker shade of the same material in folds or pipings. Most of the ladies abt the house wear beautiful & elegant clothes, not the loud kind you see at the Waldorf but just such clothes as you would expect well bred people to wear.

"I was very tired when I came up this evening but I had such a nice little dinner here in the Café that I feel quite rested now. I think I had the nicest steak here today I about ever tasted & some of the most delicious ice cream & the price for the dinner was quite moderate a trifle less than the St D. I think the prices are the same in the dining room as in the Café only in the main dining room I notice during the dinner hour they have a beautiful orchestra.

"I do not think I have ever seen a more perfectly heated & ventilated house than this it seems to be absolutely free from draughts & the temperature is just right. Most of the hotels are overheated. The St Denis has inaugurated a new feature in a 50¢ breakfast & it is a dandy for the price from their regular menu it would cost full $1.00 or more & the service & attention is the same as if the meal was served a la carte. The menu commences with the choice of four kinds of fruit – the oat meal is grits & the choice of steak lamb chops ham & eggs or half dozen other relishes cakes either wheat or buckwheat Hot rolls &c as Ben would say good enough for any dog. It is very common for me to stop there for breakfast occasionally as I have a good deal to do in that part of the town & I take a Madison Ave car down there only two blocks to walk.

"I will try to attend to all your commissions for you. They have in this room one of the sweetest clock chimes I about ever heard & as I write to you I am reminded of how the hours are speeding on as it chimes the hours quarter or half hour and it is getting almost to shut eye time – I will say good night & God bless & keep you & ours with a heart full of love. Your devoted Jack."

The next day he wrote about how he was impressed by the hotel's electricity:

"Tell Mrs. Eliza I had a good joke on myself abt her superstition on the three lights. I had noticed that the central light in my room had as I supposed two lights & although I wanted to turn on the one by the dressing table for fear of the bad luck of the three lights – but in glancing up I found that when I touched the electric button that I turned on the three lights but since then I just turn on the one light & then touch the button which gives me three making four in all & quite a brilliant illumination. Electricity is certainly a most convenient as well as a delightful light. They use it here exclusively even in the lamps. I think in this room they have 75 to 100 lights & you can read comfortably anywhere in the room.

"I wish for you so often & long for your presence more & more all the time. I think as the years go on I become more & more a lover. It is very sweet to have it so. I wish I never had the far away look my love I never want to have it. If I can do as I want you should be spared all care anxiety & trouble but alas I have the desire but not the power.

"I had a delightful little dinner here today very simple but enjoyable a deliciously cooked steak healthful fresh asparagus & a dainty little ice cream after it for which the moderate sum of 85¢ was charged. [That steak would cost $22 today, still a bargain.] Down at the St Denis the same would have cost $1.10.

Jack, again, June 3rd:

"Your letters are always welcome but that this morning was doubly so as I seemed to want just such a line of love so full of melody & so in sympathy with my own feelings of the night we spent together. How few people realize the beauty of the thought 'Two souls with but a single thought two hearts that beat as one.' Thank God we do & feel them to have no parody in them. Sharp contrasts make situations so apparent & our life has had some sharp ones lately that have shed the full daylight on our perfect love for each other. Like the illustration used by Dr. Micon (?) we always know the beauty is there but some times the light shines stronger & makes us see it more clearly & this light seems to grow in power each year of our married life."

For some inexplicable reason there are no letters remaining from 1900 but it soon becomes apparent, in 1901, things had not been going well for Jack. For more than 30 years he had tried to improve his father's business, instead of pursuing a career in engineering, at which he had excelled in school. In 1883 he married the love of his life but, as the buyer for his father's store – "Tackett & Marshall, Wholesale and Retail Dealers in Foreign and Domestic Dry Goods, Notions, Hosiery, &C, Cor. King and Pitt Streets" – he had been obliged to spend more time in New York than Alexandria, desperately trying to find the goods the public would want to purchase. He had been only marginally successful. Many marriages would have dissolved under this constant separation. Only their mutual trust and deep devotion continued to bind Jack and Nancy together. Beginning in 1901 that love would be tested even further.

Until now Jack's trips to New York had been primarily during the week and he would often come home on the weekends. That was soon to change. Jack was about to move to Norfolk, VA to join the firm of Russell & Simcoe, at 346 Main Street, as a partner. They sold the same merchandise as Tackett & Marshall. Jack made the move to improve his financial situation for Nancy and their daughters. That was his only purpose in life, to make their lives comfortable and free of financial worries. Unfortunately, though he tried valiantly, he never succeeded. Even his investments came to naught for they were entrusted to Will Fendall, who used them to line his own pockets.

The most intriguing part of this move is the lopsided logic that goes along with his moving to Norfolk and Nancy and the girls staying in Alexandria because Jack thought it was less expensive that way. There are a lot of factors in play here that are alien to most of us in the 21st Century. If the breadwinner moves because of work, generally the family moves with

Tackett and Marshall occupied the building shown as Swan Bros.

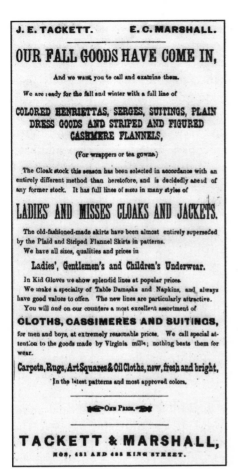

Tackett and Marshall newspaper ad.

him or her. Of course, there are exceptions. Many men come here from another country to find work and save to bring their families over later. They are not usually partners in large businesses, however, and there's a major difference between transporting someone from across an ocean or border and moving 200 miles. Perhaps the fact the Tackett household included his father and her mother made moving them all impractical. Or it may be Nancy did not wish to leave her handsome house. Whatever, for six more years Jack would live in one room, without running water, still reaching for that brass ring.

Our first indication Jack was going to Norfolk came on March 16, 1901:

"I arrived at Norfolk at 8 oclock had a good night on the boat & found Mr. Simcoe waiting for me on the wharf. We went up to his house & had breakfast abt 9 oclock which I truly enjoyed hot rolls beautiful cakes shad ros &c. He has given me a most sumptious room. I like the looks of everything very much. I expect to get back on Monday morning but if I should not don't be uneasy. Mr. Simcoe has a lovely home on one of the swell streets asphalt pavements and street as clean as a penny. He bought the house & lot for $11,000 [$282,000 now] has been offered $3000 profit on it but of course does not want to sell.

"Please give my love to Pa & say to him in case we complete the arrangement that Mr. Simcoe does not want us to say anything abt our coming to Norfolk until we are all closed up and ready to come. Your dearest Jack."

The last sentence suggests they were going to close the store in Alexandria and move, en masse, to Norfolk but that didn't happen. The store apparently stayed open because later letters mention Jack's brother, Charles, buying into the business. So Jack went alone. Now weekend visits were no longer possible; the cost of the boat trip home was too costly. Not only would Jack miss his beloved wife but his daughters, as well. Nancy Lee was now 14; Sophie was nine. He would miss their communions, graduations, high school dances, first beaus and their gradual blossoming into young women. He would now also begin to burn Nancy's letters, as she had instructed him to do five years ago. The time between visits home may have contributed to this. Packing up a few letters to bring back from New York would have been a lot easier than hauling a couple dozen from the southern corner of Virginia. As a result we can only imagine what life was like for Nancy while she took care of her daughters, her mother and father–in–law and managed the servants and the very large house Jack had bought for her.

Just like Nancy's "visits" elsewhere during the summer, she was surrounded by family and friends. Jack was not and there are those who presume he had someone "on the side." He was a pleasant looking man with the typical middle age beginning of a paunch, neither handsome nor homely. He would not have stood out in any crowd but it was not his outward appearance that set him apart. It was his unwavering, undiminished devotion to his wife, in spite of the separation that plagued them throughout their marriage. He was haunted by this and his inability to provide her with all she desired, and the anguish over this that spills from the pages of his letters attest to his fidelity.

His pleas to God to end their separation became more and more poignant as circumstances did not improve. Jack would come to believe if he had been a true Christian, life would have been easier. It's hard to imagine how much more Christian Jack could have been. He was true to his wife, he cheated no one, he preached serving and trusting the Lord to his wife and daughters and he was liked and respected by those who knew him. He may have failed as a businessman but he did not fail as a human being, which makes being privy to his slow disintegration difficult to read.

Nancy would be forced to take in boarders to make the ends meet that grew further and further apart each year but they would continue the pretense of wealth. Perhaps that's why she would prove to be totally inept in handling money matters after Jack died. The difficulties she encountered during Jack's time in Norfolk, followed by his fruitless attempt to become a drummer, may have been revealed in the letters he destroyed. Without them we can only guess what life was like for her, though a few letters did survive and they are included here. As for those from Jack, their sheer volume speaks both to his loneliness and her need to keep some reminder of him in his absence. Nancy could add those to her collection but space constraints here demand a more careful selection.

In June of 1901 Jack was living in the New Atlantic Hotel in Norfolk. The hotel had 220 rooms and was four floors tall with a fifth floor with dormers. Jack was looking forward to Nancy and the girls visiting him soon, though they "will not be able to get seats at the present table – but that will make no difference as the headwaiter will give me a nice waiter I am sure wherever we go in the dining room."

He wrote Will on August 5th, from Alexandria:

"I think Pa has at last concluded to wind up the Alexa business. I write to ask you the notice he wd be required to give Mr. Kempster – we have no regular lease on the street have paid our rent just as called for. It makes me very sad to come to Alexa & see the ending of my 20 years labor. Pa will not begin to sell til Sept 1st as things are at a stand still here. The town is dead.

"Nan said that you thought possibly in the event of Marion's marriage this fall that Mrs. C [Chalmers, Will's future wife] might take the house. I would rent it for $40 per month [$1022 today] repapering the dining room & painting the porch & after that shd put such necessary repairs as would keep the house in order reserving the right to sell but giving the tenant the right of refusal of the property in case they wished to purchase it. $40 per month would pay abt 3 pr ct after paying taxes insurance & repairs."

Will is at Orkney Springs, on the WV border. Presumably Lily Chalmers and her children are with him. On September 8th Jack had changed his mind and wrote Will:

"I have abt made up my mind under certain conditions that Nancy will talk over with you on your return to keep up the establishment that it will likely be cheaper than either renting a house or boarding in Norfolk. Of course the separation from my family is a terrible strain on me but one which I must try to bear. I realize more & more each day that the increase of the business in Norfolk and to future success depends largely on my effort but if this first year we are enabled to keep up the increase that we have made in the spring business I think that I can manage.

"I am terribly burdened down with the interest charges of over 900 pr year & the insurance of 1200 & then my own expenses in Norfolk at the cheapest abt 50 pr month or 600 per year. I tried this summer a private house & paid 30 per month. It was a mile from my business & the car fare cost 1.00 per week besides the loss of time. Norfolk is abt as expensive as NY to live in. I ought not to bother you with all the detail." Jack will end up paying $25 per week at the hotel.

October 9th, to Nancy:

"Your dear letter was a great pleasure to me as it always is. It is just like sitting down and having a little chat with you except that I never talk to you very long without holding your hand & kissing you and I miss that part of the conversation very much. You remember that Soph used to put her hand to her little fat neck & say she had a lot of kisses down there – well I have a lot some where for you and I am very very anxious to deliver them."

He reported they had averaged about $100 per day in business and they are working hard for every gain they can make, then adds:

"Simcoe has abt made up his mind that it will be best for me to go on again abt the 20th [meaning NY] & in that case I shall try to arrange to come up on Friday night the 18th & spend Saturday Sunday at home celebrating our eighteenth anniversary a little late. I hate not to be with you on the 17th but I will be in spirit if not in flesh."

Jack's next letter, October 14th, more thoroughly explains the situation with his father's business. It appears his brother, Charles, had decided to invest in it with a partner. It also gives some indication that relations between Jack and his father were not as cordial as they might have been. In a previous letter Jack mentioned he had written him but received no reply. He was also puzzled by Nancy's letter:

"I don't quite understand what you write abt the Alexa business & its going out of the family as I consider Charles very much in the family & he is going to buy it in connection with his friend Mr Baker & they employ Mr Grantz at a salary and a certain share of the profits. Charles I think very naturally does not want to put every cent of money he has outside of his house in one venture and that a venture he is prompted to go into purely through love.
"Now as to Pa's running the business it is simply impossible for any one to go to business at abt 10 o'clock in the morning come away at 1:30 and sleep til nearly five o'clock and run a retail business successfully. Of course during the excitement of the sale he has likely staid very closely at the store. He speaks of the sale as a very successful one. On that point I am utterly unable to judge as I never have been able to get from Pa how much he has sold & Charlie said when he was there that he could not tell. I don't know either if he has sold every thing for cash or has charged a lot of it.

"I left the business in Alexa May 1st in excellent shape. When I looked into it Aug 1 it has certainly gone behind as compared with Aug 1 of the year previous. Every thing and every body was out of sympathy. Mr Allen Geo said the falling off in the business was due to the absolute refusal of the old gentleman to keep up his stock, all of which he denied. Honestly my opinion is that if Pa were to run the business in Alexandria that at the end of three years should he live so long he would not have a cent.

"Of course my precious one my judgment is far from infallible and I may be dead wrong but I think if I had the choice of giving a business to a bright boy of 15 & a man of 80 that I shd choose the boy. The one can learn the other knows it all. I do not at all think Pa half appreciates the love & the motive beyond that actuates Charles in this. I can do nothing farther than I have done in this matter, all my advice has been uniformly the same I see no reason to change it.

"If Simcoe had been willing I might have been tempted simply on Pa's account to run the Alexa business in connection with the Norfolk but he thought it would take too much of my time & attention & I know he was right so on no account mention this <u>to anyone</u>. I am glad for the business to fall in Chas hands. I think it is likely it will be run under the same name & I do trust it may be made a success. I think Chas & his friends will be satisfied with an amount that it wd have been folly for me to accept.

"This has been a blue Monday. Rain nearly all day & it is the poorest Monday we have had since I have been down here & cuts into our gains but it was the same all around and misery loves company and we have been spoiled by not having a rainy Monday since Augt. We are very easily spoiled you know."

He asked Nancy to get some roe herring for him, then added:

"I have fresh fish here three times a day tho I don't eat it at every meal. I shall be glad to eat at a table where there are no <u>Dutch hogs</u> or American pigs. They take away my appetite. I am much too fastidious & fine grained for this world any how – that is with my limited means."

Jack rhapsodized over their wedding on October 16th:

"When this reaches you nearly eighteen years will have gone over our heads since that sweet October day fragrant with sweet memories linked us together for better for worse. As I look back over the long vista of years I can see so many things. The dear old Father always a sweet memory. The sweet old parlor with its decorations, ourselves so happy under the marriage bells and all went merrily. Well my precious one, I have doubtless failed & come short in many things but in my love for you there has been no variableness or shadow of turning. I love you but better with each added milestone and when we pass from this to the beautiful life beyond, then the link will still bind us and thro all the eternal life will we be one in all things, bound together by a tie softer than any cord of softest silk the strands of which are the purest refined love. May God bless you and keep you and tenderly guard you is my daily & nightly prayer."

His next letter was written on Russell, Simcoe & Tackett stationery October 30th, so he was now officially a partner. He had moved into the Granby Hotel and wanted Nancy to "send with my clothes photos of yourself & the children & a few little pictures that you can spare to hang around my room & remind me of home. Nothing breakable or expensive just a few you can spare."

November 2nd he told Nancy he saved her letters to read again before he destroyed them, then commented about his father:

"Poor old fellow [he's 79] he scarcely realizes what the conduct of a business really is and how utterly impossible it is for him to cope with it. If it were anyone else but he when he talks abt my leaving things in a tangle & his straightening them out it would worry me but his method of untieing the Gordion Knot was the old one that is cutting it. Well my precious one the talk of the dear old gentleman does not affect me one whit. My conscience is clear in this that to the success of the work there I gave the most slavish devotion. No man could have more entirely devoted his life to business than I did to that and but for it the bad would have been reached long since.

"I think if I could be at home like the darkies every Sunday that I should be about reconciled but it is rather digging to pay $7.00 for such a pleasure specially when you have so many uses for the funds. I hope my dear Nancy Lee is better of her cold. This weather is apt to make people take cold. Kiss both of the darlings for me. Give lots of love to Pa Mrs Eliza and Will. With a heart full & kisses many for your dear self."

Jack described his room as being bright and comfortable, with an old carpet and old-fashioned furniture but a steam radiator to keep him warm. He was happy he was not living beyond his means and looked forward to the "pleasure and bliss" of bringing her to New York for seven or eight days. He would then give her a credit of $10 to buy little things for Xmas but that was about all he would have to give. The trip will be her birthday (November 9th) and Xmas presents. Then he added: "Oh how I long to see

164

you & love you. Tho only a week has gone & it has passed rapidly by reason of constant occupation it seems a long long time since I kissed your sweet lips & felt the gentle touch of your hand. My visit home was one long sweet song – a poem of true love that did run smooth."

Jack also wrote he hoped Charles would make a go of it, then expressed his feelings about leaving the business:

"You cant imagine the relief to me in getting rid of the anxiety of that business is. No financial aid that Pa could have given me would compensate for the care I had in the visits to Alexa – some I left there – complaint friction & confusion everywhere & by the time I move order, I was in chaos myself & it was a week after my return before I recovered & I just began to dread coming to Alexa but now all is different, I look forward to my visits to home as a delight & can give my whole time & attention to my business here and feel that the labor is going to have its reward. Certainly if the income goes on in our business I will be able in a year or two to get myself out of any financial strain & can go on feeling on firm ground."

After attending Christ Church on November 4th, Jack wrote:

"It seems a month instead of a week since I saw you last which is very complimentary to your charms which I think increase with acquaintance. You are sweeter to me every time I am with you my own darling wife and I seem to love you better all the time. The eighteen years of married life seem to have drawn us closer to each other and all its cares are nothing as compared with the sweet love it has brought us for each other. It would doubtless seem strange to many in this practical world that you & I shd be as full of sentiment as young lovers of sixteen but what care we for the world. Our world is ourselves, beyond the pale we can see much to amuse and interest but within it is an Holy of Holies in which no one can enter save ourselves."

Jack's business report on November 15th was encouraging:

"We made a gain of abt $1000 in the first eight days of the month but this week s far behind still this is not altogether unexpected as a very large week is generally followed by a lull. Last night when I retired I so longed for you to be in my arms & close to my heart as you are always in thought. Today one week I hope to be with you and look forward to having you with me for a whole week as a joy beyond expression. This trip is to me an anniversary & Xmas present all in one & if you can just be well we will enjoy it to the full. Oh my own how much you are to me. How inexpressibly sweet & lively & your love the richest treasure that could come into my life. Few men are blessed with such love & I certainly appreciate it."

November 18th brought forth this:

"I suppose you like myself heard the Pastoral letter of the #### of Bishops yesterday. It went very strongly for the card clubs but I think none too strongly. This thing of women meeting three or four days in the week & spending the best part of the day in card playing punch drinking & feasting will destroy the moral as well as the physical notions and I can see in many ways its penurious effects. I think all things are right fun in moderation. I can see no harm in a lady giving a card party & presenting prizes because my definition of gambling is playing for something in which you have a stake and this is the case in the Centribution clubs because this is what they practically are."

On December 5th Jack reminisced about the Christmas displays they used to have in the Alexandria store:

"I enjoyed the show & the crowds. How hard it was that I had to give up in dear old Alexa after so many years of struggle. My great regret is that I did not come here years ago when the soil was virgin & I was younger, but then I did not. The past is gone the future is mine so far as God gives me strength to bear its burden and reap its benefits.

"Last Thursday was our Thanksgiving day & we were together but we are too tonight in spirit. How I would love to have you in the flesh but we must not think of this but press bravely on filling the hours of separation with thoughts – sweet loving thought of each other – and thanking God for much that he has given us. This is the only brave & true way to live. Of course we will have our moments of weakness & discomfort. They must come into all lives but we shd strive to put them aside. I feel that we may be going thro this experience for a final reward.

"I had a little too much mackerel for supper as I was helped twice. We have very good dinners. Have bacon & cabbage every day. Turkey or roast lamb or roast beef and quite good vegetables, two kinds of dessert and the table is clean and the ware very nice. On the whole it is a good cheap hotel. Of course it does not come up anywhere near that perfect ideal the Buckingham. No hotel that I have ever been to quite equals that in quiet elegance and human–like feeling. The young men at table with me are quite pleasant & in this respect things are much more agreeable than at the Atlantic where you sat one day with a Jew or a big Dutchman."

December 12th:

"I wish I had plenty of money once a year but I never expect to be anything but hard up as long as I live but I don't think of it any more than I can help and am not going to make myself miserable about it. Except that it is a great depravation to be unable to give you & the dear ones a nice Xmas present but I cannot & must not think of it. Oh my own when I think of the precious hours that we spend away from each other I some times chafe and grow very restless but I must not. I have put my hand to the plow and will not turn back – nay I cant – and if the business should ever turn out enough to give me $500 a year more than I draw I could begin to feel easy in that way. I hate to deny you anything. I want you to be free from care and all I do is for you & the dear ones. I spend not one cent on myself that is not absolutely necessary but there are so many little things to pay. Your devoted lover & husband Jack."

Jack would continue to deplore their situation, protesting he had "done his best to keep storms away and shield her" and trusting in God to bring them together. When God did not respond to his fervent prayers Jack believed it was because he wasn't a good Christian. It never occurred to him the fault lay in his putting his hand to the wrong plow. Changing professions is never easy, especially in mid-life, but Jack seems to have had tunnel vision all those years, never able to even consider an alternative. The rut he had dug was too deep. On the other hand, his dogged determination to stay with the ship was a blessing in his relationship with Nancy. No woman ever had a more devoted and loving husband. On his way back to Norfolk after Christmas he wrote: "I always knew the love was intense but somehow this separation has made me realize not only that it is intense but immense." He returned to work because he felt it was his duty.

After hearing a sermon by Dr. A. Cohe Smith on the perils of indecision Jack preached his own sermon to Nancy Lee, now 15, on January 7, 1902:

"One thought struck me that God asked us in coming to him only to forsake sin, that he asked us not to give up anything that was right, only the things that were wrong and as we pass on in life how much real joy is there in serving our Lord and Master. The service of God makes us better children better men and women better in all relations in life and the true Christian should be the happiest of mortals in this world and the world to come. I hope my precious child you read your bible every day. You will soon learn to love it as no other book and you will find much in it to comfort you. I have been careless abt this but I am trying to do better and you should think of the two beautiful Christian characters you have in your home. Your dear Grandmother & your Mother. Think of these things darling and as soon as you can unite yourself with the Church. Your dear father."

There are dozens more letters from Jack during the next six years, each declaring his love for Nancy and trust in God. One in particular, written January 24, 1902, encompasses all that and takes us into his home away from home where he sat alone each night, pouring his heart out to his beloved Nancy. The letter is 11 pages long but provides such a clear insight into Jack's lonely heart and existence it is copied here in its entirety:

"My darling wife – Your letter came to me about 1:30 today and I have just read it for the second time. I am sitting in my little room which is just abt the size of Fathers room. It has a large window with a deep seat. The window tolerably high from the floor. Just under the window is the little steam radiator and on one side of that is the wash stand & on the side where the wash stand is my wardrobe. The gas burner is between the wardrobe and the wash stand and the light is splendid. I sit generally under the gas & facing the dressing table.

"On the side next the window I have hung a very pretty little calendar. On the dressing table rest the pictures of my loves and just adjoining that my beautiful Madonna which hangs over a little table where I keep my books, bible &c next to the Madonna and over my bed is the pretty little calendar I wrote you of the Magdalena & the little picture of father taken with Soph & Nancy Lee and over the head of the bed the picture of Algernon you sent me from home. [Algernon may refer to the son of Will's future wife, Lily Myers–Chalmers.]

"The room is papered with a light paper with little garlands of blue flowers. The carpet is rather faded velvet but clean & just in front of the dresser I have a right pretty rug for which I paid 1.00 at the store. The furniture is a walnut set neat and plain marble top dresser and wash stand, rocker & small chair. The room is very high pitched, bright with a southern exposure.

"Some day I will send you the menu card to see what they give us to eat. Now for dinner today we had bisque of clam soup, boiled rock, very good roast beef, chicken coquette, several vegetables, cocoa nut pie, lemon ice and cake and a lot of other things. The dining room is large, light and bright and I think they are having now an average abt 75 people some of them very nice looking. There are several nice young men at our table which is all men. On the whole I like the place fully as well as the Atlantic and it suits my attenuated purse much better.

"I think of you every hour of the day. The sweetest thoughts and think how truly fortunate and blessed that in this lottery matrimonial that I shd have drawn the capital prize and better still know how to value it. Ah my precious one few people are so happy in true love as you and I have been and the beautiful past seems to herald a beautiful future and tho this will likely be darkened by many trials, the common lot of man, still with all of them we will be sustained by that love and trust in each other.

"I often think of the inspiration of true love, writing as I do a love letter about every day. I fear some times that the material will exhaust but no, each day brings some thought that is new and the stream goes on just as the mountain torrent and yet changing its ripples with the passing days. Shd God bless us by giving us long lives I think we would be just the same only more loving each and every day.

"Charles left us today. He was at the store for a little while. It is a great trial that I see so little of my dear brother. I love him so much and admire him so greatly. He has had his crosses full and many in this life but as surely will wear the Crown immortal in the life to come. Good night my dearest may Angels guard you. Love & kisses to the darlings & to Father, Mrs E & Will. Your devoted Jack."

In February several letters from Nancy suddenly appear. The first on the 3rd:

"It has only been a few hours my darling, since we parted, & yet the time seems long & I keep feeling as if you <u>must</u> come in & <u>speak</u> to me & say 'I love you so' as I heard you say yesterday such <u>dear</u> words to me. I am so glad you have this lovely sun shine do trust you may have very bright days while you are away for I know sunshine is always helpful.

"We have just had such a sweet visit from Lily. She brought each of us a sweet little gift she is always so thoughtful & kind, she brought me a sweet little mosaic pin, Soph a little bucket of shells and Nancy Lee a pretty box of writing paper. Said she wanted to bring Mother some little thing but cd not find just what she wanted for her but the dear old lady seemed to appreciate her thought. She & Marion [her daughter] are coming down tomorrow afternoon & be with me to entertain any callers who may come.

"I do <u>miss</u> you, my own, yr visit was like a beautiful sweet dream & I enjoyed every moment of your stay & am looking forward with such happiness to yr home coming Saturday next – am hoping you may be able to get through yr work in time to come home <u>Friday</u> night & spend Sat & Sun both with us – nothing small about me you see. Please get me from Seigle & Coopers a pair of 'PN' corsets No 21, price $1.00 & a pair of black leggings & a box of Packars Tar Soap from D & Co. Here is a heart <u>full</u> of love & kisses many from yr ever devoted little wife Nancy."

Jack was in New York on a buying trip, staying at The Buckingham at 5th & 50th Street. He wrote her a quick note to say he was safe and there was a nice room waiting for him. He put on his tuxedo to go to dinner and was "happy thinking of the two sweet days spent in the atmosphere of love so very dear to me." Nancy's next letter described the calling protocol of the day, among other things:

> "While I am waiting for the breakfast bell to ring [at home, not at a hotel] my darling I am penning a line to you. I expect about this time 8 a.m. you are having yr solitary breakfast at the Buckingham though it is in a sense lonely I am always glad to feel you are in such comfortable quarters after your hard & weary days work & I wish will all my heart I cd spend my evenings with you, but apart from the old money considerations I know I have many urgent duties here at home & I am striving so hard to live for 'today' & try & do faithfully each duty as it comes.
>
> "I made several visits while I was out yesterday. Went to Miss Chandler's but she was out then to Corses – Virginia said she saw me Sunday afternoon tripping along with <u>my beau</u> looking as happy & bright as if we were bride & groom. It is very sweet the real interest our friends take in us. From the Corses I went to see Mrs Lee & Lucy & they said the same thing. Lucy's house is <u>beautiful</u> I wish you cd see it. Then I called on 'Nellie' but she was out & from there I went to see Mrs Lewis had such a sweet visit – she is always so sweet to me. It is now a little after 3 o'clk my darling & I am quite ready to receive my Tuesday evening callers. Marion B is sick in bed & I cd not persuade Lily to come."

Now we know what Nancy does all day. In spite of her preparations, however, only two came to her party. She blamed it on the bitterly cold weather and her intention of being "at home" again next Tuesday. It was a disappointment but they had a good deal of fun over it and hoped for better luck next time. This was standard procedure then. A lady or couple would announce they would be "at home" on a certain day and others would drop in to visit. Two days later Nancy wrote she had met some friends on the street who had expressed regret they had not been able to call on her on Tuesday but hoped to do so next Tuesday. She added she had made six calls that day and done some sewing on the machine.

Jack wrote his next letter aboard the steamer, Norfolk, on February 11th, after spending the weekend with Nancy. He noted the ice on the Potomac was very heavy at times but the boat broke through it. It was an overnight trip and he was having breakfast, hoping the things he had bought would sell well. In his next letter he is optimistic he can "look forward if I am spared to be an old man to spend some of its years in comparative comfort." He will not reach either goal but Jack has been whistling in the dark for years. All of his correspondence either praised God for bringing him and Nancy together or beseeched God to help him through his tribulations. At no time was he able to face facts and acknowledge he had taken a wrong turn and then consider doing something different. Instead, like an ox with blinders, he plowed ahead doggedly, trusting God to make things right. He was a passenger on the ship of life, never taking the helm. Even when opportunities occurred later, he could not change course.

They had installed two telephones at the store for customers and Simcoe had installed one at home. Of course this meant customers could call and complain but Jack would rather deal with them over the phone anyway. He expected to change quarters in the spring. The Atlantic had burned down and consequently the Hotel Granby raised its rates by $5 a month. Jack planned on going to the YMCA, which had a "nice sitting room, all the papers, a fine bath and gymnasium." He expected to use the baths daily but not the gym. He also would not be charged for meals when he was away but it is the bath that most appealed to Jack as he did not have one with his room at the Granby, not even down the hall. He closed with his usual, but always unusual, declaration of love:

> "I have such sweet thoughts & longings for you & I know you feel the same or I could not feel as I do. Perfect love like ours is only to be compared to the beautifully tuned harp played by the touch of a divine Master with a discordant note an impossibility. May the good God that gave us this blessing preserve and increase it as he has done in answer to our daily prayers."

On February 28th he wrote:

> "Just had an almost irresistible desire to come up and spend Saturday & Sunday with you but I fear if I give way to that feeling that I will be looking back & not remembering that I have put my hand to the plow and have promised to endure unto the end so I resisted what was a sore temptation to me but the trip costs me nearly $10 & just at this time $10 is a good deal to me.

Jack went on to say their sales in February were nearly one-quarter larger than "last February" and he hoped March would do as well. His life was made up of "the hope that I may build for my loved ones so that they may be guarded from the storms, as far as I can guard them." He believes God brought Nancy into his life to teach him the value of "all that is good and fine in a woman's life" and to make reminiscence "sweeter than any

171

artists conception or poets song." If a good fairy gave him a wish it would be
to come to her every night to "find you in my arms & feel the touch of your
dear hands and have the sweet kiss you have always ready for me."

March 7th Jack…

"…hopes this time next Friday night to be on the Norfolk boat
steaming to you. One day or so with you in a month is enough to stay
the starving & the longing tho not to satisfy. But life is full of half
loaves & all concur without dissent that it is better than no bread.
This is true philosophy, the wisdom of making the best of things &
after all the sensible thing to do. Easy to preach and theorize but hard
to practice.

"I want to see as much of you as possible. My eyes just ache for
the Light of your dear face. I am afraid I should have made a bad
naval officer to be away from you three years at a time as I want to
see you very badly after three days. I am glad that the separation is
no longer or no worse. When I was in Alexa I had you but had the
terrible business strain all the time & the hopeless outlook there.

"I am glad to hear Will is better & hope he may continue to
improve." This is one of many comments about Will being ill but
the nature of his sickness is never revealed. Jack also had a letter
from Charles. "He has had rather an unsatisfactory time in NY. Bad
weather & quiet business. Said Pa had written to him at least. I don't
think he feels at all encouraged abt the Alexa business. I am sorry he
went into it."

Jack's letter on March 20, 1902, is a prime example of his snobbery. He
is at the Buckingham:

"Life is full of Contrasts & I have been through some sharp ones
today. I spent three hours in an underwriters auction sale a large
portion of the people were Polish Jews and the character of the
gathering is but illustrated by a remark of the auctioneer. One of the
habits in an auction is to bid by holding up the hand & the auctioneer
said to the crowd don't hold up your hands they all look alike to me
they are all <u>dirty</u> and then up here every one looks so immaculate
from the boys at the door to the guests in their dainty evening attire
and I feel that now I am where I belong. I did not sit down to dinner
til 7:30 & you may imagine after breakfast at 7:30 I was a trifle hungry
& the dinner tho simple was perfect – Blue points Vermont turkey
spinach & a dainty little baked apple dumpling."

Jack's plans to move to the YMCA did not come to fruition as he was back at the Granby March 27th:

"They have fixed up my room very nicely have a nice enamel double bed with brass trimmings, two very good tables, chairs &c. Last night I fixed up my little picture of the boy Christ I hung over my wash stand. The picture 'Can't Joy Talk' I always liked on one side of the room then two little card board landscape scenes from Holland framed 3 in a frame I hung in other parts of the room. For the large table I bought one of those pretty Persian covers & on that table are my treasures you in the centre the children on one side & your picture in the little gilt oval on the other side & dear little Eliza's picture just in front of yours. Nothing else is on that table. I fixed the pictures very much by arranging them with the ribbons that come around handkerchiefs. My room is just a darling & it looks so sweet with so many things to remind me of home.

"I have one drawer for my shirts one for the collar & cuffs one for underclothes and every thing in the way of outer clothing is hung up nicely in my wardrobe. In regard to the chair I thought to save expense, the little boy could take it down to the boat, that is if you found by phoning to Wattles that it costs much less than by Express. I want to try and arrange for two weeks with you at the Berrys if all goes well. How happy the thought makes me. Two weeks of love making, lying under the trees & being with each other & the darlings. God bless & keep you & ours & with love to all. Fondest Jack."

Jack's next three letters are very strange. After telling Nancy he had been denied his own "sitting" at Christ Church, to his regret, he wrote: "I had so hoped to be with you on my 45th birthday but you must leave the cake go to the 26th." What's strange is he was about to be 55, not 45. One might chalk that up to distraction of the moment but on his birthday, April 20th, he wrote: "I awoke this morning to a consciousness of my forty five years & rather uncertain sky." He then gives thanks "to those who congratulated me on passing another milestone in the journey to the beautiful beyond." Jack had an obsession about an afterlife. He constantly compared living now unfavorably with his perception of heaven. Here he continued:

"What a sweet thought that this life with all its beauties its blessings the bright sunlight the pure sweet air, beautiful trees flowers and cool green grass is only a pretaste of a land even more beautiful to those who have lived so that they can enjoy to the full the land below because the highest enjoyment in life comes only to those who love God and keep his commandment & religion in truly profitable (not meaning in a pecuniary way) in this world & the world to come.

The so called pleasures of sin are only misnomers. There can be no real pleasure in sin, true pleasure is given only to those that follow the laws of the Father for all his ways are ways of pleasantness and all his paths peace. Alas that so few are willing to believe this til they have tried the other. I would like to live my life over again to know you in its early days to give you my life as sinless & stainless as it is possible for human life to be and to be there to each other as we have been. This would be my ideal of life.

"Only two more letters after this and then the homecoming & to see your sweet face again to have you put your arms around my neck to feel your face touch mine & have you kiss & pet & love me. Isn't it strange that a great big man full 45 years old should care for all these things & yet they are my life." As far as we know Nancy never disabused him of those 10 years he subtracted.

The reader is familiar with Jack's feelings about God but there has been no clear indication of Nancy's religious beliefs in previous correspondence, until now. On May 5, 1902, Nancy revealed those beliefs, as well as much more about herself in an eight–page letter written in her large and sprawling script:

"Your dear letter telling of yr safe trip to Norfolk my darling has just been read & much enjoyed. Yes my love we certainly have a great deal to be thankful for & our kind Heavenly Father has indeed been good to us in <u>thousands</u> of ways & if we can only learn to trust & love Him more each day & thank Him continually & pray for strength from Him in all our actions we will find the way a much more easy one & the trials more easy to bear. I mailed my morning letter so it might reach you early tomorrow & now I am beginning the letter I shall send you tomorrow because I feel so like having a little talk with you.

"Yes you are just beginning yr second year in the Norfolk business world & it begins with all good wishes & such earnest prayers for yr success & such prayers of <u>thanksgiving</u> to our Father above for His help during this past year, bless yr dear, brave heart you don't know how <u>I do love & admire</u> you for the strength you have shown in this great struggle, God help you my own.

"This is our dear little Eliza's birth day [she died July 1, 1891] – 12 years old to day, a great girl she wd have grown, I doubt not, had God seen fit to leave her with us but so much safer & better <u>I know</u> she is in His keeping & yet there has never been a day in all these years I have not wished her with me, but this is natural & my Father in Heaven knows it & it helps me. I have never been rebellious but have tried always to say 'Thy will be done' but there is ever the longing in the poor human heart & the tears will come & the great feeling to have my dear child once more in my arms, just as she always is in my heart. God knows best & He is so good in sparing these other darlings to us, they are indeed treasures untold so loving & sweet & I thank Him for them each day & for the blessing of our most mutual love for each other, it certainly sheds happiness in our home darling.

"Tuesday May 6th Good Morning my love, another beautiful bright day & I hope you have the same glorious sunshine in Norfolk & may have a fine days business. I put the umbrellas in the express last evening & when I returned I found Will had his which he was most anxious to have covered too so I told him to take it to the express office & perhaps he cd put it in the same bundle but he found it had been sent off just before he arrived so I told him to send it any how & I put a little slip in saying Mrs Tackett wanted this umbrella covered with the others sent by you & all sent back together so if you have not written them you have sent 3 umbrellas to cover you can say you send 4 & I reckon it will be all right. [Nancy didn't bother with punctuation.] Will said he had been anxious for such a long time to have his covered.

"Well my love I hoped to get this letter off by the early mail but had so many interruptions I cd not & now I am hurrying to finish it & get it in by the next mail. I saw little Edith Snowden this a m & she said her Mother was going down to Norfolk tonight or rather she was going to Virginia beach with Mrs Bell Johnson but they would spend tomorrow night with Janet Woodsen, how I do wish I was going too & cd spend the day & many days with my dear Jack. Well my love I must say good night with a heart full of love & <u>kisses many</u> from your own devoted little wife Nancy."

Jack's finicky nature is evident on May 11th:

"I am sorry Chas did not let Pa know of his going to NY. It is certainly dreadful abt his clothes specially as he has a nice suit & extra trousers & as he is talking of getting a new one I cant see what he wants to wear that old tramp suit for. I wish he had my love of cleanliness – it is with me a passion & if I had money I would have a suit for every day in the week so that they must look nice & neat all the time but I try to keep the few I have clean & all around me in order."

Money, or more precisely, the lack of it, was a constant source of frustration to Jack. He frequently chided Nancy to economize in every way possible but especially by not buying new clothes. He had not bought any since going to Norfolk a year ago and didn't plan to this year. It bothered him because he did not look as nice as when he used to buy a new suit every year and he was beginning to adopt a pecuniary attitude. In June he reminded Nancy he had his life insurance to pay, then the gas bill, taxes and another quarter pew rent. No, one did not have to pay for a seat at church, unless you were trying to keep up the appearance of wealth, but he denied himself a trip to the beach, which cost a dollar, then paid for their pew.

In an attempt to provide more income Jack told Nancy to ask Will if he and Mrs. Chalmers – they would be married in November – would like to take the house "on the terms Dr. Smith offered in $400 per year & keep the property in order." Like many of his ideas, this never took flight. He did not like to bother Nancy about money matters but so far as he could see "I will be like the old man of the sea carrying a burden of this kind but I will try to carry it with a brave & a cheerful spirit, knowing that our Father gives us strength commensurate with our burden."

Jack sailed on a steamboat, the Jefferson, from Norfolk to New York. On August 24th:

"...every room was full of outsiders sleeping on the sofas – one hundred & forty first class passengers. Dinner was being served as I came on board and as I had all my things in my state room I took a seat at the Captain's table and went thru quite a nice dinner. After dinner I sat out on deck and watched the stars & the lights at the various sea side resorts and just before we passed out of the capes the moon rose & it was a very beautiful sight. I rose at a reasonable hour & took breakfast after a promenade for my appetite, had some very nice Corn Muffins roe herring & lamb chops & scrambled eggs. I ate three muffins a roll two portion of scrambled egg & 3 cups coffee so I did not have much appetite for lunch.

"The boat was as steady as a die, some of the most beautiful cloud effects one a perfect water spout which a good many watched thinking it would develop but it vanished into cloud. Another the most perfect representation of ice bergs you can conceive, and so the day drifted by. I saw a pretty school of flying fish that I watched as long as in sight. We landed safely abt four oclock & I am comfortable homed have quite a nice room with bath." The first time he has a bath attached to his room. He's at the Buckingham.

"How I have wished for you today, more than all things Sunday is our day, the sweetest of all days because for long years it is full of blissful memories beginning with the beautiful days of our love making which thank God are not over & never will be. God grant this separation cannot be for many years longer & then I trust it will never be again til God calls us to his home & I trust the call may come together."

Once again Jack has expressed his wish they die together but, regrettably, no response from Nancy is among the correspondence.

Back at the Hotel Granby in October, Jack wrote about his accommodations. "The <u>bathroom doors do not open til nine</u> [underlining by author]. I enjoyed my cold dip this morning and breakfast was very nice, boiled ham omelet rolls cakes and toast & very nice grapes as fruit." Jack gave his waiter 25¢ every two weeks. He mentioned sending money to his father for him to pay rent to Nancy, which seems a roundabout way to take care of the matter, and explained what to do with Will's check, also for his rent.

In November, 1902, the big news was the wedding of Will and Lily Twiggs Myers–Chalmers, finally, on the 20th. It was a quiet affair, held in Nancy's home. At Will's second marriage neither Nancy nor her brother, Ben, attended but by that time both were aware of Will's treachery with Jack's funds and their inheritance from their mother, Eliza Fendall.

1903 has a scarcity of letters but Jack was back in Norfolk, as evidenced by Nancy's chastising letter of April 26th:

"How I wished for you & missed you <u>this evening</u>, during the beautiful & impressive confirmation service you can never know. I just could have but one feeling, that was that you ought to be with me & witness our first born child take the holy rite & it was so bitterly hard that you cd not. I felt all during the service that yr spirit & prayers were with us but I so needed yr dear bodily presence as I <u>always do</u> & then your having to leave us at such a time was a terrible disappointment to our dear child, she had so set her heart on your being with her. She had a cry after you left, but she tried to brace up & be brave.

"She was terribly nervous & she seemed to so need yr loving strength I felt quite worried about her when we first went to church. I almost feared she wd faint, she seemed to feel so badly & I was so far from well myself but I seemed to be a comfort to her, dear little thing, and she got through the service with out any trouble. The child was not feeling well & that made her more nervous but dear uncle Will was a stay to her. My heart is <u>very</u> full of thankfulness to my Heavenly Father for His mercy in bringing our dear child & dear Will into His fold & may He give to them His constant love and care, unto their life's end.

"Dear little Soph seemed to be much impressed with the service and came to me after she came home & said 'Mother next year if you don't think I am too young [she's 11] I wd like to be confirmed.' Dear heart she is a serious little thing. I hate to think of yr sailing off all alone from us tonight for I know how lonely you do feel but life is very full of duties & you always try to do yours & to do what you think is right & I love you for it, though at times I find it bitterly hard to feel any thing which separates us is right but then I try to take up the <u>cross</u> & go bravely on, <u>knowing</u> God sends what is best for us. Good night my precious love.

"Monday – Good morning my darling, Charles is with us but goes to Winchester this after noon. He told us you just had time to make the boat & Nancy Lee & I were wicked enough to <u>wish</u> with <u>all our hearts</u> that you had, poor little heart she seemed to want you so, to say nothing of myself. Well my love I must bring this long letter to a close hoping it may reach you tomorrow. God bless & keep you my own, with dear love & kisses many your ever devoted little wife Nancy."

Jack wrote to Nancy Lee on May 16th:

"May sweet sixteen grow in sweetness and grace in the sixteen years to come as she has grown in stature in the sixteen years gone by. Is not that wishing you a large measure of happiness. This letter is rich in good wishes for you my darling child and the good wishes are all that I can send you at this time and I know that if you knew all, that you would rather have that than all else and as the years go on we all feel that human love and human sympathy are far beyond the material things of life. If your life could be as I would map it out it would be a very happy one. I would not wish that it could be one of ease and self indulgence but that you might be of the metal, the true good, that comes out of the trial of life – refined and purified. Strive to do your duty and in the path of duty you will find much real pleasure, outside of that path may be found temporary enjoyment but never true happiness. The world is made bright by ourselves. The true happiness from within. May God help you my own to be a true brave Christian woman and may our years be many is the wish of your devoted Father."

In July Nancy, as usual, fled Alexandria. She took the girls and her mother to Virginia Beach and Hattie, Charles' wife, was left to care for the house. Hattie wrote:

"…the man did not come until today to whitewash the kitchen. After he finished I gave him 75¢ according to your directions. The man has not come yet to attend to the carpets. Will has had the porch floor painted and it looks very nice. Tell Soph the cats look very lonely with out her and I haven't a crumb of comfort for them. 'Pa' seems to have <u>refreshments</u> in his room but I don't believe it is the kind that cats like. We are occupying Mrs. Fendall's room with the communicating doors of Nancy Lee's room kept open for ventilation, specially on account of father's room, which in this warm weather needs all the fresh air we can get in to it for our health's sake. Tell Miss Eliza I am trying to take good care of her room which it was mighty sweet of her to lend us and I hope she will find her things all safe when she comes back. Lovingly Hattie."

Sophie had whooping cough but it didn't stop her Sunday School teacher, Alice J. Green, from sending her eight pages of Bible passages to study and learn. Sophie was also attending the Arlington Institute in Alexandria, according to a bill from them. The bill lists Senior class at $30, Phys culture $1, French $10 and Fuel and Stationery $1.50. It also stated a "discount of 10 per cent for sisters if paid STRICTLY in ADVANCE."

On May 8, 1904, Jack wrote Nancy:

"How well I remember your first kiss to me – down in the dear old parlor of sacred memory. I think our lover days were the very sweetest another sweetest thought is that they have been a continuous performance, just as sweet now, and just as fresh as they were twenty three years ago." [Note: they've only been married 21 years.]

On November 28th he discussed a decision he and Mr. Simcoe had reached about terminating their partnership with Mr. Russell, who, "had an income from property of about 100 pr month his own home & he will get about 15,000 from the business here – besides this he can readily get a place that will pay him fully 100 pr month, so he can be very comfortable. The whole affair was most unfortunate & I bitterly regret the step we have to take."

Interestingly, penny–pinching Jack ordered his suits from New York, as evidenced by a note from ALLEY & COH, Tailor Made Cloaks & Suits, 29 Washington Place, then stamped Removed to 105 Fifth Ave Cor 18th St. They were notifying him they would be shipping his green suit on December 1st. He ordered cider from J. R. MILLNER COMPANY, at 920 Main Street in Lynchburg, VA, which was sent to Nancy by the barrel. A note dated December 5th, 1904, stated:

"Enclosed find bill of lading for the barrel of cider which I had shipped to Alexandria. I believe the barrel only contained thirty gallons, as the party from whom I got it said to me that his apples rotted very badly, and, therefore, could not send a larger quantity as he had only a very few which he could grind into cider. Hoping that it will reach its destination safely, and that you and your family will enjoy it, and with best wishes, I am, very truly yours, JRM."

On December 13 JRM followed with a letter stating he had opened the barrel that he had received and found he could not use it because it was so bitter. He was sure the tenants on a Mr. Woodruff's farm had ground "a good many specked or unsound apples." Consequently he was offering to refund Jack's money if Jack's cider was also bad. That same day Jack wrote he had taken his "plunge" at the YMCA and it took 10 years off. Perhaps that's how he came to think he was 45 on his 55th birthday, on April 20, 1902.

The stress of separation showed up in Jack's letter of January 2, 1905:

"I wish so sincerely that I had not marred the perfect visit home by my loss of control Sunday but my punishment is my conscience and my shame and regret that I should so far forget myself and wound a child that is my idol – but she like her Father has a forgiving spirit and I know that she has no atom of resentment to me but with God's help I hope that I shall never lose my temper again.

"Today has been like a spring day – all the stores were open and we did a much better business than our 1st Jany last year. Mr. Simcoe met me at the boat he was very anxious to see me, and after I got my breakfast Mr Russell was anxious to talk so we went over a few preliminary skirmishes & made Mr R an offer of considerably less than we would have given in the first flush of the affair & which he promptly accepted – and he left the store. Mr Etheridge is to stay with us til the end of the month and says that no word of blame shall attach to Mr S or I – that he entered into partnership distinctly with the understanding of preserving friendly relations with us so I hope that we will escape much that we dreaded & that both of us may make money.

"I had my cold dip this morning it was fine. I hope you will get my letter about the slippers and night dress & send them as I need them. Also the check book. I want to send you the check for the Johnson bill for liquor &c. I wish I had a fine lot of money to send you but I must only send what I can & supplement it with the fondest love for all. Your Jack."

By the end of the month Jack and Nancy were in Atlantic City, New Jersey, but it was more a trip for Jack's health than a vacation. He was evidently in a tired and run-down condition, though no diagnosis of his ailment was disclosed. Nancy Lee wrote she was glad Jack was feeling better. She, too, was better and hoping to go back to school, where she was a teacher.

During the winter months the Potomac River frequently froze over and the steamer sometimes got stuck in the ice, as Jack described on January 27th:

> "This has been a long tedious trip as I have practically been traveling for two days. I retired last night about ten o'clock & woke at a little before seven to find that we were tied up in the ice just at Indian Head. The outlook for getting out looked most unpromising & we seemed to be a regular Peary Expedition looking very much like pictures of the arctic region – but things are seldom as bad as they seem and by about ten o'clock the Steamer Anne Arundel came on and after a good deal of skirmishing pulled us out of the hole and we soon got afloat. At the same time the Steamer Washington came up & we followed in her track & were soon on our way down the river."

When he landed, Mr. Simcoe was waiting for him at the hotel. He told Nancy Mr. Simcoe was encouraging about his condition and thought he would be completely well soon, adding:

> "Oh how I have missed you my own but I try not to think about the things that cannot be helped as it only weakens me for the fight I must make to win, I hope you are well & that all is going well at home. I am going to try so hard to be brave and take a cheerful view of life and fight its battles in a cheerful spirit for that is the only way to meet the life of the world. All the last two weeks seem like a dream to me. The part when I was with you at Atlantic City like the beautiful dream we have some times – & that before like a nightmare but I hope that the trip to Atlantic may benefit us both. God guard you all my treasures fondly Jack."

Jack and Nancy's invitation to "The Literary Societies of the Episcopal High School" was for the FINAL HOP 1905 and was to be held on the 12th of June at half after eight o'clock in McBurney's Hall in Alexandria. The invitation specified "NO STAGS ALLOWED" and "DANCE STRICTLY PLEDGED." The Arlington Institute's year–end report on Sophie showed her with 8 faults, a 93 in geography, a 99 in history, a 77 in arithmetic and a 95 in English Language. She was also absent 9½ times and tardy 14 times. Her total grade for the year was 91.

October 16, 1906 Jack wrote:

"This time twenty three years ago I took my chances in the matrimonial lottery – and looking back over the long vista of years gone by – nearly half of my life more than half of my real manhood life – I can congratulate myself in feeling that to me came the capital prize – the life and love of Gods best gift to man a true pure woman. It is hard to realize that so many years have gone it seems but a few brief minutes since you and I were sitting in the dear little parlor at the sweet old home all alone the bridal party having gone to the rehearsal at the church – and just when we look at the grown daughter and the dear little Soph we are reminded that all this was not yesterday. God grant that the years to come may be as happy as the years gone by and that each year may cause our love to grow stronger – and that we may be spared for years of useful #### and that when the time comes that it may come to both and that we may walk united into that life where no parting is." Jack is apparently still under the illusion he is 49 when he is actually 59. "Tell Sophie Father wants her to get over the habit of being late at breakfast and school nothing worries me more than tardiness. I am always on time as you well know."

On November 27th Jack hoped the cloak for Soph was satisfactory and that both she and Nancy liked it. He also mentioned he would send the children money on the first of December and a check to pay the pew rent and water rent. Whether the girls were receiving a regular allowance is not clear.

On January 4, 1907, the *Alexandria Gazette* published this:

"Mrs. Eliza E. Fendall, widow of Townshend D. Fendall, died at her home on south St. Asaph street shortly after noon today. The deceased had been failing health recently, but her condition was not regarded of such a nature as to cause her relatives and friends to suppose her death was so close at hand; hence its announcement startled many. Mrs. Fendall was a daughter of the late Joseph Eaches, at one time Mayor of this city, and was the last survivor of the family. She leaves three children – Mr. B. T. Fendall, of Baltimore, and Mr. W. E. Fendall and Mrs. J.F. Tackett, of this city. She was a lady beloved and esteemed by all who knew her, and was one of the oldest residents of the city." She was 84½.

No letter of encouragement to "pour out your heart" from Will exists, such as he wrote when their father died, but brother Ben wrote:

"I have been thinking of you and the children so much since I left you Sunday. I feel certain Floy is right in her advice that you let Nancy [Lee] and Sophie come to us for awhile and that you go to Washington and have your hand properly treated. Old Mr. T. could stay at Miss Emily's or some where until you returned and I am sure it will be best for you all. Jack will be leaving in a few days, if he has not already done so, and you will be so lonely. These first days will be the hardest. In time we adjust ourselves to any environment; we must do so, even though at first we believe it impossible, and it is this transition period that we want to help you over.

"Floy and I are right my dear and we want you to reconsider the case. The girls will be very quiet with us, the park is near and if the weather is good they can walk out there and be entirely safe or they can stay in and read, bad days. The Pratt and the other libraries furnish no end of books.

"They are both in a highly nervous state, and so are you, and the only thing I know of to change such conditioning is a change of scene, if it is only for a little while it will help. Please think it over and I am sure you will agree with me and find a way to put my suggestions into practice. I am uneasy about Marian and about Lily too. I hope they are better. Will was far from well. He has not been in good shape for some time. I hope I shall have good news of them all very soon and a letter from you telling me to meet the girls in Baltimore.

"Don't brood over our sorrow Nancy, don't nurse it. We can not forget, we do not wish to forget, our mother, God forbid but let us think of her always as a dear loving mother watching over and helping us in the spirit as she did so long and so faithfully in the flesh. She has not gone away, she is still here, only we do not see her. Her sufferings are past her trials are over and in spirit she still helps and prays for her children. Think of her Nancy but not in sorrow. It is such a little while until we shall all meet again and until that time comes let us think of the bright things in the past and hope for the brighter things hereafter. Give my love to the girls. The P.R.R. is the best road for them to take and I send you the schedule. Trains leave almost any time. Fondly yours Ben."

There is no indication Nancy accepted Ben's offer. By the end of January Jack was in New York, "hard at work on the stock taking." He remembered Nancy had been with him in New York a year ago, adding: "I am getting very tired of this life apart and I fear I cannot stand it very much longer. I am sure you don't stand it any better than I do."

One of Nancy's rare letters appears, written February 5th:

"I wish I had the power to look into the future & to <u>know</u> what

was the best thing to advise you to do of one thing I feel certain and that is I want you here at <u>home</u>! I also feel it is much better not to continue a business in which you see no future success and that has not been what you hoped it would be in the past. I also think it is better to close things with a small loss than to continue and perhaps lose more. I am <u>sure</u> you can get some thing to do here or in Washington, and I will do my very best to see if I can't help you in this and in <u>every</u> way. You simply find your business down in Norfolk is not what you feel it should be & after testing it thoroughly you feel it most wise to make a change & I feel God will help those who try to help themselves & I often feel what is must be for the best if we can only look at things that happen, only <u>trust</u> in our loving Fathers care & help & do our best & all will be well.

"I think Mr S has been very nice & I appreciate it all – Oh! how I do wish I could <u>talk</u> to you my love so hard to write for fear I might make a wrong impression – God bless you I <u>love</u> you with all my heart – I read your letter to our girls and they have both written you they are plucky & <u>hopeful</u> & brave and here is a heart full of love & kisses many from your <u>devoted</u> Nancy."

Nancy Lee's letter:

"My darling Dad: Mother has just read me your letters, I feel deeply for you but I know it will all come right in the end we will stand by each other any way – Today is a beautiful snowy day, clear and cold and I have just been up to take Lily this material which came by the mid day mail – She likes it very much and is going to have it made up right away. I shall think about you all the time and I hope can find a way to help you materially – Trust in God and every thing will work out well dearest Father – With a heartful of love kisses many from your ever devoted Nancy Lee."

Sophie wrote:

"My dearest darling Daddy; I am afraid you think I do not keep my promises very well, but there has been some excuse for me, as I have really been very busy. Mother read us your letter, and I just feel, that perhaps God is using this to bring us together again. Don't please think you have failed! There's no such word as that for my Daddy, the best man God ever made! We will all help you my dearest. I only wish I was old enough to work but there are a great many things I can do to help. Don't give up Daddy. Just remember that there are three 'girls' in Alexandria, that love you will all their hearts, and who are ready to help you. I can't help feeling, that I want you to come home. Good night my dearest darling Daddy. Keep up hope. 'Never say die,' and remember that we will 'never give up Mr. Micawber.' Your devoted little daughter Soph."

Nancy continues trying to cheer Jack up while he is in New York at James H. Dunham & Co at 340 Broadway:

"My thoughts, & love, are with <u>you every moment</u> my own, <u>precious</u> Jack praying, & hoping, the strength you need in <u>body mind & estate</u> may come! to you. God bless! you – I feel brighter about you this bright day and I feel & <u>know</u> God is going to help us out of the trials that are on us now, in His own good time if we will only pick up todays work & not think of the dark side but <u>trust</u> in Him & do our work as best we can, even if we are not well & strong enough to do what we feel is our very best– that will come in time! We <u>must</u> learn to labor & patiently wait one of the hardest lessons in life but one we must learn. 'The Lord is <u>My</u> Shepherd I shall not want.'

"I still seem to feel you very very near me, with your dear loving arms about me & your dear kisses warm upon my lips & my constant prayer to our loving, kind, Father is 'please take care of & help! My own' Oh how I do wish I could write you I could get a nice fat office for you where the strain would be much less. I wish Mrs Russell Lage (?) knew how much we needed a few thousand. I know she would help us. She is so anxious to be really charitable with her great wealth, think how really happy she could make us but God knows what is best for us much better than we know our poor weak selves."

March 7, 1907, from Jack:

"Your dear letter from Washington rec'd yesterday – I am glad you are up there & hope you will be benefitted by the treatment – you will be surprised to know that I have sold out to Mr Simcoe yesterday. God only knows whether I have done right or wrong but it seems in view of many things the best for me to do but I feel very nervous over the affair but I expect I will soon pull myself together again and look around for something to do at home – God grant that I may find something perhaps Chuck Marbury may know of some one among his large circle of patients that wants a capable man of all work. Mr Goodall is all broken up about my leaving and is much tempted to leave also but I am trying to persuade him to stay. Don't you come back to Alexa on my account dearest for I will come up to see you tomorrow in Washington unless something should prevent my return. God guide me thro these hours of trial & see me safe to a haven of rest. Your devoted Jack."

Nancy obviously relayed this information to her brother Ben for on March 15th he wrote:

> "I feel sure Jack will be able to get some thing to do either in Alexandria or Washington and that you will both be all right. He is a good buyer and I should think some of those large department stores would be only too glad to get him and pay him a good salary. To–day is so bright and splendid it makes me glad to live and I hope it will do you good."

On April 1st Nancy hoped:

> "…you may be able to get some thing for future work by which you can have some <u>home</u> life as I feel it is so important, not to mention the happiness for us to be <u>together</u> & to be with your dear children who <u>idolize</u> you & <u>need</u> you so with them, we have but one life to live & for the few years which may be ours God grant we may spend <u>together</u>. I doubt not my own you will meet with many disappointments, & discouragements, but never give up, for remember 'patience & perseverance conquer <u>all things</u>' and you are <u>sure</u> to get some thing to do. Don't think of the past, it is so unhealthy & unprofitable to dwell on it and does not help the future. I wish you could have waited a little longer so as to <u>feel</u> better and stronger, before facing the trying task before you but I thought you seemed to feel you must make the start, so I did not like to deter you as you felt it was better for you. Pray without ceasing & never fail to trust in your Father's love & strength. He helps us no matter how weak & unhappy, & helpless we feel our selves to be & we all have our trials.
>
> "My dear I was just closing my letter to you when Dr. Smith came in to say he had <u>gotten a place for you</u> in the Department of Navigation at the Naval Office in Washington with a salary of $70.00 [$1500 in 2009] a month. The work he says is easy, is sure you will find it agreeable as the surroundings are very attractive, a delightful office and you will be associated with gentlemen the position is in what they call the filing office – where you have to put letters on file & place them in position – the Dr says the place is yours if you want it and as <u>long</u> as you want it, and he wants you to report at once – wanted you to be on hand tomorrow morning but says he will arrange it so you can report on Wednesday morning at 9 o'clk so just step on the train and come right home to me for I believe this offer is a direct answer to our prayers – the Dr says the salary is not large but you can be <u>at home</u>! and it may lead to some thing better later on. I tried to thank him – he seemed so anxious to <u>see you</u> – so come on home."

Unfortunately, Jack had waited too long to change directions. He would turn 60 later that month and drop dead in his yard the next year. In the interim his – and Nancy's – life would be more miserable than it had been the past 23 years. The reader is aware of many gaps in the correspondence, which would explain some situations. This is a particularly critical time for a letter to be missing for we are left to wonder why Jack did not avail himself of this golden opportunity to spend each night in the arms of his beloved wife and each day watching his daughters blossom. The pay would be steady, the commute short and the company befitting what he considered to be his station in life. But he did not take the job.

Instead, he became a drummer (traveling salesman) for a New York firm. This meant a different hotel every night as he traveled from city to city and state to state. It also meant he had to travel with a trunk, which contained his samples and clothing, along with his toiletries. No longer a young man, he had to find someone at each train stop to haul his trunk to his hotel, then back to the train the next day. He could no longer wait for a customer to come to him; he had to find that customer and convince him to buy Jack's wares.

He made about 10% on sales, but there was no base salary to close any gap and Jack would end up bankrupt. He was also bereft of companionship such as he had enjoyed with Mr. Simcoe. Now there would be no one with whom to share a conversation or dinner. In the next year he would travel as far south as Florida and as far west as Tennessee, each day seeking that illusive rainbow that would lead to the pot of gold.

A letter on Simcoe & Tackett stationery from Mrs. Goodall (it was Mr. Goodall who was so broken up about Jack's leaving) gives us some idea of the personal belongings Jack was also leaving behind. This was furniture he had added to his hotel room through the years to make the room more homelike (see letter of March 27, 1902) and Nancy was trying to sell it. On April 8, 1907, Mrs. Goodall wrote:

> "We are not just now in a position to pay the price quoted. The Morris Chair is so faded. I would not pay more than 5.00 for it. I will make you an offer and you can think the matter over and let me hear from you. The cost of packing and shiping will cost you quite a sum, judging from my experience in bringing my furniture here:

> Davenport 18.00
> Morris chair 5.00
> 1 Large table and desk 9.00
> Chiffonier 9.00
> 2 small chairs 2.50
> 2 rugs and ??? 12.00

"The comforts sheets towels we do not need at all. Mr. Goodall will attend to the packing and shiping as soon as possible. If you decide to accept my offer I will send check for half of the amount at once – and the balance in about 30 days or certainly by the first of June. We are quite comfortable in our little apartment and think I shall like Norfolk as a home very much. Hoping to see you with Mr. Tackett down during the Exposition. With kind regards from Mr. Goodall – I am very truly yours Mrs W. C. Goodall."

On August 27th Nancy wrote to Will:

"I am just sending you a little line my dearest Will to tell you we are fairly well but I can't say happy as my dear Jack leaves for N.Y. tomorrow to take a position in the Wm H. Roe Co of 491 & 493 Broadway N.Y. I hope & trust it may be for the best, but I tell you when I think of more years of separation my heart grows very sad & weary within me and yet I must put on my mask & try to be cheerful. I also have an applicant for a boarder for one of my 3rd story rooms, an Englishman, a Mr B F Brooke Lewell by name he seems a gentle man, a quiet, small, unobtrusive sort of person. I offered him one of the 3rd story rooms with board for $30.00 a month which he seemed to think most moderate he wants to come Sep 15th & when I think of all I must accomplish before that time I feel as if I was very tired & had a high mountain to climb, but I am sure strength will be given me.

"Jack had gotten desperate waiting & striving so hard to get some thing to do & he says it seems to be this place or nothing. Charles T [Jack's brother] has been trying his very best for him in N.Y. so I am hoping & praying it may help us to live & if I can only get one or two men to take rooms (I hate to have boarders) I hope we can...."

The rest of the letter is missing but that is enough to remind us that Nancy was also suffering from the separation. There were many things she could not do. She could not go dancing or out to dinner or do anything else that required an escort. Her companionship consisted of her two daughters (20 and 15), two or three servants and strangers who were rooming in her home and had to be fed and whose rooms had to be cleaned and beds made. The rest of the house had to be kept neat as well, as boarders walked through her parlor and past other rooms on their way to and from their quarters.

Her privacy was also severely restricted. She could not scold her children or servants if she was within earshot of her boarders and she couldn't appear for breakfast in a bathrobe. Then she had to change clothes to dress for tea each day. That, in itself, was a major operation for this was the time of the Gibson girl look with the S–curve silhouette, "pouter pigeon" bodices and huge puffy sleeves. Skirts still swept the floor, but the bustle was out.

Among other things she had to take care of the house, no easy task back then. The vacuum cleaner had just been invented and washing machines were not yet on the market. She had a servant to do the washing but remember, the more boarders she had, the more bedding there was to wash and iron. Females also had more underclothes to wash than males. Outer garments weren't washed; they were brushed. Being a woman had other drawbacks, too. Monthly periods were often accompanied by headaches, there was no indoor plumbing and Kotex would not be invented until World War I, by nurses, so Nancy was as confined and restricted by circumstances as was Jack.

Then there was dealing with tradesmen and contractors, as well as paying all the bills. Most women in those days left these tasks to their husbands, who had more experience in these matters. Jack held the purse strings pretty tightly, issuing individual checks to Nancy, with directions on how to use them. She was never shown how to manage finances and that would plague her after Jack died. In effect, Jack lived as a bachelor throughout his life while Nancy basically became a widow soon after she was married.

On August 28, 1907 Jack wrote on "The New Hoffman House" stationery on Madison Square in New York. It was advertised as "Absolutely Fire Proof." He told Nancy:

> "You see that I am safely landed in New York & in good quarters for the time being – tho it is rather a Beau Hickman style to take a room on 21st and date your letters from a swell hostelry but it is a harmless deception & we must put on a bold front and try to appear very bright. I am going to try to pursue this plan the other is certainly a dismal failure. I found Chas quarters very convenient to the leading places & looks quite neat & clean. I think I can be permanently located by tonight a very comfortable room for 8.00 pr week 2 meals a day as I do not want much lunch – the old lady said 10.00 but I stuck fast 8.00 & told her I expected to be here some little time.
>
> "There is a nice bath room quite near me with porcelain tub so I think I am going to be quite comfortable and I want you to feel that way about me. In my new start in life I must be more than ever economical until I pay my debts – I think if I can do that before I die I shall be very happy and I know you will be. I just hated to leave you my precious darling love but it had to be did and I hope we will both keep well and then we may surmount the difficulties and save the house.
>
> "You don't know how much I love you and our two darlings –

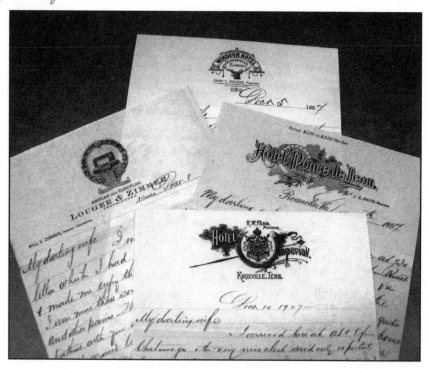

Above and below: *Letterheads from various hotels where Jack stayed throughout 1907 when he was a traveling salesman.*

190

& how I hate to deny you any thing but if these trials should bring me closer to God & make me a Christian I should not regret them & maybe God has given them to me for that purpose but I have lived a Godless life so long being only a talker not a doer of the word that it is hard to change as it is for a leopard to change his spots – But while the lamp holds out to burn the vilest sinner may return. My precious one how I long already to see you again. Last night even full of sweet sad memories but the sadness was tempered by the sweet tender love that flowed so into my heart and my dear sweetheart was dearer still in poverty & in richness you are always true to me. God grant you may all keep well."

Jack's next letter, the 31st, said:

"Tell Pa that I am hunting for something to add to the Roe business so far without much success but some parties have held out some hope but it is going to be hard to get things in good shape but I am going on trying and may get what I want at the place I least expect it. You see that nearly all the houses that I am acquainted with have already representatives in the section that I want but I may find enough to make a profitable venture and I am going all the time looking for the good things but willing to take what I can get til I get on my feet again. You asked for our number it is 43 E 21st. Things are quite as comfortable as you would expect at a cheap boarding house. I get quite as much as I think they can afford for the money."

The next day:

"I rose this morning abt six o'clock after a very good nights rest and had a bath and went back to my couch until abt quarter to eight & was ready for breakfast at 8:30. We had quite a nice breakfast Cantaloupe oat meal steak light buiscuit & for dinner chicken & roast beef creamed potatoes sweet potatoes stewed corn – delicious lettuce ice cream & cake. We have a small table of six a lady & her young daughter & four gentlemen, three being of our party. There is no style about the place but things seem clean & the food is well prepared and abundant. After dinner Charles asked me to go out to Riverside drive and Grants tomb so we took the long ride and sat out under the trees until it was time to get back for tea which was quite a nice one cold meats sardines buiscuit &c then I came over here to write you a little line of love.

"I hope that things may all soon adjust themselves so that the clouds may all be so that we can turn them wrong side out so as to show their silver linings. Tell Soph we have a cat in the dining room very much like Jim in appearance and very fond of fish. We have very nice white girls in the dining room & one white boy. I like the girls better they seem very good natured & accommodating."

On September 3rd Jack wrote on WILLIAM H. ROE COMPANY, IMPORTERS AND COMMISSION MERCHANTS, NOS. 491–493 BROADWAY, NEW YORK stationery:

"I have had plenty of exercise today. Tramp tramp all the time I do hope to get fixed up soon but it is hard work to get the right things in shape to pay me but I must go on very patiently – which you know is hard work but I hope to learn the lesson.

"Yesterday after dinner Chas joined me at the museum of natural history which we both enjoyed til they closed – I spent a good deal of time in the forestry division and was specially taken with the specimens of the big trees of the Pacific coast – very wonderful they are. Then I was much attracted by the meteorites – one specimen weighed over thirty one thousand pounds. You could easily spend days in this place looking over the wonder of lands & seas and the mineral specimens are beautiful. I thought it best to take this time at some place of interest as it is very dull staying around the boarding house, it is pretty hard to come down to these second rate houses but we must try to be content in the state we are in as it only makes the lot harder when we fret. I hope Sallys find of the cook will turn out a good one & also that you will be able to get another boarder as the two will cost but little more than one & be double pay."

Jack now began his life on the road. All of his letters tell Nancy how much he misses her and the children and are signed "Your devoted Jack" but we will skip those comments. His first hotel is the Exchange Hotel in Fredericksburg, September 24th. "I find some very nice stores here and am doing some little business, sold three bills two quite small, the largest one I think was more a complement to Chas than to myself – but it all goes – better shine by a reflected light than not at all." References to bills will continue but without any explanation as to what that means exactly. "I have done my best to day & angels can do no more but I don't think I always do my best. The spirit is willing but the flesh alas is very weak."

Two days later he was at Murphy's Hotel in Richmond:

"If I continue travelling will be away from home for several weeks. My trip here has not been good but Jordan is a hard road to travel & I am very green at this work but I hope I am not too old a dog to learn new tricks. I wish you would try your hand on a letter to

Morgan if I can get a place at 100–125 a month none of this travelling for me but if I cant I will try very hard to make this a success."

Jack was displaying all the symptoms of a martyr. Ever since he graduated from VMI he had been denying himself. Instead of pursuing a career in engineering, at which he excelled, he joined his father to help him in his dry goods business, for which he was ill-suited. By the time he had married the love of his life, the pattern was set. His letters explode with self-denial or reasons why he can't do this or that. Somehow he has come to believe he was not worthy for if he were God would make it possible for him to be with Nancy and be a success. Jack's major shortcoming was his lack of self-esteem. Otherwise he was a decent, honorable man. His last year was heartbreaking to read.

On October 2, 1907 he wrote:

"I expect to be landed in Norfolk and I hope to pick up some of the money I lost there. I arrived safely [he's in Baltimore] had some little delay in getting my trunk as I do not hesitate to say there were thousands piled up there. I checked it through to Norfolk as I could buy a ticket thro almost as cheap as one from here."

The Haddington Hotel in Norfolk, October 5th:

"I am going over at 9 o'clock to Newport News & will spend Sunday & Monday there at the hotel Warwick so you might write me if you get this early tomorrow. If not send your next letter to Suffolk Va general delivery. My friends here have been most kind to me in their manner & two of the best bills I sold were to them. I hope in time I may pick up this business and make it a success. I am sure if I can do so that I will grow to like it. I did not want to spend Sunday in Norfolk as there are many things to remind me of my wrecked hopes but I am learning to recognize many of these as just my misfortunes & I expect I have only what I deserve in the eternal fitness. But if I can only win enough success to do for you my dear ones I shall be content."

From The Stratford Hotel in Petersburg, VA, on October 9th, Jack wrote:

"This is an old hotel made to look like new. The rooms are very nice but the table on the European plan is far from good but I struck another where the meals are much better & next time I think I will stop at that they serve club meals and I got a very nice dinner for 35¢ – cream of tomato soup – roast beef mashed potatoes sweet pickles & cup Coffee – plenty to work on. They had all priced dinners from 25¢ to 1.00 – you pay your money & take your choice.

"I wish we had a sweet little country home somewhere near the town where we could raise chickens & early vegetables &c and make a living – & I could work out in the garden &c but I guess I will stick to the road unless I can get a good position thro some influence & it seems very hard. I just long to be with you as I am so lonely without you. Well dearest we must think of His appointments and accept them as right. If I could have just kept my health I don't think I would have ever been in this fix but as Elizabeth would say I am not the only one.

"Oh how I long to see you my love and how deeply I am grieved that I have brought so much trouble on my loved ones by my misfortunes, looking back it all seems to me so strange that I could not have made more of my opportunities and have protected those I love so dearly – but certainly for many years I was able to give you all that money could buy in the way of comforts and when I had the money it was yours."

Nancy responded with:

"I am hoping and praying <u>all</u> the time my love that the much needed help may come to you but <u>please</u>! don't keep looking back and grieving about what is past it does <u>no good</u>, but unfits you for the present heavy burdens. <u>I know</u> you <u>did</u> – you <u>have done</u> & you <u>will</u> do <u>all</u> in your power for the three women you love & who love you & be thankful to God for this love that <u>nothing</u> can change – & let us try to go <u>most</u> patiently on & be glad & have a smile & a bright word whether we have dark days or bright days – this effort can most certainly do us no harm and it may do us great good.

"I know how troubled I feel, that you have met with no success & feel so discouraged with this new work, and I know it is much greater trouble to you with all your hard work but I do hope the bad beginning may mean a good ending we will <u>hope</u> so at any rate. With a heart full of love and kisses many from your ever devoted Nancy."

Jack's next letter, October 12th, came from the Hotel Carroll in Lynchburg, VA and gave Nancy his upcoming schedule:

"I think I will be in Danville on Monday & Roanoke Tuesday so you can direct your letter tomorrow to the hotel Ponce de Leon Roanoke Va & next letter to hotel Lexington Lexington Va then to c/o S D Timberlake Staunton Va. I expect to go to Staunton Harrisonburg Winchester [VA] Martinsberg [WV] Hagerstown, Cumberland then Frederick [last three in Maryland] & home. Will be home in abt two weeks. I have done some little business here & hope to do a little more this is a fine town beautiful stores. My impression is that it is far ahead of any town in the state. Three stores here would do credit to Washington – thoroughly modern & up to date. I am trying to do my best but am not setting the world on fire still I am not entirely doing nothing but not much with some accts."

Two days later Jack, now in Danville, apparently changed his mind about his schedule. He sold two bills to one party in Danville but said he was still struggling, adding he was now going to Greensboro, NC from Danville. On October 15th Jack was at the Hotel Zinzendorf in Winston–Salem, NC, which boasted of a long distance telephone and hot & cold running water in every room. Jack certainly delighted in the running water but as Nancy had no telephone at home he could not call her:

"This evening after my days work was done my trunk packed, I took a walk around Greensboro [30 miles east of Winston–Salem] which is a crude new town showing much that has been done but leaving yet much to finish up. But this is apart from what I started to write for as I wandered around in the sweet autumn air my thoughts were with you my dearest heart. Yesterday at Danville they had a phonograph, ordinarily I do not like them, but this was a very sweet instrument and as the song, the old song, darling we are growing old and the sweet sentiments of a love always young came forth – I could not help feeling that freshness of our love and that great longing for you.

"A party in Greensboro today was talking to me and saying something about some developments of 50 years and I said that I would not live to see them & he said why you would not be more than 90 – then – & I laughed and told him I was 45." That would mean Jack has not aged at all during the past five years, as he proclaimed himself to be 45 on his 55th birthday in 1902. Now he's 60.

"I seem to have been away from you so long yet I think it is only two weeks tonight since I spent at home – it seems so much longer tho the days have been full & striving and the nights have passed away in sleep yet the time is long. I hope to be home in two weeks or less tho I cant tell. I must work while it is yet day.

"I want to write you of my impression of North Carolina. I like it the people are full of energy. My first two receptions were a trifling bit chilling this morning but the third attempt was more encouraging. I sold four bills all small in Greensboro & if I could do as well each day in NC would feel fairly well satisfied. I arrived at Greensboro last night abt 7:30 as we were late. The hotel looked very bright & there was a bright open fire in the lobby. When we were ushered in the dining room we found the attendants all young white girls – the one that waited on me was just about Soph's ago. They are so gentle quiet almost noiseless in their motions and excellent in the service.

195

"We were to have left Greensboro at 6:30 but our train was delayed in leaving & we arrived here just before the dining room closed for tea but we managed to get in. This is the finest hotel in the state. I expect good service all around. They say this is a nice town abt 3,000 people or abt twice the size of Alexa. Looks very busy and bustling. I cant tell what it has in stock for me but time will tell."

The next day he told Nancy:

"I have sold to day & yesterday in the two towns abt $1000 – abt 800 of it in kid gloves & in abt 10 days abt 150 dozen Satine Skirts but I cant get people to buy dress goods. There are some very nice stores here. One of the best stores is kept by a Syrian & nearly all the employees are minhen of the same family. I did not sell them anything but think I will. They have a new store here just opened and they seem quite busy.

"I do so miss you darling as the shades of night come on and I feel like I would give a great deal to be with you this night on the eve of our anniversary. I hope to get an anniversary present in the shape of a letter at high Point. I will likely spend Sunday at either Salisbury or Charlotte. I may go to Asheville and several other towns but cant tell. This is a great state. I wish I had my life to go over with and get in one of these live towns – but no if I had to live it over again I shd be a professional man. I have had my hair cut & look very much younger in Consequence."

On October 17th he is at The Elwood in High Point, NC:

"Just about this time twenty four years ago you were saying the words that bound you to me for so large a part of your life. Years that are gone and looking back over a beautiful vista like all the views of life with sunshine and an occasional shadow, but I can say that in no year day nor hour of that twenty four years have you failed in any way to live up to my highest conception of a wifes duty and your love for me has been of the highest purest type. I only wish that I had been as worthy of it as I shd have been.

"I did not realize that I was so far away from you today til I saw 302 miles to Washington on the Station here. Today has been delightful but I think we are on the eve of a change in the weather. There is now a bright coal fire in the big grate in the lobby of the hotel. This is the highest point on the Southern road between Washington & Atlanta. It is a new town the main street very broad & no street cars. This is said to be the largest furniture mfg place in the country. The hotel is quite nice, nice rooms they charge full enough for everything but there are few extras and I manage to keep expenses fairly well

196

down. They have girl attendants in the dining room & they are quite attentive. There are a great many handsome modern homes here but the streets are very dusty. In the early spring I should think it would be very pretty here."

That same night Nancy was writing:

"At this time 24 years ago you & I were standing before the altar at dear old St Paul's Church – pledging our faith each to the other in holy marriage my own hearts love. I loved you very dearly then but with each year my love & faith in you have <u>increased</u>, not only in the years when you were prosperous, but since your trials came for in the trying hours I have seen how hard you have tried to do for me & it all makes me love you the more my hearts choice. God bless you.

"Your long sweet lovely letter came to me 'on time' this a.m. and I was so glad to get it for it certainly added to the sunshine of the day which has been very bright. Nancy Lee [20] gave us as an anniversary gift a lovely little green jardinière which is on the table as I write filled with the most lovely white flowers Mary Beny brought. Sophia Ford [15] gave us the lovely little salt cellars which you saw. Agnes Crawford sent us a bunch of Irish <u>potatoes</u> & apples, some of which you shall enjoy when you get home. Oh! how I wish you were here tonight my love true, I can never quite tell you the words all your devoted love has been to me.

"Well darling I must say good night as it is mail time. I am glad you sold the little bills in N.C. The letter I sent you to Lynchburg was returned to me to day but I think I will have to send it to you again as I don't want my written words lost. Will & Lily have just come in and brought me a bottle of delicious Bay Rum which I will let you use it when you get home. I will count the days until your return. The children Will & Lily send love to 'Jack' with a heart full of love & kisses many from your own devoted Nancy."

Obviously Nancy's "written words" were not lost, as evidenced here. Not only are you reading them, but so did her daughters. On the envelope, addressed to "John Ford Tackett Esq, c/o The Berkley Hotel Staunton, Virginia" was a note in the corner: "Don't destroy this from my dear mother to father." Letters were delivered the next day and cost 2¢ back then. A century later letters cost 44¢ and take several days, especially across state lines.

Jack was at The Selwyn in Charlotte, NC on October 19, 1907, which catered especially to commercial travelers:

"I feel like I am in New York in this splendid hotel. Their prices are just 50¢ pr day more than the hotels at Salisbury &c and the accommodations fully equal to the Buckingham – a beautiful lobby with splendid writing room lovely dining room &c. I felt quite for a little while like a millionaire but then I came down kerchunk and know I am just a tourist making barely expense. Salisbury is the dirtiest town I have struck in NC with rather a rough population but I think that it is going to be a good business point. In fact if I can get the right kind of accts I am sure if I can get enough Southern territory that I can make a big success & be at home three or four months of the year. It seemed quite strange this evening to dine with people in evening dress & see the fair sex in their bright attire. I brushed the dust well out of my clothes had a bath & felt quite spry. I certainly needed the bath. I am going to write you more abt this town in my tomorrows letter as I have only had a very brief view of it. I have left forwarding orders all along the route for your mail. I certainly have missed your letters. I have written every day and am glad you have gotten my letters. I want to always try to do this as I am sure it is a comfort. I have seen a great many fields of cotton this evening, all of them hand picked over once but they have lots of the staple in them. How I would love to be with you at church tomorrow but we will both say the same prayer & the same service & may God give me such reasonable success as may bring comfort to my three sweethearts."

Jack was still playing the "if only" game while desperately trying to keep up his spirits, as well as Nancy's. Having spent over 20 years in one place, traveling at least provided a change of pace and scenery and his correspondence now revealed an acute awareness of his surroundings, a constant yearning for his beloved and his obsession to be a success. These final scribbled letters were full of minutia, describing every detail of his daily life, from the time he woke up until he fell into his lonely bed. He would drop dead in his garden in five months, bankrupt, but between now and then his letters provide an unmatched tour of the south in 1907, along with the death pangs of a dying man.

Still at The Selwyn, Jack wrote:

"I woke abt 7:30 this morning or rather I arose at that time and was ready for breakfast a little before nine o'clock. We had a most elaborate menu – I think all the meats – steaks chops – two kinds of Fresh fish, sausage, eggs in all different ways Fruits – six different kind of cereals and about seven or eight kinds of hot bread. I never saw a more beautifully served breakfast at any hotel, then we had a very nice lunch to which I did but slight justice. The late dinner was as elaborate as the breakfast and I wished that you might enjoy the sweetbreads as I never eat them but with an association with you as I associate all things that are sweet with you.

"After Church I took a walk around the town the street the church is on is a very handsome one it is a typical Southern street, the houses are set back about fifty feet from the street and the yards are full of trees flowers &c there are many original growth oaks as large as those at Bonneville and a great many Magnolias and a large sprinkling of live oaks and the greatest profusion of roses, the bushes are just gorgeous with them it almost reminds one of June the frost seems to have scarcely touched anything. Even the Cannae are gorgeous in blooms & fresh as August. It has been almost too warm for walking out, in fact the fall has been very mild.

"I went to YMCA rooms and read two little love stories you know I always like to read love stories it is living over again my love with you. Oh if I can only have success to crown my efforts for you for everything has so gone against me this year but I think the tide will turn & that I may win something & lay it at your feet.

"There are some very peculiar coincidences today. I was reading an article in the rooms of the Christian assoc on Lincolns last day on earth and just as I came out there was an iron plate on the street marking the fact that Jefferson Davis here heard of Lincolns death and after I came to the hotel there was some trouble about the electric lights & we were sitting in semidarkness & I had mechanically opened a copy of Scientific American – when suddenly there was a flood of light in the room & I found that I had opened at an article on the illumination of Niagara falls by electricity made from its own power and the article was of great interest depicting its beauties.

"How I wish I could see you tonight, I was reading an article on kissing & its necessities this evening, and the writer seemed to think that after a long married life it became just a form but tonight entering into the twenty fourth year of my married life I long to kiss you just as much as I did when I had the right Oct 17 –1883."

October 24th, Hotel Ponce de Leon, Roanoke, VA:

"This place is a wonder. When I first came here twenty seven years ago I think I could have bought all the land & buildings for $150,000. I am sure today there is 15,000,000 in property here & land from 500 – to 40,000 inhabitants splendid stores. If I get every thing I sold shipped this will be my best day. It is all right about the samples from Norfolk they are some goods that I want in Washington.

"I expect to be in Charlottesville tomorrow at Colonial Hotel and in Staunton tomorrow night at Beverly Hotel. I expect to spend Sunday in either Staunton or Harrisonburg. I just long to see you all. I am working pretty hard & considering I am a new man doing fairly well. You cant think how very hard it all was at first tho but if I can get good things to sell every thing will work out well."

October 28th, The Kavanaugh in Harrisonburg, VA:

"If you have any one that needs the rest cure advise them to take the 8–22 train from Alexa to Harrisonburg. Train stops every two miles & the Conductor pays social calls & gathers chestnuts on the road side – with all that there is a beautiful panoramic view of mountains &c. This is a fine little hotel. I ate all my lunch before twelve o'clock & had chance to get a good lamb at Strasburg & dinner at same place but I thought I could get on all right til supper time. We had nice broiled trout steak tomato omelette hot rolls biscuit & corn cakes.

On November 15, 1907 Jack is at the "Absolutely Fireproof" Hotel Fairfax in Norfolk, VA:

"I do not get my supper til after eight tonight as I had some work to do in Portsmouth & tomorrow morning I expect to remove to Newport News & to Elizabeth city [NC] from here tomorrow afternoon. [Remember, this means he had to pack up his trunk, arrange to have it delivered to the train station and be aware of the train schedule to each town he wanted to visit. He also had to wire ahead for reservations at a hotel in each of those towns.]
"I sold Mr Simcoe [his former partner] two bills today one from my silk house & one from kid glove house. Sold in all eight bills today. I went around to where we used to go & had some lovely broiled bass & I knew you would have enjoyed it, had my dinner there today cost 30¢ – had a nice breakfast here for 40¢ this hotel is very nice & I have a very comfortable room. Small but very beautifully furnished – full length mirror door to closet &c. I stopped tonight on my way from supper for entertainment at a sale of the Japanese art exhibit from Exposition some beautiful things sold at a song but I did not have a verse so I did not buy. All my money must go to pay my first debts. When they are paid I will be ready to say now lettest thou they servant depart in peace but I fear if I want that I will be a very old man. God keep you & with fond love for all Your devoted Jack."

November 19th found Jack at The Gaston in New Bern, NC:

"I had good luck today the best being getting your letter of yesterday just before I left the Louise at Washington it must have made a good connection and it was very sweet to get it and made me feel nearer to home. I am always near to you, you are with me every where and my sweetest reveries are of you and your beautiful loving presence. I have ordered my mail and some samples sent to me at Rocky Mt NC Hotel Cambridge you might write me just a line there Thursday morning when you receive this and Friday morning drop a postal to the Briggs Wilson NC. Then you might mail me a letter Friday night to the Yarborough Raleign NC so that I can get it by Sunday. [Yes, there was mail delivery on Sunday.] I expect to go to Raleigh so as to be there on Sunday.

"This hotel is a dream. You cant imagine the effect of coming our of the night into a beautiful modern hotel & being ushered into a dining room all furnished in red & gold. The menu most elaborate I am afraid your little Jack ate almost too much supper. Well my advice from all the traveling men was to turn back but I am picking up some little trade. I have no doubt it wd seem very small to many but I made nearly $20 in commissions today & yesterday and received the most courteous and cordial treatment. This was specially so in Washington where the buyers are all young men. I am only looking for small returns do not expect as well the balance of the week but I am thankful for the beginning."

The next day he was in Kinston, NC at The Caswell:

"You see I am a veritable bird of passage no two nights under the same roof. We left New Berne after quite a sumptuous supper to arrive here at 8:30. This town has the handsomest paved street in North Carolina it is as wide as Washington St as level as a floor with the most beautiful side walks. New Berne has some very attractive houses it is just at the intersection of two broad rivers the Neuse and the Trent and they have an abundance of fresh fish & oysters. Tonight at tea we had oysters raw & stewed two kinds of fresh fish steak broiled ham eggs all style hot rolls buiscuit cakes ice cream cake &c. [Jack apparently doesn't like commas.] Now I do not eat all these different things or I would not have been able to tell the tale.

"We had a lovely seat commanding a full view of the river and altogether the day was quite pleasant and am glad to say profitable as I sold a nice bill of silks to a party who told me he had bought but would look at mine & after looking he bought about $500.00 and I over heard him tell his partner that he would countermand an order he had given another party which showed that mine must be O.K. The business part of New Berne is just opposite the Episcopal Church which occupies a whole block with its grounds and makes the street look very attractive – it must be lovely in summertime. I found the people all most courteous & hope I will continue to do some business.

"The men all seem to like me. I tell them I am forty five [still!]. I had an ex confed from Balto who is I think abt 70 & he steps along like a boy & enjoys traveling. He knows all the Alexandrians like Mr Ramsay Mr Warfield & others. Well my precious one I hope this town will treat me well but I don't expect much & then I am not disappointed."

From The Cambridge in Rocky Mount, NC, November 22, 1907:

"Your dear letter mailed to this point at 3 o'clock yesterday was waiting me when I arrived here at 3 today so it made me seem very near to you. You can direct your next letter that is Sundays to The Carolina Durham NC Mondays to Fayetteville NC general delivery. Don't know the name of hotel there and Tuesdays to the Orton Wilmington NC where I expect to spend thanksgiving. I expect to be in South Carolina probably Florence and spend Saturday & Sunday in Charleston SC but I will write you more fully later on. I have sold four small bills today and have an engagement for tomorrow morning. I will be in Wilson about 2 tomorrow & go to Raleigh tomorrow night.

"This town is a great railroad point. The main street is about a quarter of a mile wide [remember his 150 foot long room at the Buckingham in New York in January 1899?] & the mud galore but you know it is not very nice in muddy rainy weather anywhere. The hotel is a new one have not sampled the table yet but I may get enough to eat at all of them. I am doing so far much better than I expected but cant tell when the tide will stop. Dont think it will pay to travel after abt 1 or 2 Dec & wish I could get something to do between that time and Xmas so as to make the extra boodle for you. Love to Father and the darlings. Your devoted Jack."

A letter from Nancy appeared, written November 24th:

"This is a rainy, dreary, gloomy Sunday but I weathered the storm and went down to service at St Pauls, and glad I am I went for the service was very sweet & impressive, followed by a splendid sermon from the Rev McDaniel of St John's in Georgetown. Subject 'The Golden Rule' a large subject & he most certainly managed it in a masterly manner I do wish you could have heard him darling, for I know you would have kept well awake, & been interested in all he said. 'Do unto others as we would have them do unto us' oh! if by our thoughts words & daily acts we could so live!! how much happier we would be & how we could daily & hourly by our own living extend God's kingdom upon Earth.

"I have missed you & wished for you so today, I did not get your letter today but as I had two yesterday I would not worry. I have so enjoyed your nice satisfactory letters lately telling me all about your dear self, I am glad you find good hotels & very glad too you find some trade when other traveling men discouraged you. I know your sweet manners & courteous <u>insinuating</u> ways have a <u>charm</u> that helps you, it is a gift God has given you so use it well. I am glad you find N.C. so kind & appreciative and hope they may so continue. It is sweet to feel you will be with us before Christmas so many things about the house you can do and attend to for us & perhaps who knows you may be able to get some little position to help you on a bit during the dull time in your traveling business." She then brings him up to date on the activities of Nancy Lee and Soph.

On November 25th Jack was at the Hotel Corcoran in Durham, NC:

"The bird of passage left Raleigh at 6:30 and arrived here to late supper only twenty six miles away. Tomorrow I take a long jump into Wilmington one of the longest I have to take. I found Raleigh a beautiful town (tho I did no business there). It is most beautifully laid off streets all wide good sidewalks. The Capital building is old and stately just such a building as you would expect in North Carolina. The Senate & house have the same desks solid mahogany & chairs covered with hair cloth that were put there over seventy years ago & things look just like they did then all in perfect keeping. The grounds are beautiful full of grand old oaks magnolias & other trees & in summer the yard must be a mass of shade.

"All around the sides of the square are beautiful residences. One whole block being occupied by a very beautiful Episcopal Church with a Colonial rectory adjoining. The Steeple of the Church is made of solid blocks of a redish granite and is finished at the summit by a fine looking rooster – probably a type of the biblical bird that made Peter feel so badly. Facing down one of the streets is a Colonia Confederate shaft surmounted by a gallant Confederate full life size. The inscription on the shaft – First at Bethel – Last at Appomatox – on one side of the Square is a superb statue of Senator Vance Thrice Governor of the state and Senator for four terms – a superb face and splendid pose – just near the Capital building is the statue to Ensign Worth Bagley. Facing the main st entrance of the Square is a statue of our Geo Washington. The Governors mansion is somewhat removed from the Capital building occupying a beautiful position in the Center of a highly ornamented square.

"The city is full of beautiful residences altogether it is outside of Richmond the prettiest town I have been in. If my plans work out right I shall spend next Sunday in Columbia the Capital of South Carolina & most likely the following Sunday in Atlanta but it all depends. I am feeling very anxious to see you but that begins from the night I leave you and lasts til the home coming. Just think only a month from Xmas. We must try for the darlings to make it as happy as we can & God grant ere another one comes some of our clouds may have rolled by."

Jack would spend Thanksgiving, November 28th, at The Orton in Wilmington, NC:

"You will be surprised to receive this at Wilmington but just after I had checked my trunk & gotten on the train I had a letter about some business here for the silk people and tho I was tempted to come back to the hotel I concluded to go on hoping to find the stores open in Marion SC as they are in Alexa half a day. I arrived there at breakfast & found all closed & that the town was not my kind at all so I concluded to pocket the loss of the RR fair & came back to Wilmington & finish up here & go to Florence SC tomorrow evening & Columbia Saturday evening – the only loss is the RR fare over 4.00 but I am wiser that much.

"I arrived here abt 1:30 and went in to dinner and my waiter who has only one arm said just take your old seat and I had just finished my fish with lettuce & celery and I glanced around to see a very familiar face looking back & there was Algie [Lily's son] sitting about four feet from me so I got up to shake hands & as we both had the same waiter we finished our dinner together and we had a royal one. I send you the menu. I never saw a much finer dinner I have crossed under the things I ate so you can see I was moderate and do not feel at all uncomfortable.

"I bought the enclosed little hymn from a blind man on the train, and an old gentleman travelling in the interest of Coca cola gave me a very nice watch fob, a pencil & the little match safe and mirror which I send to you. This old gentleman is an American citizen a citizen of the United States & not born in the US – now where was he born. Guess & write me to Columbia. I found Marion a quaint South C. town just like some of our old towns would have looked in the revolution. We had fried chicken for breakfast as I had been up since 4:15 at 8:30 I was a trifle hungry.

"I so wish you could be with me on these trips I think I shall like the sunny south very much certainly I like its people. Well I hope my trip back here will amount to something. Kiss the darlings for me. I am just longing to see you all sometimes I get a bit homesick but I know that means death to me and my work so I strive against it."

On November 29th Jack received a cable from Goessling & Ferre, Importers of Kid Gloves, 350–352 Broadway, New York, saying:

"We are in receipt of yours of November 26th, enclosing orders, and wish you would let us know by return mail when you are coming to New York, as there are some things we wish to talk to you about, and we merely want to know when you will be here, so that we can go accordingly. Very truly yours, Goessling & Ferre." A handwritten note was added at the bottom of the page. "You are doing fine. Malone of Miller & Rhoads was in & I sold him several hundred dollars."

Jack's letter to Nancy on December 2nd, from the Hotel Jerome in Columbia, SC, explained the above letter:

"I worked myself out of a job here at 10 oclock this morning in other words I finished all I could do by that time & have to wait for 3:50 for a train to Charleston. I made abt 10.00 commission by 10 – on kid gloves & petticoats. I enclose you a letter from the Kid glove house to let you see that all of them don't think alike. The M. Malone they refer to is Miller & Rhoads buyer in Richmond & often I get the commission on the bill he went in on my work. Miller & Rhoads do a business of nearly a million dollars in Richmond & I can sell any of them that will give me a show – from the right kind of houses."

He went on to describe people he had met, then added:

"Don't you get tired of reading these long letters of mine but I just feel that it is like sitting down & having a sweet little talk with you but I miss very much having you in my arms & kissing you. I think I would rather have one of your kisses just now & to feel the touch of your hands in loving carress than all the wealth of the Indies. But God grant that before many days I will have them."

Jack now headed for Jacksonville, Florida, which will be as far south as he went. His trip back from there provides a travelogue through the South of a century ago. It is especially fascinating if you follow his journey on a map. He would have made a great tour guide. In Jacksonville he stayed at the Windsor Hotel, which, oddly, had a moose head for a mascot. His train arrived there late on December 5th and there was no porter at the train to help him with his trunk. He told Nancy it was "about as far from the street car as from King to our house on St Asaph to walk." That's only about two blocks but he's carrying a trunk, not a suitcase. He was rescued by a "big fellow who insisted on sharing my load," a traveling man from Chattanooga, TN. Jack then added:

"If I had a little more time I would take in New Orleans & other places but I am going to turn my face homeward tomorrow next Macon then Atlanta Birmingham [AL] then Chattanooga Knoxville [TN] Bristol Roanoke Lynchburg [VA] & next stop in Alexandria Hotel De Tacquette, 211 S. St Asaph St. Mrs Jno F. T. owner & proprietress."

The next day Jack wrote:

"I am taking a little time off so that you may have a long letter for your Sunday reading. I am only going to give you my impressions of Savannah and reserve Florida for a later letter. Savannah is a beautiful city. Charleston is unique it stands alone, and somehow even in its hotels it is distinctive. The negroes even are different tho in that respect I have little to complain of but to return to the subject of Savannah. You enter the city to the large union station erected in 1902. Very beautiful in exterior design semi Moorish as to architecture. The general waiting room is most commodious & convenient, in its centre is a very large fountain & basin & in this are a dozen alligators of all sizes of the young they were too lazy & sleepy to tell me their ages & except for their slick well cared for looks they might have been specimens preserved in Alcohol, but they were evidently alive, and changed their positions quite frequently during the day.

"The hotel deSoto I imagined to be a very modern structure but I was informed that it was built before the war, & occupied by Sherman as a hospital during his march to the sea – it is built in the form of three sides of a hollow square and banked against its spacious porches are palms & tropical plants and a beautiful green lawn in the Centre. The halls & office are very spacious just off the office is a circular lounging room or sun parlor in the centre of this is a large double open fire place extending nearly to the ceiling & the days & evenings I was there blazing wood fires were burning. The dining room is a beautiful room & the table most generous & sumptuous. The hotel is situated in the fine residence section with broad streets parked in the centre with double rows of trees – growing in many instances four rows of trees in a street.

"Not very far from the hotel is the park full of splendid live oak trees beautiful fountains & monuments, Savannah has preserved some of the great events of the war of the revolution & the war between the states in one of the Squares are bronze busts of Barston killed at first Manassas and M Laws – a later period. A splendid shaft to Genl Nathaniel Green an adopted son and a revolutionary hero the gallant pole Pulaski, a splendid bronze to the heroic Sergeant John Jasper. Savannah unlike Charleston strikes you as a progressive modern city it is beautifully laid off, looks solid & prosperous.

"I wish you could go over the ground with me. Tonight I turn my face homewards tomorrow morning I will be in Macon 250 miles nearer to you than today. Sunday in Atlanta 83 miles nearer still. I will write you again tomorrow night from Atlanta or from Macon it all depends on the trains."

The Lougee & Zimmer Hotel in Atlanta was Jack's location on December 8th. He told Nancy:

"I am in hopes that I can get thru with my business and get back to you next Saturday night. I fear that I will not be able to make expenses the balance of the trip but it is much better for me to make the towns that I pass through on my way home. But for the financial depression I think I could have had a profitable trip but I hope that I will have gained much in many ways that will bring me future results.

"I came over from Macon to Atlanta on the Central RR of Georgia this is a very fine road and runs all the way in a ridge of land so that you get a good view of the Country and it is quite a different one to that I have been passing through a good deal of it is the peach growing section, and large orchards are on the route. We pass thru several manufacturing towns very nice ones. We arrived at the Union Sta Atlanta about six o'clock & had to take a cab [probably a horse–drawn vehicle] to the hotel this is an enormous hotel there are a number of fine ones here, but this is first in the centre of the goods–shopping district. I had heard a good deal of Atlanta but it is really a revelation it is a busy bustling miniature New York – lots of tall office buildings & altogether most citified."

Jack then spent the next four pages of his seven-page letter describing: going to Church, where a lady shared her prayer book and the rector said he was glad to have had Jack, which impressed him; walking out to see the Capitol building and grounds; taking a streetcar ride up Peachtree Street to see the splendid residences; going to the YMCA to read; calling on friends, where he was greeted "cordially"; what was served for tea; the beautiful hands and feet of his host (yes, host, not hostess) and how much he enjoyed the evening. He closed with, "Wont you please take to the laundry for me any good collars & cuffs & white shirts I have at home."

The Hotel Imperial in Knoxville, TN, was the site of Jack's letter of December 10th but he began by describing Chattanooga…

"…a fine city of abt 60,000. Two very large department stores. Loveman & Co reminded me very much of Woodward & Lothrop before the large new addition was made & Miller Bro is much larger. I did some little business there & hope for more. It is a fine town very broad streets & many fine buildings – it is situated in battle scarred territory & was constantly changing occupants during the late war. Lookout Mountain is quite some taller than the Maryland hills. The Read house is quite old fashioned as to lodging rooms but up to date down stairs has an excellent café good service & fair prices. I had quite a good dinner there today oyster soup lamb chops & cup of coffee 40¢.

"By the way I weighed today 166 lbs against 152 when I started on the road. I would have been heavier than this but for the financial panic which has made trade so light that I have nothing in my pockets to make me weigh but as soon as the atmosphere clears I will have the shekels rolling in. I wrote to Mr F [his father] to send you the rent check – pay the children the interest I think abt 19.70 for the two they will remember & buy out of the balance any little things you want to send for small remembrances to Cousin Jim & others. Our presents will have to be light this year.

"Please God tomorrow night I will be on dear old Virginia soil at Bristol and next night Roanoke Friday night Lynchburg, Saturday night in your dear arms feeling your caress & having yours & the dear childrens kisses to gladden my heart. Nearly five weeks & when I get back about three thousand miles of travel. I have seen a lot of the dear South land & it rejoices my heart to see its scars grown over and the crown of its prosperity. The bounty of its cities & towns linger as sweet memories. Charleston stands out first for its quaint aristocracy & the air of the old South that will never never fade. Savannah by far the most beautiful city & Atlanta a veritable New York in miniature. This seems a very substantial city – well paved streets. I have not yet been to my room and came in late for tea. I am still on central time 10 pm – really 11 – & so I must close. God bless you all."

December 12, the Hotel Ponce de Leon in Roanoke, VA – again:

"I arrived here at 7:30 after a long ride of six hours from Bristol Tenn. I slept last night in Bristol VA and sold two bills on the other side of the street in Bristol Tenn, one of them quite a nice bill of silks to a large jobbing house the best in the town – and the buyer was a young son of the head of the house & one of the nicest young men I have met – the other was to a very sweet woman who buys the silk gloves &c in another large house & who by the way thinks a lot of our G & F gloves.

"I met at East Radford where we changed cars for Roanoke. Mr Hutchinson who was in the room with me when I was last in New York & we had a very pleasant ride as far as Roanoke, he reports business as very dull here and at Lynchburg but I will try to pick up a few crumbs. Blessed are they that expect little for they shall not be disappointed.

"I expect to arrive in Alexa on one of the late trains Saty night abt 12. I may get there earlier. My darling I am just longing for you. I

think at night of the happiness of having you in my arms & feeling your
tender loving caresses & the touch of your lips. God grant that we may
all have a sweet Xmas, not a merry one but happy in being with each
other and we will feel that all the dear ones that are resting in the sweet
fields are looking into our lives & being with us. Last Xmas to me was
inexpressibly sad. The shadows were falling – not only the shadow of
the fading love and light but that of my bad health seemed to be on me.
But thanks to God I begin to feel that I am yet to be spared to years of
usefulness." Jack will drop dead in three months.

A letter from Ben, Nancy's brother, appeared, written December 27,
1907:

"Just a line to say that we have all survived Christmas and are able to
sit up and take nourishment. We are all especially pleased with the various
presents you and the children sent us; speaking for myself I am delighted with
my book. I am devoted to Joel Chandler Harris because he takes me back
to the dear south of my childhood, where there were no colored ladies and
gentlemen and where the negroes in most cases had the love and respect of the
white people. It was all very sweet and beautiful but is gone for ever, nothing
can bring it back. The whites have changed as completely as the blacks &
all have new ideas new aspirations and new points of view and when our
generation passes away not even the memory of the old south will remain. I
hope you are all well. It is a great pleasure to me to see Jack so much better. I
feel sure that he will be successful next year and that his dark days are behind
him. Hope I shall hear from you soon. Affectionately Ben."

From the Hotel Albert, 11th Street & University Place in New York, on
December 30th, Jack wrote:

"I just made my train this morning in Washington as everything
was late and I had to get over on the electric. Just after we started
for Washington the track got blocked and we lost about an hour so
I was quite late getting into New York but I went right to Goessling
& Ferre we had quite a satisfactory talk and altogether the interview
I think was agreeable. They have had a fine business & are in good
humor about it. I think that I am going to make a good success in
another year with their gloves. I concluded not to go way up to the
Buckingham & tried for a Dollar room at St Dennis but they had
none & so I came around here & secured a very nice room at 1.00.
This is really a very much nicer hotel than the St Dennis has nice
writing room &c. I enjoyed my ginger cakes & apples for lunch and
had a very nice dinner. I hope as Dr Smith says that we have our
dark days behind us. I hope to see you before the old year goes out."

On January 7, 1908, Jack was in Fredericksburg, VA:

"I had your dear letter at breakfast this gloomy rainy morning and it was as near your presence as it could be a ray of sunshine. What a beautiful conception of a human life a ray of sunshine – verily any one who has lived such a life has not lived in vain & when the light is transferred from a world like this to one where there is all light and receives the reward of talents not buried – the well done good & faithful servant, it is sweet to think of association with such a life and feel that God has greatly blessed me in my precious wife. Fredsbg looks duller than Sunday – Merchants taking stock some having special sales – others sick so that the drummer's lot is not a happy one but I picked up two small orders & the promise of others later on & so I am thankful for so much and am on to Richmond."

Three days later Jack was still whistling in the dark, at the Haddington Hotel in Norfolk:

"I recd your letter with the gloves late tonight when I returned to the hotel. I have been hunting all day but so far have found no game – perhaps I may bag something tomorrow. I am trying very hard not to go up & down but to hope that the law of averages will adjust things. I hope I have made an opening to get the Suffolk matter adjusted as if I do I think it will lead to some good business. If I can just have my people to be a little patient I think I can make the thing go – that is I can pull enough out of it to make both ends meet. They all seem to think down here that I have improved wonderfully & I trust it may continue."

On January 14th Jack's letter from Martinsburg, WV contained his upcoming itinerary:

"I may run a day ahead of this as I may get off here in time to make this point & Cumberland [MD] tomorrow & be in Grafton [WV] Thursday so you had best after tomorrow just write me to Marley Fairmont WVa Friday morning & Saturday morning a line to Waldo Clarksburg WVa. Then if you have time until Saturday night & mail early Sunday morning to Chancellor Parkersburg WVa. Monday McClure Wheeling WVa Tuesday Frederick Huntington WVa & Wednesday to Ruffin Charleston WVa from that point I will be working homeward and I may get back by Jany 31st but it all depends on how things go & the prospects.

"It is very sweet to have you miss me my lovely children and I pray that I may have strength and health to succeed so that we can keep up our lovely home in a simple way. By the way as I was going over to Washington I met the Acetelyne gas man and he is going to send me some advertising matter on that gas. It is the finest out & much cheaper than the illuminating gas. I had my hair cut in Hagerstown 15¢ I pay 25¢ at home. I met a travelling man just from the Baldwin $2.00 house. If I had have stopped at the Baldwin I would have gotten a very nice hair brush as a souvenir. Last year they gave a very pretty soap case."

"I have been in three towns today," Jack wrote on the 16th, "Cumberland Md Keyser & Piedmont WVa. The two latter are right in the mountains and this hotel [the Kenny House] is built right on the side of a mountain. It reminds one of the old time hotels that you read of. We had for supper tonight Stewed Oysters Stewed Chicken scrambled eggs fried potatoes hot rolls coffee all cooked like home. An old fashioned butter dish on the table with the butter cut in golden cubes and ice on it.

"Had several letters from my silk people. Don't think the silk business is very good in New York but I hope to do some business there & before I go on I have to keep trying all the time. I am very well and trying to keep a stiff upper lip & whistle to keep my courage up. I bought six 12¢ collars today in Cumberland for 9¢ they were my usual size 16½ but I can wear 16 all right but think of it – six nice collars for nine cents. I went to the YMCA building in Cumberland last night and read the Washington papers & Life & a few magazines. These rooms are quite a resource to one in a strange place.

Jack was in Fairmont, WV, on the 20th. He…

"…took the trolley ride over to this beautiful little mountain town abt eight thousand I should say but with a fine department store that would not be ashamed to hold up its head in Washington. I only sold one bill and find it will not pay me to go over to Morgantown so I will go on to Wheeling arriving there about 5 o'clock.

"The ride over was beautiful on the trolley and I had a charming companion that is spiritually tho not physically for I felt your dear presence near me all the time. You must have been thinking of me. I wonder if any one ever thinks of me as I do of you. I know they cannot for I am not worthy of such thoughts as I give to you my precious best loved one. But the all Seeing Eye records for you many quite loving unselfish acts and when you are called to him there will be many deeds to your credit that you have long since forgotten.

"As I passed along the trolley line this morning I could not but drink in the beauty & grandeur of nature. The sun should have been up but it was hid behind the everlasting hills. The ground & the trees fairly glistened in their coating of frost and the moon still lingered – reluctantly abdicating after a struggle to the more manly rays of the Sun. We ran along a swift little river spanned every few hundred yards by tiny suspension bridges & stopping ever once and again to take on the sturdy looking mountain children bound schoolward. I was sorry when the hour and a half ride was over and we dashed into one of the pretty avenues lined with beautiful homes that told of wealth & progress every where. I look out opposite on the Court House a splendid building looking almost like a state capitol, finely paved streets & side walks & all of this coming from the bowels of the earth for but for coal this country would be a waste & a crow would have to carry its rations. But the Maker of all things not only makes the surface of the earth to bloom like the rose but for the toiless gives rewards below. I passed a fine farm house coming over this morning & they had fail'd to turn out their gas lights & four immense torches were burning – at night they must be visible for miles."

On January 24th Jack at last had some good news to report, from Hinton, WV:

"I sold my friend Mr Richardson about one thousand dollars in silks & kid gloves & he not only bought the goods as if he wanted them but seemingly took a sincere pleasure in doing all he could for me in every way & then sold another new account. Mr R insisted that I should go up & dine with him. He lives in a sweet home built when his circumstances were much more moderate than at present. He had told me that if I would go to dinner I would likely get left overs as Mrs R had given a lunch yesterday. So we had delicious cold turkey – asparagus on toast stewed celery in cream creamed potatoes cranberry jelly just like you mold it and for desert a delicious spongy cake and a rich sauce.

"Mr Coyle & Richardson are just finishing a magnificent store three floors & basement they will occupy – and the balance they rent out as office – have already rented five thousand dollars worth per annum. The building costs abt one hundred & thirty five thousand dollars and is a great credit to their worth & energy. I will go from here to Ronceverte tomorrow."

The next day Jack was at the Hotel Ronceverte, which was electric lighted and steam heated:

"I woke this morning away up in the clouds mountains all around

212

and quite a stiff climb to get to the hotel. I just thought I would stop off at Hinton & this place to see what was there and I picked up abt five to six hundred dollars in sales as a reward for my effort and I think I am going to make a pretty good a/c of the one at Hinton. I leave here at 8:40 & will land on Virginia soil at abt 10 o'clock in the very comfortable 'Gladys Inn' at Clifton Forge owned & operated by the C & O RR.

"The scenery around Hinton is wild in the extreme the town is built just in the Moutains and above two rivers that make a junction there. There are quite a number of fine buildings erected and in course of erection, but my it is a fearfully rough place. The Hotel is modern only opened a few months 2.50 & up a day & abt 1.50 accomodations but most of the hotels leave nothing to complain of save that it all tastes alike & the sweet home cooking is a delight.

"The scenery along this C & O is grand just around Charleston the grand Kanawha Valley is a superb panorama for miles and the stately hills immediately opposite Charleston are capped with some magnificent residences. After leaving that valley you dash in a wild country almost all Mountain & you see the almost perpendicular side of the Mountains covered with miners & wonder how people can live there & be happy – But the Lord in his all wise provision seems to fit the back for the burden. I have missed your letters sadly, did not get one at Wheeling or Charleston tho I was in those towns on scheduled time but I will hope to get straight at Roanoke. Just write me a line or a postal in the morning."

It will be another five days before Jack received word of Nancy's trouble with her teeth. In the meantime he was beside himself, not knowing if she was ill and needed him or not. He kept imploring her to write or have Nancy Lee write to tell him what was wrong. While he waited for word he traveled to Staunton, Harrisonburg, Winchester and Charlottesville before he finally heard in Lynchburg on January 30th. From there he headed home. His pockets, however, were still empty.

While Jack was struggling to make a living, Nancy's brother, Ben Fendall, is fighting City Hall in Baltimore. On February 13, 1908 he wrote Nancy:

"I am sending you this as your Valentine. I am mighty glad you and Soph are better but sorry that Jack could be with you such a little while and that his business prospects are not as bright as he had hoped for. But I am hoping and believing that things will pan out better in New York than he expects and instead of picking up a little he will pick up a whole lot.

"Well! I have beaten off the 'Gray Wolves' again. They tried to prove that a big bridge I am proposing to build was faulty in design, would not stand with its own weight and a whole lot of other pleasant little things. The whole pack took up the cry following the 'Sun' as leader but I cleaned them up. I have been fighting these devils and whipping them for two years and I hope they have enough. I am a bit weary of it myself but if they want some more I'll try and give them another run for their money. I am not hunting trouble but if it comes I am not all in yet and when they come I shall try and give them some of the same. I am enclosing some comments from the papers which will give you an idea of the case and as you may imagine I am feeling all right. Affectionately, Ben."

Unlike Jack Tackett, who joined his father in the dry goods business after he graduated from the Virginia Military Institute with distinction as a civil engineer in 1868, Ben Fendall pursued his engineering career from the bottom up. In 1869, Ben began laying track for the Baltimore & Ohio Railroad. Now he was Chief Engineer in Baltimore and his bridge would be a multiple–span, 540–foot–long arch bridge of ferro–concrete over Gwynns Falls on Edmondson Avenue in Baltimore. It would be constructed by the Baltimore Ferro–Concrete Company between 1908 and 1910 and would stand into the next century, when the street was widened to six lanes.

If Nancy ever wondered how much better things would be for them and how much happier Jack might be if he had followed the path of a civil engineer, there is no record of such thoughts. Still, it would be hard to avoid them, as Jack was not quite four years older than Ben. Jack would be 61 on April 20th, but would drop dead before he reached that milestone. He was dying a slow death, which was tearing him apart. Partly it was a tumor on his heart from being separated from his beloved wife for so many years, but no x-ray would show this. Partly it was a cancer of his spirit, eaten away from years of struggle to make the proverbial ends meet. And partly it was a malignancy that was destroying his soul, bit by bit and day-by-day as one failure followed another, yet no physician could identify any of this.

In February he was back in New York, hoping a Seventh-Day Adventist would prove a comfort to Nancy as a servant. Then, on the 15th he sent Nancy a note to sign from the New York Life Insurance Company. They had agreed to lend him money for 12 months on his life insurance, which he planned to use to pay his premium. He told Nancy the amount would be deducted from the $3,000 policy payable to her should anything happen to him.

Obviously, Jack was broke. Still, Nancy had hired another servant. We do not know, however, how many other servants she had but Nancy Lee is almost 21 and Sophie will be 16 in June so they should be of some help in taking care of the house and boarders. Sophie was not well at the moment but was Nancy robbing her of school to pay for another servant? A letter from Ben on February 17th suggests as much:

> "I am sorry things have not 'panned out' with Jack's business as I had hoped, but, be that as it may, Sophie must not be taken from school. As soon as she is well enough to resume her studies, send her back and when the bills come in send them to me and I will send you the funds with which to pay them; later on, if Jack is in a condition to refund, well and good, if not well and good also. The vital proposition now is to educate the child and that proposition must not and can not be interfered with or delayed in any manner, shape or form. Please let me know what the payments will be and when they fall due so I may arrange to meet them promptly. Three months now are worth twelve months next year." The tuition was probably $100 a year.

Jack's letters are now desperate pleas for help and apologies to Nancy for asking her to take care of some money matters. He needed her to go to Burke & Herbert Bank to find out when $150 was due, for which he would have to borrow $53 to pay one third of the note. He managed to get $35 from his brother, Charles, which was all he could afford. Nancy Lee was making clothes for Sophie out of Jack's old things. He claimed he was glad but that was another blow to his pride. In hindsight he wished he had held on "to the bitter end in Norfolk" and particularly regretted he had brought "great sorrow to you all." He was lonely and homesick but still trying, out at the hotels until nearly 10:30 at night, looking for business but finding it hard to get at the buyers.

He had been in New York for three weeks when he wrote on March 5th:

> "I hope you can get a nice boarder or two of course it does not seem to help much but there are certain things to be provided in the house such as servants lights & fuel that are not added to by the addition of one or two persons and so all that you get for the boarder or boarders can go on the table. I do hope that my part of the affairs will soon show up better and if I can make money arrangements to get out soon on the road I feel that I can do some business.
>
> "It does seem so hard that the question of money or rather the lack should separate us. I sometimes wish that I had some friend that could help us just at this time but I don't know of any one to call on. Thank the children dearest for their sweet messages and love and tell them their Father misses them even more than they miss him."

And the next day:

"I had one customer today from Hagerstown he bought all he could from me. I think the days are quite long in the waiting as I do not have much to do. I went out last night with Charles and Mr H – to the hotels and we did not return until nearly 10 o'clock. I am far from accomplishing what I hoped here in New York but I hate to give up. I would if I had something to turn to at home but you know that I have tried very hard to get something to do at home without success."

His desperation shows clearly in his letter of March 10, 1908. It was written on W. M. Alford & Son Broad Silks stationery, at 119 Spring Street:

"Your letter came to me in good time this morning. I am greatly troubled about my money matters and what you write brings them more forcibly to my mind tho to tell you the truth they are never absent from my thoughts. I have exhausted all my resources. I am just sending a check for 35.00 to Aitchison to pay part of his note of 150.00 due on 11th tomorrow. This money I had to borrow from Chas for a few days and I hope to be able to return it as soon as I get a small amount due me by this concern for sales last month they are generally not made up & paid til about the 15th of the following month that is 15th March for Feby sales. You know the needs at home taxes for State due in Dec not paid – pew rent bills &c.

"I hate to suggest the following but I know that Will if everything is put before him will divide the personal assets of your dear mother. I mean the water stock & bonds let you have your third so that you can use them as security to borrow money on for absolute daily needs. Of course in the general distribution the note I owe your dear Mothers estate will be charged. Of course this suggestion if followed out only provides the temporary relief that we have been using in bridging over the daily needs til I can make a business that will pay. You know full well that the past month has been a great disappointment to me and I do not even now know that I can get the money advanced for the spring trip. I don't know dearest what to write further on this matter and I thought you might want to show the letter to Will. Give him my love. Your devoted Jack."

The next day he wrote:

"I am so troubled that you have to borrow the money but just get Pa to let you have a little for the pressing needs of the house until I get back & we can try to make some arrangements. I do not know exactly what they will be. I applied to my Kid glove house to advance me 300.00 for travelling expenses which I thought would about carry me thro most of my spring trip and they have agreed to let me have 150.00 now conditioned on how things turn up for the balance of the trip. Of course this money does not help me personally as I can only spend it as travelling money. Mr Roe wants me still to take his line and I cannot refuse as I have not sold enough to make my commissions. I am trying to get everything together so that I can be at home Saturday afternoon [it is now Thursday] but you can never tell exactly about these things. May God keep you my darling may he soon scatter the clouds that are so thick around us & let the sunshine in on us."

There is no evidence suggesting either Will or Pa helped out with any funds. It is doubtful Will let Nancy have anything from their mother's estate because he had been embezzling it for years, as Nancy discovered after Jack died. There is a gap of eight days between the above letter and the next, which was sent from Petersburg, south of Richmond. Jack was still hoping things would get better. He would be happy if he, "could know that I had some nice little place with just enough to keep the wolf from the door where I can be at home with you never more to leave." His next letter came from Frederickburg, where he wrote about his visit with Hattie, Charles' wife.

Jack was drowning and all of his cries for help were going unanswered. Hindsight is always 20-20, as they say, but did it never occur to him he could stay home for less than it was costing him to be on the road. Not only would he be with his beloved wife and children, but that would eliminate hotel and transportation costs, as well as laundry bills for his collars and cuffs and the expense of those daily letters, even though postage was only 2¢. Eating at home would also be far less expensive, though he might not get the fancy fare to which he had become accustomed. Still he struggled on blindly, like a gambler trying to recoup his losses by playing another hand, making one more bet or rolling the dice one last time.

Nancy's letter of March 24, 1908, did not demonstrate any understanding of Jack's desperate situation. She rattled on about a visitor of Nancy Lee's, Will & Lily inviting her to tea and going to church with Nancy Lee, then added she thought the "old cook is inclined to stay with me." She also related having the "promise of a young house girl tomorrow." So Nancy seems not to be helping those elusive ends to come together by cutting down on expenditures at home, though Jack was still trying to cut down his expenses on the road, as evidenced by his letter of March 26th. He was at the Colonial Hotel in Norfolk:

"I came to this hotel on Algies recommendation as both he and I knew the clerk who used to be at the Atlantic at the time I first came to Norfolk it is very near the one I used to be at when I had the room in the YMCA building, one thing I like abt it is the price is moderate. I am trying to make the money go as far as I can this is one of the new houses and I expect I will like it all right and I think it suits me better to stop on the American than the European plan. I hope I shall be fairly successful here. Norfolk looks on the streets rather busier than some of the other towns. It seems a bit strange to me always coming to Norfolk under such different circumstances but then I must try & not think too much of these things."

His last letter was written the next day. Nancy had gone on one of her trips:

"I am glad you are enjoying a little rest out at Malvern – thank you for the little violet. I expect things are beginning to look very sweet in the Country – they begin to be quite Spring like down here in fact it is quite warm. My darling my ears did not burn but I thank you all for saying sweet things of me. I am not sure that this letter will reach you much before I do so I am just chancing a line. Kiss the darlings for me & give all lots of dear love. Your devoted Jack."

That same day Ben wrote:

"Unless you want the money at once it will be more convenient for me to send check next Wednesday. I have the necessary funds in the Savings Bank but not in the bank I check on and if necessary can make the transfer but assume a few days will make no difference, if it does, write me and I will fix you up. Let me know a little in advance of the next payment and I will be 'Johnnie on the spot.' Hope I will hear in your next that Jack is doing better. Love to the girls and Will and Lily. Affectionately, Ben." The funds were probably for Sophie's schooling.

Three days later Jack dropped dead in his garden.

The *Alexandria Gazette* of March 31, 1908, page 2, said it all:

Death of John F. Tackett
The many friends and acquaintances of Mr. John F. Tackett were shocked and grieved yesterday evening to hear of his sudden death which occurred at his home shortly before five o'clock. The deceased was in the garden adjoining his residence when death overtook him. He was seen to fall by passersby who hastened to his assistance and carried him into his house. Dr. Arthur Snowden, who had been summoned, arrived as soon as possible, but upon making

an examination he found life was extinct. His death was caused by heart disease.

John Ford Tackett was born in Fredericksburg sixty years ago. He attended the High school taught by Cuthbert Beckner and at the age of 16 years entered the Virginia Military Institute where he graduated with distinction in 1868. He was in active service with the cadets during 1864 and part of 1865 in the valley of Virginia and in front of Richmond and was with the corps when they disbanded in April, 1865. He returned to the institute in September, 1865, and was graduated, as stated. He was educated for a civil engineer, but owing to the great losses of his father he entered the manufacturing business with him. In early manhood the deceased removed to this city and engaged in the dry goods business at the northeast corner of King and Pitt streets. Later the firm name was changed to Tackett & Marshall. Shortly after the death of Mr. Marshall, Mr. Tackett removed to Norfolk where he conducted the dry goods business for a time. He subsequently returned to Alexandria, and of late he had been connected with a large dry goods house in New York.

Mr. Tackett was elected a Police Commissioner from the Fourth ward in 1895 and served in that position for four years. Besides his father, Mr. Tackett is survived by a widow, daughter of the late Townshend D. Fendall, and two daughters and a brother, Mr. Charles E. Tackett whose home is in Fredericksburg. The deceased was justly popular with all who knew him.

Nancy Tackett

Nancy Tackett was now a widow, with very little experience as a wife. Though she and Jack would have celebrated their 25th wedding anniversary the following October, they had not really lived together for any extended period of time. Within two years of their marriage, in October 1883, the letters began. This was because Jack was a buyer for his father's dry goods store, necessitating many trips to New York City of a week or more. Back then weekends together were probably frequent but also hectic, as they had to catch up with what had gone undone during the week. When Jack joined Simcoe in Norfolk, in 1901, the cost of travel and his need to improve his financial situation cut down considerably on those weekend trysts, and by then there were many more things to take care of while he was home, leaving less time for Jack and Nancy to just be together. Then his last year was spent almost entirely on the road, each day unpacking, going from place to place trying to sell his merchandise, then repacking and catching the train to his next destination.

Jack's sudden death, especially at home, had to be a devastating blow to Nancy but after the first few months, as heartless as it may seem to say, it did not change her life very much. She still had to generate her income through her boarding house, for Jack had not been making any money while on the road. She still had to care for his father, as he was living in her house. There were no fewer places to set at the table, for Jack had not been there for a very long time any way. And, of course, she had been sleeping alone for years, the place of the biggest void when a husband or wife has died. She undoubtedly missed his letters, though, and so will we, for they kept us abreast of what was happening.

When Nancy's father, Townshend Fendall, died in July 1893 her mother, Eliza, came to live with her, but here it was the reverse: Nancy's daughters were already living with her. Nancy Lee would be 21 in May and Sophie 16 in June. Nancy Lee was teaching but still living at home. She would remain single, though she was an attractive young woman and had beaus, and eventually run the boarding house. She took care of their mother when she was dying and Sophie was living in San Francisco, unable to join her. Sophie would also become a teacher but would marry, have two sons and move around with her husband, a captain in the army. Both of them were deeply devoted to Nancy. She had been, after all, both parents to them, as they barely knew their father, seeing him only on occasional weekends.

Both girls wrote dozens of long letters. Nancy Lee, like her father, wrote about what was happening <u>around</u> her, describing her surroundings, events she attended, people she met and interesting things she did. Sophie, like her mother, wrote about what was happening to her, regaling Nancy with how many boyfriends were pursuing her, the many parties she attended, what she wore and always mentioning how pretty someone had told her she was. Nancy's directive to burn her letters applied to her daughters as well as her husband. Unlike Jack Tackett, however, Nancy Lee and Sophie obeyed those instructions so there are only a few letters from Nancy and they are mainly to her brother, Will, asking him what he did with the money Jack and she had given him to invest for them. This means sometimes there are many years between letters and other information, since including Nancy Lee's and Sophie's correspondence would fill another book.

Will was living at 219 South Alfred Street with Lily. That address was originally purchased by Will's uncle, William Eaches, for whom Will was named. Eaches bought the property with financial help from his brother–in–law, Townshend Fendall (Will's father), turned it into rental property but died before he could reap the rewards of his efforts. Will was living in it with Lily now, but it also shows up in a lawsuit in 1919, filed by Will's second wife. He conned her out of five grand to improve the property, claiming to be the sole owner of it when he knew he was not. It appears there was no limit to Will's larceny. But that's in the future. For now there was a letter to his present wife from his step-daughter, Marion, written on July 13, 1909, which somehow appeared in this still accumulating pile of letters. She was in Maryland and wrote to Lily that Will had promised to pay a couple of her bills, but then claimed he could not find his checkbook. This was not the only time he used this excuse.

Will must have thought his magical disappearance act with others' funds would continue to go unnoticed for he still wrote letters as if nothing was amiss. On August 7, 1909, he wrote from Yellow Sulphur Springs:

"Lily seems to be better. I keep her in the open as much as possible. She is drinking the water faithfully & has more relish for her meals and sleeps better than she has for years. The most impossible people as usual are at this place but as we do not come in close contact it is rather amusing to watch them. There are several agreeable people that we are thrown with in the evenings (for the mornings are spent walking & sitting under the shade of these beautiful trees reading or talking.) One elderly maiden lady got to talking to Lily a few evenings ago (we had noticed she was out of the general run) and we found she was the daughter of Genl' Stokes an old army officer who had been sent to New Orleans to investigate the conduct of Butler & Banks and among other things the stealing of the valuables etc in the Twiggs Mansion & she said the things they did were so atrocious that the U.S. Gov locked his report up among the archives & they are there still not allowed to be seen by any one. When she found Lil was Genl' Twiggs

Granddaughter & that her Father was Genl' Myers they had many things in common.

"I think Lil sent a letter (from a young man who wishes board – a friend of Mrs. Belle who wrote to her), to Nancy Lee today. I think he will be in Alex in about two weeks he is a Lawyer. We only know him through letter and Mrs. Belle. You can judge best when you meet him. I trust darling you are still improving. Kiss my dear Sophie for me & with many for yourself & much love in which Lil joins. Ever your devoted brother Will."

There is a 12-page letter from Nancy to "My dearest Will" in Charlottesville. It is dated August 22, 1909. Nancy related local gossip and told Will about Ben's wife being unhappy at Orkney Springs, where the "table" was bad but which Nancy Lee would find delightful. She then added:

"I went over with Nancy Lee, on Friday, to Dr. Rust and while there, phoned to Charlie Marbury [Nancy's cousin]. He said he & Mary were at home, and as soon as I was through at the dentists, he was coming around for us in his automobile and wanted us to stay to lunch. We went and had a very sweet little visit but we did not stay, as we had told Sophie we would return to dine at home – they both thought I had improved and invited me to go to Atlantic City with them this week but I told them I had to stay at home now, and let my dear big girl go away, as I felt she needed a rest & change very much. She sends her best love to uncle Will and aunt Lily and thanks you for your letter, which she says she will answer after she reaches Orkney on Tuesday next.

"Waddy has been several times to see me about the furnace he says our old one is in a most dilapidated condition and it will not cost a cent less than $75.00 and perhaps more & he does not then guarantee satisfaction, and seems to be rather in favor of putting in a new furnace this price almost took my breath away, & I don't know what a new one would do, he is coming tomorrow to take the size of the rooms and let me know about heating all the rooms, and when he does let me know I don't know what to tell him, for I am all at sea as to my income, and don't want to go into a large thing I may not be able to pay for, for the bills I am now owing are heavy burdens – if I only knew I was to have some certain boarders this winter I could save up and pay a little at a time but every thing is uncertain.

"Mr. Bryan brought a Mr. Wilbour to see me the other night about board. I showed him the 3rd story front room, but he seemed uncertain. I have not heard any thing from Mrs. Bell's friend yet but I am trying to hold my soul in patience.

"You said the morning I left you were going to leave me a little written statement of how you had invested my money and what you

223

had paid out in taxes, insurance & other bills but Nancy Lee said you had not left any thing with her, so I am afraid you were too hurried before leaving home to fix things up – and I want you to let me have my portion of the little <u>personal</u> money our dear little mother left, her own little savings, that she said she wanted equally divided between her three children – You see the interest has been accumulating for two and a half years and it would be an immense help to me at this time as my account at the Citizens Bank is very low and the $8000 I got you to deposit in the National Bank the day I left, I don't want to touch you know why – by the way have you my bank book or did you leave it at the bank – I do hate to worry you about those things when you are away for a rest but I feel so anxious to know just how I stand, before I attempt to do any thing – and it keeps me so nervous. I know you are doing the very best you can for me and I do appreciate it more than I can ever tell. It is bed time and I must say good night – with Dear love for you and Lily in which the girls join Your ever devoted Nancy."

There is no answer from Will to the above questions anywhere in the collection, which does not seem surprising, considering he is notorious for dodging difficult questions, such as those from his step-daughter. But could there be another reason for the silence? Is it possible Nancy did not mail this letter? Will was in Charlottesville, a long way from Alexandria. He would have had to bring the letter back and give it to Nancy in order for her to add it to the collection. Did she, after penning the letter, hesitate to send it, perhaps in fear of irritating Will? Or was correspondence collected individually by each family, then, at some point, all of it was dumped into the same receptacle? They certainly arrived at the library mixed together. One of the many mysteries in these letters.

Will did send Nancy a check for $25 from The Red–Land Club in Charlottesville on September 17th. He and Lily did a lot of traveling throughout the state, seemingly for her health, which appeared to be delicate. It does raise the question, however, as to who was minding the store. Will was supposed to be a lawyer in Alexandria but if he was seldom there, how could he serve clients? Was Lily paying the bills or was Nancy, unbeknownst to her? In his letter Will advised Nancy:

> "I think the idea of hot water heat is the best & it seems to me very reasonable. Ned Dangerfield can advise you as he has been through it – don't bother about the money we can fix that all right – about your money at B & H [Burke & Herbert Bank] let it stay for the present. If you need any thing else at once let me know."

More on the subject on the 23rd:

"Trust you have had a talk with Ned Dangerfield & have settled about the Heating of your house as I wrote you I thought the Hot water was best & not very expensive. The estimate on mine some years ago was $950 but evidently they are less now – I wish I could be there to help you but I can not leave Lil just now. I trust you will soon have your house maid again & your house filled with agreeable people. God knows Nancy I would love to be near & give you real help but my hands are tied. Affectionately, Will."

On December 30th brother Ben wrote:

"I am sorry the steam heater uses so much coal. Yours is a very large house and very expensive to heat but, notwithstanding, a ton a week is too much. I hope the people who installed it will be able to show you the trouble.

"I had a letter from Will last night in which he said Nancy Lee was quite sick and had been since before Christmas and was threatened with jaundice all of which was rather alarming. I trust it is not as bad as he thinks and that she is better now. Give my love to her and to Sophie. Isn't it wonderful how old Mr. Tackett holds out? I think of him so often. Hardly suppose he remembers any one except those with whom he is in daily contact but give my regards to him any how, whether he knows who I am or not. Affectionately Ben." John Edward Tackett, Jack's father, will die the following February, four months after his 87th birthday.

On February 24, 1910, Lily Twiggs Myers-Chalmers Fendall, Will's wife, died after an illness of several weeks. Some time after she died Will moved in to Nancy's house at 211 South St. Asaph Street as a boarder, but subsequent letters from Nancy indicate he didn't always pay his rent. Judging by a list Nancy compiled in 1921 of his belongings still at her house, he moved in lock, stock and very large barrel. Among the items, which were located in every room – hall, front and back drawing rooms, library, smoking room (for meats, not pipes), dining room, kitchen, back room, second story front, little front room, back room, third story front and third story back – were Fendall and Eaches portraits, including a portrait of Lord Townshend and paintings by Hector Eaches; mahogany bureau, tables, side board, desk, chairs and sofa; a grandfather clock, in Fendall family about 300 years; brass andirons and shovel; a walnut bed, bureau and mirror; and Lily's personal property, a large dressing table, large wardrobe, wash stand and commode stand. The latter, of course, was a seat for a chamber pot.

With his furniture all over Nancy's boarding house, it must have seemed like home to Will, though he no longer needed to pay any servants of his own. In fact, as a boarder he didn't have to pay for any upkeep of the house at all, except for the monthly boarder's fee, thereby saving a substantial amount of money while he looked around for another rich widow.

In 1910, Nancy Lee was still living at home, though she occasionally traveled to visit friends. She and Nancy seemed to trade off trips for Nancy still took various vacations elsewhere, always for a rest, at which time Nancy Lee ran the boarding house. Both she and Sophie encouraged Nancy to stay away as long as possible so she would recuperate but from what is never clear. Sophie was in Charlottesville, having a ball, falling in love with Jimmy Slee, a Yankee, but he thought, "Robert Lee is the greatest man the world has produced." Both girls sewed their own clothes, including their undergarments and nightgowns, though they could no longer just order cloth from their father's store. Dresses were still ankle length, the zipper had not yet been invented, the hobble skirt came and went, fur trim was on everything, feathers were mandatory on hats and no self respecting lady would go out without wearing one.

Both girls were also artists and intrigued by spiritualism, especially Sophie. Nancy Lee was more skeptical but both reported making the "table" move, even "waltz around the room." Sophie related she had a guardian named Utopia Tacquette and she was a Hugenot ancestress. The spirit also told her it was Tom Eaches and he was Nancy's guardian spirit. Tom was Nancy's uncle. A Quija board is not mentioned so there is no clear indication of how they moved a table or communicated with spirits but there were many mentions of this in 1910.

Nancy Lee was in Eastville in July, on the Chesapeake Bay side of that tail of Virginia, which hangs down below the eastern half of Maryland. She related going over to Cape Charles in an automobile. The Tacketts got around on horsepower that had four legs or by streetcar, except for extended trips, in which case they went by train but even then they needed a conveyance to haul them and their trunks to the station. Electricity was installed at 211 South St. Asaph in 1922 but gas light is still present today in the flickering flames that burn on either side of the front door.

On August 6, 1910, Jack's brother, Charles, died after a very brief illness. The girls and Will went to the funeral in Fredericksburg but both girls insisted Nancy not come back from Haymarket, Virginia, but stay there to rest. Nancy was 47 at the time and while the house had lots of rooms and three floors, she had two servants to cook and clean so why she needed all this rest and recuperation is impossible to fathom. It is more likely she was escaping the heat of Alexandria, as she had always done, while feigning exhaustion. Whichever, it may have helped in the long run for she lived to be 86½.

In February of 1911 Nancy received a check for $78 from a boarder, which gives some idea of her income. The check covered $64 for four weeks board, $6 for the month the writer was absent and $8 for reserving the room for a month. In addition, Nancy had received $11,731.66 from Jack's life insurance, from which he had borrowed $3,000 one month before he died. After paying off the loan at Burke & Herbert Bank and other bills she had $7,831.66 left. That should have provided a nice cushion but, unfortunately, she gave it to Will's charge, thereby letting the fox in the henhouse. It would be another five years before she realized Will had been systematically stealing from her for years.

Sophie was having a grand time in Charlottesville during 1911, and she regaled Nancy with reports of her conquests of many beaus. She reported she played cards with the son of "one of Uncle Will's many flames," thereby verifying his reputation as a ladies man, which he had promulgated himself in his letters to Nancy during his bachelor days. Nancy Lee spent October in Norfolk, where she related she had engagements for every night in the week. She went to see "The Goose Girl" and enjoyed it but had to stay home one night because her "troubles" arrived. It was not unusual for women to remain at home during their period. Kotex would not come on the market until 1921 and then it was embarrassing to ask for the product. Stores finally solved the problem by putting a box on the counter where ladies could drop in coins and pick up the Kotex without asking for it.

Sometime early in 1912 Stanley Blanton moved into Nancy's house for what would turn out to be a long stay. He was Sophie's future husband, but not until after a very rocky six years. None of his letters – of which there were not enough for Sophie – were returned to whatever receptacle was holding this voluminous correspondence, but her lamentations about his not answering her letters, forgetting about her, never wanting to see him again, convinced he cared nothing for her, then asking Nancy for news of him, these were kept. Stanley was obviously behaving the exact opposite of all the beaux Sophie kept saying were courting her. Whether this was intentional or not, it worked.

It seemed strange to find a letter written to Lily, from her daughter, among the personal letters of Nancy, Jack and the two girls but even more strange was the letter to Prof S. G. Blanton written by his mother. Yes, Stan was staying at Nancy's boarding house, but why would he give his mother's private letter to Nancy? He and Sophie were barely acquainted at this time. Were they found in his room and automatically added to others or did he add them? Nancy was paranoid about having her letters destroyed, yet she apparently had no qualms about keeping those written by someone else. There would also be two more letters to Stanley from his mother, long before he married Sophie. How they came to be included here we'll never know but we do know she wrote the following from Richmond on June 19, 1913:

> "Well I have sold our home & will have to vacate in 30 days this seems dreadful to me; and I do feel perfectly at sea to know what is best to do, & when to go. I sold it for ten thousand seven hundred & fifty, but had to take two small brick houses on Leigh St. at four thousand, but this is good renting property in the Negroe district. I have been looking for a house for ten days but have found nothing as yet. When I look around and see so much that is sacred and dear to me & to know I will so soon have to give it up it nearly breaks my heart. I feel it was the best thing to do & I hope every thing will turn out all O.K. It will be a job to dispose of the furniture & carpets I will have no use for. I have written for your Sister – she can help me so much.
>
> "Hoping to see you soon & with a heart full of love & best wishes for a most delightful little outing from a devoted Mother. I have had several good weaping spells, since I have been homeless."

Another "Private" letter appears, this one from Sophie to Nancy, pouring out her broken heart on September 27th. She and Nancy Lee were in Williamsport, PA with friends. Sophie wrote she had not had a single line from Stanley since she had been gone and had never had anything hurt her as much. She was "more and more deeply convinced that he cares nothing for me," but she still wanted Nancy to find out all she can. She left a note and her address for him when she left home so felt there was no excuse for his behavior. Three days later she wrote about a trolley ride, shopping, going out to dinner and a bridge game, then very casually mentioned she got a letter from Stanley Blanton. There would be four more years of this rollercoaster ride for Sophie, during which time she would flit from one boyfriend to another.

In August of 1914, Will is wooing another rich widow, this time at the Beach House on Nantucket Island in Massachusetts. He calls Katherine Atterbury Brastow his "dear little friend" and raves about the location being "the cutest place you can imagine, like being on ship board." Every moment he feels like falling on his knees and thanking God for the blessing he is enjoying. His "friend" has all sorts of wonderful surprises for him each day, is full of music, plays divinely and will be a great help to "our little Sophie" some day. Will went on to relate her mother is lovely to him and says he has been the best medicine she has ever had and she feels stronger each day he is there. It appears Will is once again weaving his web of deception.

In December, Will drops in on Ben with Katherine, now his fiancé, according to a letter from Ben to Nancy. He found her to be very pleasant. Ben also enclosed a check for a small amount, wishing he could increase the amount but, "when I take a thousand dollars out of my salary for house rent and Life Insurance I must sail mighty close to the wind to keep clear of the shore." On January 4th Ben asks when Will will be married.

On January 17, 1915, the Washington Post published the following:

"A wedding of interest to society not only in Washington and Virginia, but in New York and Philadelphia, took place at noon yesterday, when Mrs. Katherine Atterbury Brastow, daughter of Mrs. John Colt Atterbury, of New York, became the bride of Mr. William Eaches Fendall, son of the late Townshend Dade Fendall, of Virginia. The ceremony was performed at the home of the bride in the presence of a small gathering of friends of the bride and bridegroom, principally from out of town. The house was simply but very tastefully decorated with palms and American beauty roses, and a breakfast followed the ceremony. The Rev. Dr. Samuel Wallace, of the Theological Seminary, of Alexandria, officiated. The bride, who was escorted by her brother, Mr. J. Francis Atterbury, of New York, who gave her in marriage, was very handsome in a gown of green panne velvet, the upper part of gold lace, with a hat of white lace trimmed with pink roses and carrying pink roses. Her son, Mr. F. Addison Brastow, and Dr. Edgar Snowden acted as ushers, and Mr. Morgan Beach was best man. Little Miss Schuyler Dunlop and Master Carl Hjallmar Oberge were ribbon bearers. They were picturesque little figures, the former in a white ruffled frock, with pink ribbons and carrying pink roses, and the latter in a white suit with a wide page's collar. Mr. and Mrs. Fendall left Washington in the afternoon. They will be at home after February 15 at 2013 N street. Among the guests were Mr. and Mrs. J. Francis Atterbury, of New York; Mr. and Mrs. George Oberge, of New York; Mr. W. W. Atterbury, Mr. and Mrs. Lawrence Wetherill, Mrs. Kate Eaches Ridgely, Mr. and Mrs. C. W. Collins, and Mr. and Mrs. E. C. Felton, all of Philadelphia; Miss Tillinghast, of New York, and Col. Robert E. Lee and Mrs. Lee, of Virginia."

It is interesting to note that Will was married to Lily at Nancy's house, followed by a reception Nancy had for them, but there is no mention of Mrs. John Ford Tackett or her daughters, Nancy Lee or Sophie Tackett, nor of Mr. Benjamin Fendall and his wife, Florence, among the many guests attending this wedding of Will's. There is, however, an announcement of the wedding among the letters which includes a card stating "At Home after the fifteenth of February at Twenty thirteen N Street N.W."

On March 20th, Nancy wrote this to Will:

"I saw Ned Daingerfield this morning and he said he was very anxious to see you about 'that little bank matter' he had written you he said some days back but had not heard from you and as there were some matters of importance coming up he would be glad if you would step into the bank Monday or Tuesday next (March 22 and 23rd) to see him about it. I could not tell him anything because I don't know – except that Ned invested $2,000 for me, which has been paying me $80 a year and I know you have brought me from time to time a note to sign saying something about collateral. I never understood for what, and you would say you would explain it to me when you had time & I do hope you can make it convenient as soon as you possibly can & tell me quietly about my affairs.

"I know I had after Jack's death from his life insurance $11,731.66 out of this $1,900 – paid his debt to the Feds & to bank – then $2,000 Ned D invested for me leaving $7,831.66 which you took charge of – to pay what little was owing & the rest you would invest &c – on June 1st 1908 you got a cheque from me on the First National Bank for $300.00 to invest but you did not tell me in what then July 31st 1908 you got a cheque for $100.00 on First Nat Bank – and on Dec 14th 1908 a cheque for $500.00 & Jan 7th 1909 a cheque for $400.00 (making in all $1,300.00) then in April 1909 – when I was in N.Y. you sent and asked me to send you a blank check payable to cash, I think you said, & you would fill out the amount as you were going to invest it for me – but did not tell me in what & when I came back you said you would explain it all to me when you had time and said you had the papers &c in your box in bank & would go over them with me – so please as soon as you can let me know what the investments are & what they pay so I may not be under such a great strain & be able to pay what I owe outside.

"I have tried to manage to the very best of my ability up to this time, with what I have gotten from my boarders but you know I have had very little in that way this winter & even with the very strictest economy, could not make both ends meet. Hoping to see you soon & quietly talk over matters I am with love for you & Kitty in which the girls join yrs affectionately Nancy."

Sophie was now at State Normal School in Fredericksburg. She was 23; Nancy Lee was 28 and still living at home. In June, 1915, Sophie wrote: "Mr. Blanton came down, bringing perfume, two boxes of candy and a bottle of whiskey for mint juleps." Sounds like Stan knew what to do, he just didn't do it often enough to satisfy Sophie. By March of the next year she was teaching in Staunton (pronounced Stanton) and telling Nancy Mr. Blanton was "too busy to write letters. Maybe he had better not trouble himself to write me any more if it is such a burden to him." So the rollercoaster ride continued and it will be two more years before Sophie became Mrs. Stanley Blanton, during which time she would blow hot and cold over the relationship, alternately praising or damning Stan. It's too bad we don't have his letters to tell us his side of the story.

1916 seems to be the year Will's web of deception began to fall apart, judging by a letter from Ben to Nancy on June 27th. He wrote:

"I have been hoping to hear from you for some time with regard to any steps you may have taken in the matters discussed when I last saw you. Not having heard from you I fear you have not taken any steps so far. My own judgement is that the sooner you act the better and I most earnestly recommend that you proceed at once and whether you have or have not taken the matter up with John Johnson to keep me posted as to the status of things.

"The first person I met when I got to Warrington, after leaving you Sunday, was W, and I rather expected he would see you the following day to find out why I was in Alexandria."

It could be considered circumstantial evidence to suggest the above letter indicates Ben is referring to Nancy learning about Will's devious ways, but what follows in 1917 gives credence to the statement. Before more evidence appears we learn Sophie is homesick and sorry she missed Gypsy Smith's meetings. He was a fire and brimstone Evangelist who was very popular at the time. Sophie didn't miss much, though, as her letter of October 5, 1916, indicates:

"I have just had the most thrilling, exciting, wonderful time I ever had in my life. The Buffalo Bill Wild West Show was in town today, and I went. Mr. Braxton (the father of one of my pupils) took me, and his two children and Margaret Hatt, one of my last year's pupils. We did have the best time. We went at one o'clock and took lunch with us. We saw the parade before we started and it was fine. You never saw such lovely horses and they did the most wonderful things. They did marvellous tricks with lassoes. One man lassoed five horses when they were going at a full gallop. Then he got his lasso going very very fast, and jumped through it. I sat on the edge of my seat the whole time. The only thing that bothers me is that I know I must have missed something, because there was so much all going on at once.

"I am enclosing some newspaper clippings about Mary Gertrude that Eve's aunt Annie Johnson sent her. I am sorry Mary is coming out anti Wilson. But I hope and pray he is going to get the election. The New York Times seems to think he has a very encouraging out look in the middle West.

"I am much thrilled over the C.B. hat. I'd love to have a small hat, and I've been walking by all the store windows with closed eyes. Tell Nance she needn't look with eyes of love upon it. I let her have the Mary D. dress when I really wanted it, and I can't be unselfish again so soon. Well darling, it is supper time, so I must stop. Here is dear love, and kisses many from your devoted baby Soph."

By October 15th Sophie had…

"…long ago given up expecting anything from Stanley. He just isn't that kind of a person. I did get a letter from him on Thursday, but I don't intend to hurry about answering it. It seems silly to keep up this farce of correspondence. I think the letters are a burden to him, and the pleasure to me is hardly great enough to make up for all the disappointments of looking for the letters that never come. He just forgets all about me as soon as I have gotten out of sight. I wish I didn't care anything about him, but I'm fool enough not to be able to entirely help it. Maybe I may before I get old enough to depart this life."

Eleven days later she wrote Nancy she cried when she saw "*The Birth of a Nation*," but the box of roses sent by Stanley cheered her up. She is terribly homesick for her mother, who writes every day. This compounds the anguish Sophie feels over the sporadic letters from Stan. No matter what the poor guy does, it's never enough. By the end of November he leaves Nancy's boarding house for a new job of some kind, to which news Sophie responds, "He has so absolutely gone out of my life now, that I could scarcely be expected to feel any other emotion than surprise over his leaving." In a little over thirteen months they will be married and then she will apologize to Nancy for all the mean things she said about him but for now she still rides that rollercoaster. Shortly after the above comment she is putting Stan's initials on some handkerchiefs and hoping for a white comb, brush, mirror and powder box with her monogram in black or dark blue from Stanley.

1917 is the year President Woodrow Wilson and Nancy Tackett would declare war, though in different areas of combat. World War I would be over, however, long before Nancy's war with Will. Due to Nancy's directives to her daughters they destroy her letters and the absence of letters from Nancy Lee at this time (due to her living at home), the history of the latter war comes from

Sophie's and Ben's letters and trips to the courthouse in Alexandria. The first letter to Nancy is from Sophie, on January 6th.

> "I am so glad uncle Ben came and I do hope he is going to stick by you and be some help and comfort. Just when is the suit to be tried? If you want me I will come home next week end, or if it were really necessary I think Miss Howard might give me leave of absence for a few days. Let me know dearest if there is any way in which I can help, for if there is, you know there is nothing in the world I would not do for you. I hate so for you to have all this trouble, but I am sure this is the best and only course to take. You have given him every possible chance to defend himself, and by his own conduct he has left no other way open. It is only fair and just to you and to us that he should be called to account. And even if we find there is nothing left it is better to <u>know</u> and have all this uncertainty cleared away."

On January 8th Ben sent the address of someone to help with the suit. "In reply to your inquiry the address is Wm L. Marbury [their cousin], 700–704 Maryland Trust Building, Baltimore, Maryland. Better mark 'Personal' on the envelope."

In spite of yearning for Stanley, Sophie did not lead the life of a wallflower. Far from it. She was always mentioning a different escort or suitor for trips to the movies, a dance or a party. She described her attire at a country club dance, where she related she got quite a rush, "I really looked nice. I wore my suit, my new gray waist, my gray fur, gray spats and little red hat." Yes, the ladies also wore spats over their shoes but tripping the light fantastic in all that finery today would be considered gauche. Today the dress code seems to be to wear as little as possible.

Her next letter, January 14th, mentions going to see *Intolerance*, D. W. Griffith's second silent masterpiece, after *The Birth of a Nation*. She wrote it was marvelous but so terrible she wished she had not seen it, then described it to Nancy.

> "It pictures the sufferings caused to humanity by intolerance at four different periods of the world's history. One part was laid in Babylon at the time of Belshazzar's reign, and portrayed the fall of Babylon and the incidents leading up to it. Another part was drawn from scenes from the life of Christ, dwelling mostly upon the intolerance of the Pharisees. It pictured the marriage at Cana, the story of the woman taken in adultery, and finally the supreme intolerance, the Crucifixion.
>
> "Another story was woven around a pair of Huguenot lovers at the time of the Massacre of St. Bartholomew. And the fourth was a modern story, showing the Intolerance shown from Capital to Labor,

233

and vice versa. But there were scenes of such horror in all the parts that I came back perfectly limp and sick, and I fear I shall be haunted by some of the scenes for weeks."

While Sophie undoubtedly taught history to her young pupils, she was also inadvertently recording the history of her family and the times. She was glad Nancy's new maid was a help but wished she was there all day to wait on table at dinner time. On January 18th she related they were having a half-day holiday and a celebration on the morrow in honor of Lee's birthday, then was enraged there was not going to be any holiday on Washington's birthday. She resisted going home because it would cost $8 ($132 in 2009), was chauffeured to a dance, took aspirin for her "troubles" for the first time and it worked wonders, got a letter and a bunch of sweet peas – Special Delivery – from Stanley. He was now a sergeant of the High School Cadets Light Infantry unit but Sophie doesn't indicate where.

By February Sophie was all a twitter over the trouble with Germany. Afraid it may mean war but presumed, for some inexplicable reason, it would be naval warfare. She wished Stan would give up teaching night school and worried about Nancy working in their cold kitchen. (It had a cobblestone floor, so would have been cold if the oven was not on.) Her main concern, though, was over Kitty (Will's wife) having the nerve to invite Nancy over after all that has happened. She wondered if, "uncle Will has kept her in ignorance about it? And has he ever made any answer to Mr. Johnson? Seems to me Mr. J might push matters a little more. Do let me know if anything happens."

Something did happen, on April 3, 1917. One day after President Wilson asked for a declaration of war, Ben Fendall declared war on his brother, Will, judging by Will's answer to a Bill of Complaint. Ben's battle with Will was over property, whereas Nancy's was fighting him primarily over money she and Jack had given Will to invest, though she also had a stake in the distribution of three properties. The answer to the complaint was classic Will. He begins by acknowledging Ben's one-third undivided interest in a house and lot at 309 Prince Street, but denied:

"the plaintiff [Ben] has any interest in the property described in the bill of complaint as house and lot No. 219 South Alfred Street. [This is the property William Eaches developed with Townshend Fendall's financial assistance.] Respondent is the absolute and sole owner of the Alfred Street property. The facts in relation thereto being as follows: The father of plaintiff and respondent had made quite extensive advancements to the plaintiff in the way of education and otherwise, and partly on that account gave respondent the said lot on South Alfred Street, and executed a deed to the respondent therefor. There was an old dilapidated house on the lot which was almost valueless, not producing enough income to keep it in repairs, and meet taxes, and insurance. Respondent's father executed and delivered to Respondent a deed in fee simple to said lot and old building about the year 1893 [Will was 37 then]; that the deed was burned up some years ago when a fire took place in respondent's office in the City of Alexandria, Virginia, and respondent since the institution of this suit has found, <u>to his surprise</u> [author's underlining], that he had neglected to record the deed. Both the plaintiff and respondent's sister, however, knew about the transaction and knew that respondent was the owner of said lot and old house. That from the time he received a deed for the said property it was assessed in the name of respondent, and he paid all the taxes and insurance thereon.

"That many years ago, the old house was so dilapidated that it was impossible to derive sufficient revenue therefrom to keep it in a habitable state and to meet the taxes and insurance; that the plaintiff, thereupon, erected a dwelling upon the said lot at a cost of between $2000.00 and $2500.00, and received the rent therefrom until he occupied it as a dwelling for himself. That after respondent ceased to occupy the new house as a dwelling, and found it hard in that location to be rapidly rented, he turned the house into two flats, or apartments, at a cost of about $4000.00 and has been receiving the rent since. The respondent has been in notorious, quiet, peaceful and undisputed possession of the said property on South Alfred Street from the time his father executed a deed to him about the year 1893 until the present time, without a suggestion from the plaintiff or respondent's sister, that there was any question of respondent's rightward title, and respondent has a good title to the said property by adverse possession even independent of the deed from his father to him. Both the plaintiff and respondent's sister are also barred by latches from setting up any claim for an interest in the south Alfred Street property. They both knew that respondent erected the building on the said property, and he believes they also knew that he had spent large sums in later converting it into two apartments. [Actually, his wife, Kitty, spent the large sums on the property in 1915, as will be evidenced in her law suit in 1919.] The Alfred Street lot, at the time respondent built the house on it, was not in a good location. The lot was not worth probably more than about two or three hundred dollars, and the old house practically worthless. Respondent admits that the Prince Street property and the Fairfax and Wolfe Street [alternately referred to as Fairfax and Wilkes, which is correct] property cannot be partitioned in kind. Respondent admits that he received what rents were derived from the Prince Street property and the Fairfax and Wolfe Streets property, but he avers that the rents have not been sufficient to pay repairs, taxes, and insurance. That he spent large sums of money on the Fairfax and Wolfe Streets property and spent considerable money, from time to time, on the Prince Street property, but it was almost impossible from the location and condition of the property to derive much therefrom. A good class of tenants could not be secured for the property, and the tenants would generally leave in default in the payment of a great part of their rent, and, as stated, the respondent has paid far more in taxes, repairs, and insurance than he ever received from the property, and respondent denies the right of the plaintiff and his co–defendant to call upon respondent at this late date for an accounting of rents and profits.

"Nearly all of respondent's papers and receipts were burnt when there was a fire in his office, and it would be impossible for him at this date to make an accurate account of what he received and paid out. [Or 'my dog ate my homework.'] He paid out far more, however, than he received, and in addition to this has at times advanced some money to the plaintiff and more frequently to his sister and co–defendant. Respondent denies the right of the plaintiff or his co–defendant to call upon him for any accounting at this late date, as they have known all these years that he was collecting what little rents he could from the property, and was keeping up such repairs as were made and taxes, and insurance, besides spending other large sums in repairs.

"Respondent has no objection to the partition of the Prince Street property and the Fairfax and Wolfe Streets property, and he is perfectly willing to convey the same to any agent with authority to sell the same and divide the proceeds equally between those entitled."

It is interesting to note Will declared he had, "advanced some money to the plaintiff and more frequently to his sister," since it was his lack of refunding any of the money Nancy and Jack entrusted to his keeping, much less accounting for it, which brought about this and subsequent suits. On October 18, 1918, the court decided the above properties (now Fairfax and Wilkes Street, where their grandfather and father lived) could not be conveniently partitioned in kind and that all the property should be sold and the proceeds distributed, "among those entitled to share therein." Lest you think that was a quick resolution, it will be over a dozen years before the sales take place.

On June 2, 1917, Ben wrote Nancy:

"Have you had any conversation with John J. with regard to getting the cancelled checks whereby the Life Insurance Companies paid you the various amounts due you under the policies in which you were beneficiary? You no doubt recall we talked the matter over when I saw you on May 11th. I carry several policies in the New York Mutual and know the agent here very well and have had a talk with him on the subject, without mentioning any names, and he informed me that he thought there would be no trouble in getting the original cancelled check, with all endorsements, from the Washington Agent, who is our cousin Thos. P. Morgan; my friend said that the application

236

for the check for use in the Courts must be made by you. So far as the other New York policy is concerned I assume that you should pursue the same course. Tom Morgan would know and I am sure would help you in the matter. George Uhler can tell you how to proceed with the Royal #### policy. If you need me let me know, but the first thing to do, as I see it, is to submit my plans as outlined to you to John J. and let him determine if there is any thing in it."

During a lull in the court proceedings Sophie and Stanley finally got married, on January 12, 1918, She would be 26 in June and he was 28. They were married at St. Paul's Episcopal Church, which was – and still is – a block east of Nancy's house. Stanley was now Captain Stanley Gifford Blanton of the 319th Infantry, stationed at Camp Lee, Petersburg, VA. Sophie's Uncle Ben gave her away but Uncle Will was not present. Nancy Lee was her maid of honor and Stanley's brother was his best man. The reception was held at Nancy's house at 211 South St. Asaph. The wedding was held on a Saturday at 6:00.

Sophie made a detailed list of their wedding presents, which filled six 8½ x 11 lined sheets of paper. Uncle Will and Kitty were not listed among the wedding guests but sent a "fitted bag." There were a number of silver utensils, dishes and trays; soup, berry and coffee spoons; oyster forks; dinner, dessert and fruit knives; champagne and other glasses; several cut glass serving pieces; a number of handkerchiefs; candlesticks; a coffee pot and tea pot with tea balls, tea cozy and tea strainer; chafing dishes; money; a framed invitation; an electric stove and, from Sophie's girlfriends, several crepe de Chine negligees, two boudoir caps, a blue garter and grey silk stockings.

Among the other mementoes of her wedding, Sophie kept a small marriage booklet provided by the church. In it is the following, from The Epistle. Eph.v.22:

"Wives, submit yourselves unto your own husbands, as unto the Lord. For the husband is the head of the wife, even as Christ is the head of the church; and he is the savior of the body. Therefore as the church is subject unto Christ, so let the wives be to their own husbands in every thing. Husbands, love your wives, even as Christ also loved the church, and gave himself for it; That he might sanctify and cleanse it with the washing of water by the word, That he might present it to himself a glorious church, not having spot, or wrinkle, or any such thing; but that it should be holy and without blemish. So ought men to love their wives as their own bodies. He that loveth his wife loveth himself. For no man ever yet hated his own flesh; but nourisheth and cherisheth it, even as the Lord the church: For we are members of his

body, of his flesh, and of his bones. For this cause shall a man leave his
father and mother, and shall be joined unto his wife, and they two shall
be one flesh."

By the end of the month Sophie had settled into a room at 725 Sycamore
Street in Petersburg and was writing Nancy how dear and sweet Stanley was.
He had to take a para–typhoid shot, which was stronger than the regular, and
he became very sick from it. This was probably given to all military personnel
at this time because of the war in Europe but Stanley never went overseas.
Instead, he trained others wherever he went.

Sophie had shown an artistic talent in the drawings she had made for the
shows she put on with her students and the costumes she had fashioned. Here
she was obviously enjoying improvising in her limited quarters. She wrote
Nancy:

"You ought to have seen how cute our little table looked. I used
the service, had my little lemon dish as a butter dish, put toast on the
Love's cheese dish, & used our fruit knives for breakfast knives. We
had grapefruit first, then corn flakes & cream. I toasted bread fairy
well on the little gas heater, and then we had the funniest time fixing
coffee & bacon & eggs on the chafing dish. I had to boil the water and
make the coffee first. I got the instantaneous kind. Then I managed to
cook the bacon and eggs before the coffee got cold. We enjoyed our
breakfast lots but I hope the little electric stove will get here by next
Sunday. Then we can have a wonderful breakfast. I fixed Stanley a
cup of coffee before he started out this morning. I did hate to see him
go, for it is sleeting, and an awful day. He has to leave by 5:40, and it
is pretty hard these cold mornings, I think, though he doesn't ever fuss
about it."

On April 8th, Sophie related the display put on by the army. Stanley was
now a Major:

"The exercises were very interesting. They started out with a
physical drill, which all the training camp men took part in, and it was
just as interesting and pretty as could be. It was really wonderful to see
those five hundred move as one man. Then they had numerous other
drills – Guns Drill, Signal Drill & Bayonet Drill, which was really
exciting. Then they had Grenade Practice & a Trench attack, which
was thrilling. After all this we went to Stanley's company and had a
delicious lunch – hot coffee, lamb, turkey, salad, pickles, hot biscuit,
ice cream & cake. After lunch there was a Baseball game, and then
a grand review and parade. Col. Love & General Cronkhite and his
staff reviewed, and I nearly burst with pride when the 5th Company
marched by, keeping a perfect line. They looked splendid. Then we had

supper, hot biscuit, cold ham, turkey, potato salad, coffee & ice cream. After supper we went to a Vaudeville Show given by the Training Camp men, too. It was fine."

It had been over a half-century since residents of D.C. and Alexandria packed picnic baskets and trotted out to Manassas in their horse–drawn carriages to watch the Battle of Bull Run, then turned tail after the first shots were fired. Now Sophie found watching the soldiers demonstrate how they went about killing other soldiers with bayonets, grenades and a trench attack exciting and thrilling. At least it was not the real thing but it is interesting to note this grisly performance of the latest weaponry is no longer staged for civilians.

By June Sophie, now four months pregnant, prepared to leave for Augusta, Georgia and Camp Hancock, where Stanley had been ordered to take command and organize the entire Division. He would be given carte blanche to choose his men. The camp was a machine gun training center, with 22,500 men and 600 machine guns. Sophie would live in a cottage there – at 2116 Walton Way – though Stanley stayed at camp except on weekends. This was the first of several moves they made.

Sophie's letter to Nancy, on June 11th, gave a very graphic description of her visit to a doctor:

> "I went to the doctor this morning and I am so glad the examination is over. He is perfectly fine, and so kind and gentle. He made a most thorough examination but he didn't hurt me as Edgar did, and was even more careful, I think, for he used a sterilized rubber glove. He examined my heart and lungs, and took my blood pressure, and a blood test. I took a specimen of urine which he tested, and said was absolutely healthy. He doesn't think it at all necessary to take the frequent doses of calomel. Said I wasn't bilious and didn't need it. I was glad of that, for it made me so sick, and left me so constipated each time. He couldn't find anything at all wrong with me. It certainly is fine to know I come from a sound healthy stock, and haven't any awful inheritance of disease. I am going to take just the best care of myself, for I want my baby to have every chance." Sophie has already named her child John Stanley, who is due in November.

After years of Nancy's letters being diligently destroyed by her daughters, one finally appeared in the collection. Nancy was helping with her new grandson and wrote the following to Nancy Lee, back in Alexandria, minding the boarding house. It was dated November 5, 1918:

> "I have been dreaming so much about you lately. I go to bed about 10 P.M. never later than 11 – but I have the bad habit of awaking too

early, the R–s don't have breakfast until 9 o'clock & I cd so well sleep until 8 but I wake early & think & think & say Nancy has to be up now giving the early ones breakfast & I cd so easily help her if I was at home.

"I was just counting your house hold over this a.m. Miss Hattie & Evie the Critchers the Love's the two boys Miss A – Eugenia Philis – Mrs. Bailes & Miss Pollock – 15 counting yourself quite a number for you to handle. I am thankful Lizzie hangs on – does Mrs Cockran come to dinner, and has Mrs. Besson begun her house keeping yet? My love to them all. I miss my big family and am glad they miss me.

"Have you been able to find out any thing about fuel, soft coal for our furnace & did the man from the country ever bring the two loads of wood I ordered. Have you been able to make any Bank deposits yet be as economical as you can dear for I dread the expense of the winter & I hope the L.A. man will be economical with the fuel."

After reporting on Sophie and the new baby Nancy closes with:

"The weather has been simply lovely sunshine all day – but the nights & early morning are <u>very</u> cold. Stanley really suffers out at Camp. He says he will be mighty glad to get his heavy dressing wrapper & slippers. I think you better send them in a separate package for Sophs suit, heavy coat, furs & dresses will be too much in one package, then too I really think it is safer these crowded times not to send such big packages. Well darling I must close with a heart full of love & a God bless you from your ever devoted Mother."

In January of 1919 the court ordered the 309 Prince Street house and lot, 219 South Alfred house and lot and the Northeast corner of Fairfax and Wilkes Street to be sold, either at private sale or public auction. This battle continued for several years, so this seems like a good time to describe the property, based on maps, records and other information in the Local History/Special Collections department of the Alexandria Library on Queen Street and in court records at the court house.

Prince Street runs parallel to the main street, King, and 309 is four blocks from the Potomac River and faces south. The earliest picture of the property was taken in 1959 and is probably not the original. Today it is listed as having three baths and 2,000 square feet. It is two windows and a doorway wide, has two stories and a dormer and is wedged between two other similar houses. Alexandria has dozens of these kinds of dwellings, painted in yellow, blue, salmon, gray or white. Today 309 is gray brick. In September 1919 Mrs.

Minnie E. Wright offered $2,200 for the property, which was approved by the said owners, according to court records.

Now let's tackle the property Will so adamantly insisted his father, Townshend Fendall, bequeathed to him because he liked him best – 219 South Alfred. That address shows as 217 on the maps and is next to an alley. Today it looks like it was built by a committee. It has three full stories in front, covered with yellow brick. Then there is an addition tacked on to the rear of the building, of red brick and smaller than the front. It has outside stairs so may not be accessible from the front section. It came to Towny by the back door, so to speak. According to Timothy J. Dennée's *A History of 219 South Alfred Street*, written in 2000, Towny had loaned William Eaches (for whom Will Eaches Fendall was named) $900 to purchase the house, but Eaches died before paying off the loan. In 1883 the property was sold at auction, and Towny was the highest bidder. According to Will, his father delivered a deed in fee simple to the property in 1893, which Will subsequently tore down and replaced at a cost of between $2,000 and $2,500. He then rented this property until he and Lily moved in after their marriage in 1902. After they moved out (date unknown) Will claimed he "turned the house into two flats, or apartments, at a cost of about $4,000." An offer, in writing, of $6,500 was made for the property in September. Both Nancy and Ben accepted this, but Will refused to sell.

Amidst all this "I did too," "You did not," Kitty suddenly filed a petition proclaiming it was her money that covered the repairs and improvements. On October 1, 1919, she stated her…

> "husband represented himself to her to be the sole owner of the house and lot known as 219 South Alfred Street. That believing him to be the sole owner of the said premises, she loaned and advanced during the months of July, August and September, 1915 [they were married in January], the sum of Five Thousand Dollars to be spent entirely upon the improvement and repair of the said premises, and to be refunded to her, with interest, out of the rents and profits issuing therefrom… That neither the whole nor any part of the said loan of Five Thousand Dollars has been repaid to her."

That same day the court rejected Will's claim of sole ownership and declared the property was owned jointly so on the 11th Will filed a "Bill of Particulars" claiming, basically, he had not been represented by counsel (but he was an attorney), he never had the opportunity to testify, the Commissioner in Chancery was never told in whom the title was vested and the order to Will to seek counsel was not issued until "the decree confirmed a sale of said property." Germany had surrendered last year and the Treaty of Versailles had been signed four months ago but Will was neither surrendering an inch nor interested in any treaty.

The third property, frequently listed as the Northeast corner of Fairfax and Wolfe by court papers, was actually 219 Wilkes. The 1877 map clears this up by listing T. D. Fendall as the owner and the house is shown to be fairly large. There was a railroad tunnel, now a bike path, that started one block west of Fairfax and ran under Fairfax (photo on page 118.) The house currently located at that corner now faces Fairfax and is a large brick extending almost half a block down Wilkes. The original house was bequeathed to Mary T. L. Fendall, Towny's sister, by their father, Benjamin T. Fendall III, in his will on June 15, 1848. Mary never married and at some point she, Towny and Eliza all lived together in this house. When Mary died she left a half interest in the house to Towny but the other half to a John Coe, so Towny only had a half interest.

On June 7, 1921 Ben wrote Nancy:

"As usual that scoundrel has presented a pack of lies. John Johnson knows that you can not take any part of a man's life insurance, where his wife is the beneficiary, to pay a debt he owes to his father or anyone else, especially so when the father left all his property to his son's children: that policy never was your husband's it was yours from the beginning. Be the foregoing as it may no one may pay out money belonging to another without a full showing that such payment <u>was</u> made & was <u>legal</u>. The trouble, my dear, about your insurance is this, suppose you prove that the wretch took your money and spent it on himself, he has nothing that you can get your hands on in the shape of tangible property, all that any court could do would be to send him to the penitentiary as a thief. All these statements he makes as to furniture and stuff that pa gave him is all rot, a base statement from him would never be considered by any one. While we are on the subject of gifts has Marion ever had her mother's will recorded? If not I think she or one of her brothers should give the matter attention and <u>forthwith take possession</u> of what she left, then let the wretch bring suit if he thinks he can recover. I am awfully sorry I can not make any helpful suggestions, but when you get down to real facts your money has been taken from you by a trick and all spent by the party who took it, which party has absolutely nothing, in the shape of property, real or personal, that can be attached."

Ben was now 70, Nancy 68 and Will 65. It was the time of running boards and rumbleseats, prohibition and bathtub gin, Al Capone and Bugsy Siegal, flappers and the Charleston, silent movies and vaudeville, indoor plumbing and electric lights, telephones and typewriters but stores closed on Sunday, television and computers were pipe dreams and cellphones of any kind had yet to be imagined. The stock market crash was still almost a decade away, but it was already a time of hardship for Nancy, due to Will's treachery. By now the town knew of his actions but he was living in Washington and no law office is listed in the Alexandria Directories of that time.

Nancy had been borrowing money, probably for some time, though records of this aren't found in the collection until 1915, other than the $10 and $15 checks she had been writing to herself since 1912. These were undoubtedly for cash, though probably not for groceries. Those she would have paid for by the month. On July 2, 1915, however, she took out a six-month loan on the Citizens' National Bank of Alexandria, VA for $922.86, which included the interest. Copies of promissory notes show Nancy borrowed over $10,000 between then and 1929.

Nancy wasn't the only one having trouble. Sophie and Stanley were at Camp Meade, MD in December 1921, where he was suffering from dizziness and constant pain and pressure in his head, making him nervous. He had recently finished a long siege at Walter Reed Hospital, which both of them felt was wasted. This was the start of Stanley's slow but steady deterioration. He would spend the next twenty years being miserable, finally becoming so ill Sophie would be afraid to leave him alone.

On September 18, 1923, Ben Fendall died. Following is the obituary, which appeared in the Evening Sun in Baltimore, on that date.

BENJAMIN T. FENDAL, P.S.C. SECRETARY, DIES

Held Position with Commission Since 1912 – Had Been Ill Health for Year.

Benjamin R. Fendall, 72 years old, secretary of the Public Service Commission and former city engineer, died early today at his home, 141 West Lanvale street. He had been in ill health for a year, but was at his office up until two weeks ago.

Mr. Fendall had been secretary of the Public Service Commission since December, 1912, when he was appointed to that office to succeed the late Louis M. Duval. Prior to his appointment Mr. Fendall had been a member of the commission.

The late Governor Crothers appointed Mr. Fendall to the commission in 1912 to serve out the term of Commissioner Phillip D. Laird, who was promoted to the chairmanship.

Prior to Mayor Preston's term of office, Mr. Fendall served as City Engineer, having been appointed to that office first by Mayor Thomas G. Hayes in 1900. He was at the head of the city engineering department for 12 years. Prior to his connection with the city government Mr. Fendall was in the engineering department of the Baltimore and Ohio Railroad.

The Baltimore American added: Under his regime many cobblestoned streets were replaced by modern pavements.

This was, of course, a blow to Florence and their children, Benjamin Mason and Mary Gertrude, both in their 30s, but it also had to be devastating to Nancy, for she had now lost her protector and advisor. Ben had always looked after her and been there when she needed him, even before Jack died. He had stepped in and paid for Sophie's education, without hesitation, when Jack was unable to do so. He had stood beside her when she had to take Will to court, joining her in that endeavor. He had scolded or praised her when she was growing up, depending on her behavior at the time. Now he was gone, but the lawsuits continued.

Florence subsequently filed suit March 9, 1925, to establish she and their children were Ben's legitimate heirs, that he had died intestate and that they wanted to have the court proceed with the original case, filed in 1919, to have the three properties named therein sold and the proceeds divided between "those legally entitled thereto." She was trying to start a fire under the court. There is, of course, no record of how Nancy felt about this, due to her letters being destroyed, but the case continued to move at a snail's pace.

Two years later other property was added, such as the capital stock of the Alexandria Water Company (where Towny Fendall worked) and several West Virginia bonds. All of this was to be sold and equally divided. The suit also asked that the claim of Katherine Fendall be rejected. That, however, was far from the end of it.

The rest of the activity before the court fills over 30 pages of legalese, making it impractical to add here. The bottom line, to use today's vernacular, was: Will had to cough up the bonds and whatever else he had; he was denied his petition he was the sole owner of 219 South Alfred and it was sold for $7,500 (over $93,000 in 2009); this amount was to be divided between all of them and; the property at Fairfax and Wilkes was sold for $1,000. Nancy also turned over to the court the names, addresses (if known) of all the heirs, devisees, and next of kin of Benjamin T. Fendall Sr. Money then seems to have been doled out to everyone in Alexandria, from the *Alexandria Gazette* (for advertising) to the City Collector for taxes, to the Clerk of the Court, the Commissioner, attorneys and all the Fendalls and Marburys within earshot. Nancy received around $4,000, which was only a fraction of what Will had stolen from her.

One of the rare letters from Nancy appears dated October 5, 1929. It is actually two almost identical letters to her daughters, and is a will. As they are the same, except for mention of Sophie's children, Nancy's is quoted here:

"My own precious Nancy Lee I feel I am perhaps very sick tonight but I want you to <u>know</u> how <u>I love you with all my heart</u>. You have been and are the most loving, faithful, devoted child to me. You have never failed me in any way & I know & believe God will bless you my darling child. You have been so brave through the many trials you have had to pass through & I am proud of you. I am glad you have our <u>beloved</u> Sophie & her precious boys & hope they will <u>always</u> love & look after and comfort & help you and that Stanley will be a brother to you.

"I have not much in material things to leave but I want you & Soph to share equally except in the actual money & of that I want you to have two thirds & Soph one third as she has her husband to protect her & you are alone – take care of what you have & I feel you will get along, if you can have someone to help you in your work, like dear Miss Baldwin. You can keep the house for awhile until you can get things straight for I know how you love your house – Soph can help pay the taxes as half the house will be hers. You two share alike in that & 1 of the Montgomery Ward Stock is for you and one for Sophie. 1 thousand each. I want my precious John & Joe to each have $100 put in Savings bank for them & Stanley $50.00 to help on his automobile.

"I'm sorry to write on such paper all I have near & the pain's bad & I can't move from my desk. God bless & keep you my darling Nancy Lee and think of me always as your devoted Mother and my precious Sophie too I do dearly love & she is always so good & sweet to me God bless her – your devoted Mother."

This, of course, is only a partial will, since it doesn't spell out exactly what Nancy has. There may have been also a more formal will but on April 23, 1930, Nancy obviously has recuperated from whatever was ailing her, above, and so she sets down some specifics of what goes to whom. This list is written upside down, sideways and every other direction on a sheet of paper. Whether it was used as the official will is unknown but her division of her belongings is fascinating.

The Montgomery Ward stock, mortgage, liberty bonds and savings were divided as she indicated above, with Nancy Lee receiving $6,611 and Sophie $5,550 but both getting a half-interest in the house. Then Nancy sets about carefully doling out the mementoes that have accumulated. To her son John she gives Jack's watch fob and seal, scarf pin and one pair of cuff buttons. Son Joseph gets the same except for the watch fob. To Stanley and Benjamin Mason (Ben's son) she gives Jack's other scarf pins. Ben's daughter, Mary, gets a gold bracelet marked, "N Fendall."

The division of her jewelry is the most interesting, for she leaves <u>one</u> diamond ear ring to each daughter. Presumably they would not need to wear them at the same time so they could pass the single earring back and forth.

Then Nancy Lee got her diamond engagement ring, a handsome bracelet, Uncle Langhorn Dades Miniatures and Jack's class ring at V.M.I. to use until John was 21. Sophie got her topaz ring that was set in the original setting of her engagement ring, her turquoise and pearl ring, one little pearl ring and pearl pin, a handsome bracelet and Uncle Langhorn Dades miniature in breast pin.

Will died on March 27, 1936, in Washington, D.C., rating only one paragraph for his obituary, naming his parents and wife and adding, "In former years Mr. Fendall engaged in the practice of law in this city." He was 79½. Not surprisingly, there was no further correspondence from Will since the first law suit was filed and the obituary does not indicate the cause of death or location of his burial.

Though the war was over, Stanley stayed in the army and was constantly being transferred from one place to another. Their second son, Joseph, was born in Puerto Rico in 1925. Sophie's letters were full of reports of Stanley's deteriorating condition. By 1933 he slept several hours after lunch on a cot in his room and the boys made him nervous. He had arterial sclerosis (hardening of the arteries) and coronary thrombosis, but it wouldn't be diagnosed for another six years. By that time he was in very bad shape, as indicated by Sophie's PRIVATE letter to Nancy Lee, who was caring for their dying mother. The letter was dated April 28, 1940 and was from San Francisco:

"This letter is just for you to read, of course. I can't write freely when I think you & mother will read it together. It nearly <u>kills</u> me to be away off here, and know you are going through all this, and that mother is suffering so, and feeling so utterly wretched – while I am doing nothing. I hope and pray the new nurse may be some real help to you – and help to make mother more comfortable. The nausea is the most trying symptom of all I think for it makes her so weak and exhausted, I know. It seems so cruelly hard that she has to go thro all this and I feel as if I want to just <u>push</u> the days along, so I can be back there with you both.

"Things here are moving along about as usual. Stanley has a mean cold in the head, was in bed Thursday & Friday but he got up yesterday and went over to the hospital for a treatment and went again this morning before we went to church. The violet ray treatments they have been giving him <u>have</u> done him good, and he looks better.

"I want to get mother something for 'Mother's Day' and am wondering if she wouldn't like one of those bed pillows that are almost like an arm chair. They are made of three pillows – one at the back, and two smaller ones like chair arms and look very comfortable. Do you think she might like one? Please let me know. I would call up again but it is so terribly expensive – that phone call we made, even after hours, was eight dollars – of course we talked six minutes and it was

<u>more</u> than worth the money to hear your dear voices but we can't do that very often.

"Nance darling I haven't written you a single letter that has said what is in my heart. They all seem to be just a string of words, and I feel like tearing them up & writing another – but I know it wouldn't be any better. Just know I love you, and am with you every step of the way. God bless and keep you, darling. Always your devoted sister Soph."

On May 10th Sophie adds:

"They won't issue Stanley's travel order until after his retirement order comes through, May 31st. They have set June 13th for the date for the packers and we are planning to leave June 15th and if there is any way we can get away sooner we will. Stanley has been so miserable all week – pain and gas and indigestion. Today the doctor is keeping him in bed with the lightest possible diet. His fears run rampant whenever pain comes, and he is frantic with worry – thinks of cancer or gall bladder – and then decides it <u>must</u> be his heart and that the doctors don't know what they are doing.

"At times he hardly seems normal and then again he will be like the old Stanley, & I feel almost as if I must have dreamed the bad times. Nights are the worst, for he begins to be afraid when darkness falls and I dare not leave him alone for fear he might do himself some injury. I am telling you things I have never told before and of course they are for no one else but you but I must let you know <u>why</u> I don't come – the true underlying reason. But promise me you will destroy this after you read it and make no mention of this part of it in your answer, for Stanley wants to read every line of the letters from home.

"Nance, I can't bear to think of our precious little mother suffering so! If only the medicine can help to relieve the swelling and if the organs of elimination will function properly and my constant, fervent, hourly prayer is that if <u>only</u> I can get back to her! Kiss her for me & tell her there isn't a moment when she is out of my thoughts. Devotedly Soph."

Nancy succumbed to cancer on May 26, 1940, before Sophie even left San Francisco. They held her funeral at St. Paul's Church but withheld burial until Sophie could return. Within a year-and-a-half Sophie would also lose Stanley, who died on November 18, 1941 and was buried in Arlington National Cemetery. Sophie would join him there in 1985.

Nancy Lee Fendall Tackett had been spoiled all her life by her parents, her older brother, her husband and her daughters. She had cajoled and connived to get things to go her way and had usually succeeded but she had also run a boarding house for over 50 years, though she always seemed to be elsewhere during the summer. She loved that house. 211 South St. Asaph Street had three full floors and at least seven bedrooms. There had also been a room on the second floor used as a smokehouse, with meathooks to hold Virginia smoked hams. The front part of the house had 12-foot ceilings, which added four feet to the stairs to the second floor. This had a Victorian façade, which had been added to match the adjoining house. The original house had the normal eight-foot ceilings and there was also a screened-in porch and a huge garden. Each room contained a fire place, which meant it had to have wood or coal brought up and the smoke would soil the wallpaper and furniture.

Nancy Lee would now completely take over the management of the boarding house, as Nancy had willed, and run it with the gentle manners of an earlier age. Her grand nephew remembers Sunday lunch with the "little old ladies," where the tablecloth was linen, the linen napkins were arranged in napkin rings, there were crystal salt holders and he got to ring the bell announcing dinner was ready.

The house was sold after Nancy Lee died on September 7, 1959, and was restored to two floors with dormers on the third floor, making it much more attractive. It has been remodeled and enlarged many times since then, transforming it eventually from a genteel elderly lady into a lady of high fashion, dripping with jewels. Where crossed swords of Jack Tackett's used to hang above the large fireplace in the front room, now a row of red and white Staffordshire cats are crowded together on the mantle. The screened-in porch has been expanded into a huge room with a television the size of a billiard table. Outside, the once open area now resembles a Greek or Roman patio, with a dozen pillars and wisteria vines twined above it. The house sold for $4.5 million in 2005 and is on the market now, in 2010, for $5.7 million. It is a sign of different times.

The Eaches, Fendalls and Tacketts lives cannot be duplicated. The days of the horse and buggy are long gone, though wars are still with us. The harnessing of electricity has harnessed us to the "Information Age." Now we no longer have time to stop and smell the flowers, and are leaving no record of our passing to our descendants. Our inventions and gadgets wear out before we do and instead of passing on our history, thoughts and feelings – as these families did – we pass on pollution and landfills.

Jack and Nancy Tackett's great-grandchildren are still around to read about them and know what their lives were like, but their great-grandchildren will not have the same privilege regarding their lives. There will be, and are, some exceptions, but basically none of the great-grandchildren yet to be born will ever hold a letter in their hands that was written by their ancestor, and that is a tragedy.

Eaches Family Tree

JOSEPH EACHES
B. July 18, 1794, Loudoun Co.
D. December 19, 1857

Married November 27, 1816
Children all born in
Alexandria, Virginia

ANN MCCORMICK
B. September 1797
D. July 4, 1850

JAMES MCCORMICK EACHES
B. May 25, 1817
D. September 3, 1847

MARY EACHES
B. 1820 (1950 census)
D. January 2, 1858 (obituary)

ELIZA EACHES
B. July 7, 1822 or 1823
D. January 4, 1907 (obituary)

Married January 15, 1849
Children listed under Fendall Family Tree

TOWNSHEND FENDALL
B. May 15, 1813
D. July 23, 1893

THOMAS EACHES
B. 1824
D. Between 1867-1870

Married

MOLLY OR MARY
B. Unknown
D. Unknown

HESTER - B. 1857 D. Before 1863
EWING - B. March 13, 1863
KATE - B. 1867

WILLIAM B. EACHES
B. 1826 (1850 census)
D. February 26, 1856 (obituary)

DANIEL B. EACHES
B. 1832 (1850 census)
D. After 1864 (letter)

JOHN M. EACHES
B. January 1, 1835
Buried May 1, 1868

CAROLINE (CARRIE) EACHES
B. 1837 (1850 census)
D. August 16, 1866

Married August 30, 1860
in St. Louis, MO

THOMAS G. RUSSELL
B. 1833
D. Unknown

DORA - B. July 1861
HECTOR BRADEN - B. Feb. 1863
ELIZA FENDALL - B. March 1864 (per Carrie)

HECTOR BRADEN EACHES
B. April 8, 1840
D. July 2, 1875 in New York

(Birth and some other dates from Thomas Katheder, Esq. *The Virginia Genealogist #42, Number 1, Jan-Mar 1998*, and from the letters. Obits from the *Alexandria Gazette*.)

Fendall Family Tree

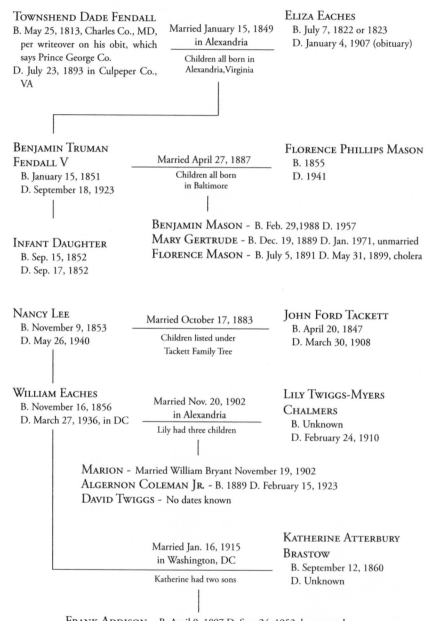

TOWNSHEND DADE FENDALL
B. May 25, 1813, Charles Co., MD,
per writeover on his obit, which
says Prince George Co.
D. July 23, 1893 in Culpeper Co.,
VA

Married January 15, 1849
in Alexandria

Children all born in
Alexandria, Virginia

ELIZA EACHES
B. July 7, 1822 or 1823
D. January 4, 1907 (obituary)

**BENJAMIN TRUMAN
FENDALL V**
B. January 15, 1851
D. September 18, 1923

Married April 27, 1887

Children all born
in Baltimore

FLORENCE PHILLIPS MASON
B. 1855
D. 1941

INFANT DAUGHTER
B. Sep. 15, 1852
D. Sep. 17, 1852

BENJAMIN MASON - B. Feb. 29,1988 D. 1957
MARY GERTRUDE - B. Dec. 19, 1889 D. Jan. 1971, unmarried
FLORENCE MASON - B. July 5, 1891 D. May 31, 1899, cholera

NANCY LEE
B. November 9, 1853
D. May 26, 1940

Married October 17, 1883

Children listed under
Tackett Family Tree

JOHN FORD TACKETT
B. April 20, 1847
D. March 30, 1908

WILLIAM EACHES
B. November 16, 1856
D. March 27, 1936, in DC

Married Nov. 20, 1902
in Alexandria

Lily had three children

**LILY TWIGGS-MYERS
CHALMERS**
B. Unknown
D. February 24, 1910

MARION - Married William Bryant November 19, 1902
ALGERNON COLEMAN JR. - B. 1889 D. February 15, 1923
DAVID TWIGGS - No dates known

Married Jan. 16, 1915
in Washington, DC

Katherine had two sons

**KATHERINE ATTERBURY
BRASTOW**
B. September 12, 1860
D. Unknown

FRANK ADDISON - B. April 9, 1897 D. Sep. 24, 1952, heart attack
JOHN COLT - B. October 5, 1904

250

Tackett Family Tree

JOHN EDWARD TACKETT
B. Oct. 1822, Fredericksburg, VA
D. Feb. 19, 1910, Alexandria

Married Sept. 8, 1845
in Fredericksburg

Children all born in
Fredericksburg

SOPHIE FORD
B. 1818-same
D. Sep. 3, 1853, childbirth

**JOHN (JACK) FORD
TACKETT**
B. April 20, 1847
D. March 20, 1908

Married Oct. 17, 1883
in Alexandria

Children all born
in Alexandria

NANCY LEE FENDALL
B. Nov. 9. 1853, Alexandria
D. May 26, 1940, Alexandria

NANCY LEE FENDALL - B. May 17, 1887 D. Sep. 7, 1959, unmarried
ELIZA FENDALL - B. May 5, 1890 D. July 1, 1891, cholera

SOPHIE FORD
B. June 3, 1892
D. February 6, 1985

Married January 12, 1918

**STANLEY   GIFFORD
BLANTON**
B. April 7, 1890
D. November 18, 1941

JOHN STANLEY - B. Nov. 11, 1918 in Augusta, GA D. Oct. 31, 1899 in MA
JOSEPH WARREN - B. Oct. 13, 192 in Puerto Rico D. Unknown

CHARLES E. TACKETT
B. 1848
D. Aug. 6, 1910

Married Oct. 11, 1888
Fredericksburg Marrige Records

HARRIET M. SLAUGHTER
B. Unknown
D. Unknown

Harriet had a son but name, etc. not known

SOPHIE TACKETT
B. August 31, 1853
D. January 26, 1899 (obituary), unmarried

(Birth, marriage, death dates other than obituaries found amongst collection of letters. Obituaries found in the *Alexandria Gazette*.)

Bibliography

History of Charles Co, Maryland, Tercentenary Year, 1958
Margaret Brown Klapthor & Paul Dennis Brown

Portals to Hell: Military Prisons of the Civil War
Lonnie R. Speer, 1997 Stackpole Books

Beefsteak Raid, by Edward Boykin
Funk & Wagnalls Co, NY 1960

Northern Virginia's Own: The 17th VA Infantry Regiment,
Confederate States Army – William M. Glasgow

Slave Manumissions in Alexandria Land Records, 1790–1863

Alexandria County (Arlington) VA Marriage Records 1853–1895
Wesley E. Pippinger

Eaches of Loudoun Co, VA – Virginia Genealogist 42, Number 1
January–March 1998 – Thomas Katheder

Alexandria Gazette – newspaper – dates designated in story

Eaches, Fendall, Tackett Collection – Boxes 237–237F
Local History/Special Collections Alexandria Library
717 Queen Street, Alexandria, VA 22314

A History of 219 South Alfred Street Alexandria, Virginia
Timothy J. Dennée Alexandria History Services
September 2000

About the Author

When Barb Winters volunteered to sort, read and organize the six boxes of old letters, photos, diaries and other records dropped off at the Local History / Special Collections Department of the Alexandria Library, she had no idea she would become so involved with the lives of three families from her adopted home that she would devote three years to telling their stories. But she did and she has, relating the fascinating lives – in their own words – of the Eaches, Fendalls and Tacketts, their loves and losses, betrayal and survival, from before the Civil War to post World War I.

Photo by Elza Photography

Index

254